CONFRONTATION '51
The 1951 Waterfront Dispute

confrontation '51
the 1951 waterfront dispute

Michael Bassett

A.H. & A.W. REED
Wellington Auckland Christchurch Sydney Melbourne

First published 1972

A.H. & A.W. REED LTD
182 Wakefield Street, Wellington
29 Dacre Street, Auckland
165 Cashel Street, Christchurch
51 Whiting Street, Artarmon, Sydney
357 Little Collins Street, Melbourne

© 1971 MICHAEL BASSETT

This book is copyright. Except for purposes of private study, criticism or review, no part may be reproduced by any process including stencilling or photocopying without the prior written permission of the publisher.

ISBN 0 589 00681 9

Typeset on IBM Composer by A.H. & A.W. Reed Ltd
Printed by Dai Nippon Printing Co. (International) Ltd, Hong Kong

CONTENTS

	Page
ACKNOWLEDGMENTS	7
INTRODUCTION	8
CHAPTER I	
Post-war Difficulties with the New Zealand Waterside Workers' Union	13
CHAPTER II	
National Party Attitudes	34
CHAPTER III	
The February Dispute	61
CHAPTER IV	
Summoning Up Support	86
CHAPTER V	
Deserted by the Union Movement	113
CHAPTER VI	
The Later Stages of the Dispute	136
CHAPTER VII	
Government Triumphant	167
CHAPTER VIII	
Finale	196
BIBLIOGRAPHY	213
FOOTNOTES	215
INDEX	256

LIST OF ILLUSTRATIONS

		Page
1.	Peter Fraser *(Auckland Star)*	17
2.	The National Cabinet *(Auckland Star)*	36
3.	William Sullivan *(Auckland Star)*	39
4.	Jock Barnes and Toby Hill *(Auckland Star)*	44
5.	F.P. Walsh *(Auckland Star)*	47
6.	S.G. Holland *(Auckland Star)*	50
7.	Union leaders *(Auckland Star)*	63
8.	S.G. Holland and John Foster Dulles *(New Zealand Herald)*	66
9.	Servicemen on the wharves *(Auckland Star)*	96
10.	Servicemen unloading coal *(Auckland Star)*	96
11.	Auckland Union members	106
12.	Walter Nash *(Auckland Star)*	153
13.	New union members *(Auckland Star)*	160
14.	Police at the gates of Princess Wharf *(Auckland Star)*	160
15.	Police and demonstrators *(Auckland Star)*	163
16.	A procession of watersiders *(Auckland Star)*	168
17.	Barnes addressing union members *(New Zealand Herald)*	172
18.	Deregistered watersiders *(Auckland Star)*	177
19.	Holland campaigning *(Auckland Star)*	199

CARTOONS

A.	IT'S THE SAME WAR (Minhinnick, *New Zealand Herald*)	88
B.	"HANDS UP ALL THOSE WHO VOTE FOR A STRIKE!" (Minhinnick, *New Zealand Herald*)	89
C.	"The Police have been very lenient . . . . " *(Illegal Information Bulletin)*	140
D.	"I am here, Madam, under Section 18B of the regulations." *(Illegal Information Bulletin)*	140
E.	"The Country is right behind the Government." *(Illegal Information Bulletin)*	140
F.	WHO'LL WIN? IT DEPENDS ON YOU, BROTHER *(Illegal Information Bulletin)*	141
G.	The Silent Three are McLagan, Nash, and Semple (Minhinnick, *New Zealand Herald*)	157

ACKNOWLEDGMENTS

This study began a decade ago as a master's thesis at the University of Auckland. Since 1961 when that thesis was completed I have consulted what additional material has become available and have re-lived 1951 with many of the leading actors who were involved in the drama. Many debts have been incurred, the heaviest being to the late Professor W.T.G. Airey who supervised the original work. I must thank Professor Robert Chapman for years of encouragement in the study and Professor Keith Sinclair for arranging access for me to Sir Walter Nash's papers. My thanks are due also to the trustees of the estate of Sir Walter Nash for allowing me to see his papers. Mr H.O. Roth of the University of Auckland kindly lent me many documents from his personal collection on labour history and read this book in manuscript. Messrs H.L. and A.E. Bockett generously agreed to read and discuss an early draft, and many ex-watersiders, among them Harold ("Jock") Barnes, Toby Hill, Jack Basham, Ron Harrington and Ron Jones, lent me material in their possession and willingly answered my questions. My thanks are due also to the Federation of Labour and the Labour Party which allowed me to consult their records. My wife, Judith, has read and re-read with infinite patience drafts of this work. My thanks are due to them all, as well as to the New Zealand University Grants Committee for providing me with a small grant to facilitate the travel connected with this work. All should feel free to dissociate themselves from this study, or from any part of it. The opinions expressed in it are my own.

INTRODUCTION

New Zealand's system of industrial conciliation and arbitration was established in 1894, fifty-seven years before it sustained—and survived—the onslaught of the militant unions in 1951. The unique act that was introduced by William Pember Reeves was designed on the one hand to strengthen labour, on the other to save it from itself, by limiting the likelihood of strikes.[1] The Industrial Conciliation and Arbitration Act 1894 promised the protection of the law to any group of fifteen workers who registered themselves as a union under the Act. As a consequence of registration, a union had to accept that a strike was illegal while any industrial dispute was being considered by a Board of Conciliation or by the Court of Arbitration.

In the first few years of the new system workers improved their position within the economy, while employers, most of whom had opposed the passage of the IC & A Act through Parliament, viewed the system with disfavour. However, in time attitudes were reversed.[2] By the early years of the twentieth century the number of unions in existence and their total membership were increasing rapidly. To a growing number of unionists the protection of the IC & A Act seemed unnecessary; the strike weapon looked like a more effective guarantor of progress. The Federation of Labour that was formed in 1908 had contempt for compulsory arbitration. During the next five years its member unions cancelled their registration under the IC & A Act, in order legally to pursue a policy of strike action.

Employers, previously sceptical about compulsory arbitration, began to perceive in it unforeseen virtues. Not only did the Arbitration Court appear to be keeping wage rises to a minimum; the provisions in the Act restricting the use of the strike weapon by those registered under the Act had also ensured a measure of stability in industry from 1894 until 1906 that looked worth trying to recapture.

A later and more conservative Liberal Government than the one that had brought in the arbitration system in the first place proceeded to help the employers "save the unions from themselves". At first all strikes by arbitrationist unions were made illegal. And then in 1912-13 the Reform Government aided the employers in crushing several non-arbitrationist unions belonging to the Federation of Labour. This was both a victory for the employers and a warning to those unions that might in future try to operate outside of the system of compulsory arbitration. In the Labour Disputes Investigation Act 1913 strikes by non-arbitrationist unions were not made illegal, but they did have to follow a carefully detailed procedure if legal penalties were to be avoided.[3] New Zealand's labour legislation was becoming increasingly constrictive.

During the next twenty years the country's economy fluctuated; the rapid inflation of 1919-20 gave way to the depression of 1921-22; the uncertain twenties wound down into the Great Depression. Attitudes towards compulsory arbitration of industrial disputes gyrated accordingly. In the boom times of 1919 the newly-formed Alliance of Labour denounced arbitration and lauded direct action. A decade later Alliance spokesmen were defending the Court against the attacks of employers who, in declining circumstances, believed compulsory arbitration to be the prop for artificially high wage rates. Between 1932 and 1936 employers and farmers had their way; the provision for referring an unsettled dispute beyond conciliation to the Court of Arbitration was deleted in the IC & A Amendment Act of 1932. Weak unions were allowed to grow weaker and wage rates were depressed as the Coalition Government heeded the advice from deflationists.

After 1935 economic conditions improved, unemployment vanished, and the welfare state arrived to take care of many of society's basic insecurities. In the IC & A Amendment Act of 1936 there re-emerged Reeves' twin aims: strengthening labour (this time through the introduction of compulsory unionism) and saving it from itself (through the restoration of compulsory arbitration). Once again the labour movement in its moment of weakness favoured compulsory arbitration, while employers opposed it. And once again opinions altered with time.

Twelve years after the IC & A Act had been first introduced, attitudes to it were being reversed. By 1948 the same thing had happened again. Those unions possessing a tradition of dislike for arbitration were vocal, stressing their belief that the labour movement would be stronger without the Court, and without compulsory unionism. Beset by a period of inflation once again, employers were anxious that industrial activity be confined rigidly to the system of compulsory arbitration. And governments, once more, were prepared to assist them to that end. The Labour Government believed that its introduction of the welfare state made strikes unnecessary; it was conscious also that strikes threatened its policy of economic stabilisation, and therefore its political survival. In the tradition established by all governments before it, Labour was expanding the powers of the state to deal with strikes. An IC & A Amendment Act in 1939 gave to the Minister of Labour the power to deregister a union operating under the arbitration system in the event of its striking. In place of the deregistered union a new union could be registered. And now that compulsory unionism was in force, all workers wishing to continue working in the industry covered by the new union would be compelled to join that union.[4] Governments now possessed the powers to break arbitrationist unions trying to pursue an illegal policy of direct action. The actions of unions not registered under the IC & A Act were by now covered not only by the Labour Disputes Investigation Act 1913, but also by the Strike and Lockout Emergency Regulations 1939. The Public Safety Conservation Act 1932 could also be invoked in case of a strike. Governments possessed virtually limitless powers to deal with any strikes.

Yet, although it became increasingly dangerous, industrial unrest continued. After World War II the number of working days lost through strikes rose; in 1949 more were lost through strikes than ever before in New Zealand. Two years later a conservative government embarked on a crusade in the name of eliminating strike action and restoring the supremacy of industrial conciliation and arbitration. A smaller proportion of the labour movement required disciplining than had been the case in 1912-13. Yet the 1951 waterfront dispute was, in the words of one observer, "full-scale industrial battle, the longest, costliest and most widespread in New Zealand's history".[5]

Differing attitudes to arbitration were at the core of the 1951 upheaval. Yet there were other factors involved as well, some political, some personal. Disillusionment with the modest reform programme of the Labour Party; concern about the rightward drift in New Zealand's foreign policy; growing rivalry between the personalities on the right and left of the trade union movement; the desire of conservatives to restore a harmony of interests more weighted towards capital and "gentility" after an age of fierce egalitarianism; all these were involved in the waterfront dispute of 1951. Conservatives came to see the dispute as "the most outrageous challenge ever issued to the authority of the State."[6] Many of the workers involved saw it as part of an international struggle by working men to introduce a new and more just system of bargaining between capital and labour. And although the dispute involved only 20,000 workers at its height, and although the watersiders lost, there were few New Zealanders indifferent to it. The dispute lasted more than five months, interrupting transport and the supply of some essential goods and services. It involved the only early termination of a Parliamentary term in this century. And it provided the National Party with a golden opportunity to convert a shaky political base into a solid foundation built on aggressive anti-unionism. Frustrated at having to administer the welfare state inherited from Labour, Nationalists took some satisfaction in humiliating the trade union movement on which their opponent's political power was based.

In retrospect it seems clear that the core issue of compulsory arbitration was lost sight of in the midst of these wider issues. It is true that in the legislative aftermath the penal sections of the IC & A Act were strengthened. All strike action became hazardous as well as illegal. Yet industrial unrest was not eliminated in 1951 any more than it had been in 1913. The number of days lost through strikes declined only temporarily. By the mid-fifties there were again signs of dissatisfaction with—even contempt for—the system of arbitration. Persistent full employment and an actual shortage of labour gave a growing number of unions the opportunity to negotiate ruling rates of pay above those fixed by the Arbitration Court. For many workers the Court's deliberations became more and more irrelevant.

In this context 1951 appears as an effort by Government and employer to achieve by one means (toughness) what another aspect of Government policy (full employment) was bound in the long run to defeat. Insofar as 1951 was about the maintenance of compulsory arbitration the achievements were ephemeral. On the wider political issues which, initially, were less central to the battle, the winners' accomplishments were more enduring. 1951 consolidated F.P. Walsh's position within the labour movement and it opened up the prospect of a lengthy period in office for the National Party. Moreover, it pointed to what was to become a persistent problem for the Labour Party—its relationship with its parent body, the trade union movement. For the political, social and economic development of New Zealand the waterfront dispute was a portentous event.

CHAPTER I

POST-WAR DIFFICULTIES WITH THE NEW ZEALAND WATERSIDE WORKERS' UNION

"Industrial unrest," says L. F. Crisp in his biography of Australia's prime minister, Ben Chifley, "has been characteristic of capitalist economies during post-war transitions the world over."[1] After World War I the United States, Britain, and several European countries as well as Australia and New Zealand, were plagued with strikes during the period of readjustment. After World War II most governments took elaborate precautions to minimise dislocation. But industrial stoppages occurred again. In the United States, the steel, rail, automobile, electrical and mining industries were all affected by disputes during 1945 and 1946,[2] and early in 1947 the British transport industry was paralysed. In Australia there were troubles in the iron and coal industries between 1945 and 1949, and early in 1951 there were stoppages on the waterfront. Post-war America saw labour baron John L. Lewis rise to greater prominence, while Australians felt the impact of watersider Jim Healy's militancy. Clearly there was nothing unique in the fact that New Zealanders experienced troubles with militant unions and their leaders after World War II.

In terms of days lost, New Zealand actually suffered less from post-war industrial disputes than many other countries. Australia, Canada, Finland, France, India and the United States were all hit more severely by strikes between 1946 and 1954.[3] Yet strikes in New Zealand had more serious repercussions than elsewhere, partly due to the country's unique system of arbitration which involved the state directly in the handling of industrial disputes.[4] In New Zealand, more than elsewhere, governments had always been held directly accountable for the state of industrial relations, and the waterfront crisis of

1951, the most serious in the country's history, lasted longer, involved more complex legal issues and had more serious political consequences than any comparable crisis overseas.

In most countries the prime cause of post-war unrest was inflation. Governments were anxious to retain reasonably full employment at the same time as their spending on capital works was expanded to make up for wartime cutbacks. Consumer goods were usually in short supply, but demand for them was high. With such inflationary pressures already present most governments tried to avoid the further problems which would follow from rising wages. Unions, for their part, were worried by inflation and wished to make use of the increase in their bargaining power afforded by full, or near full, employment. Demands for substantial wage rises were frequent, and in many western countries it was clear that governments and unions were set on collision courses within weeks of VJ Day.

New Zealand, like other countries, emerged from the war "taut with suppressed inflation".[5] Savings were high, but there was a shortage of raw materials and finished goods. Government works such as state housing and hydro-electric development which had been cut back during the war, were speeded up and by 1946 Government spending was running at an unprecedented level. Peter Fraser's Labour Government continued to control imports so as to give priority to raw materials and capital equipment, and consumer goods remained in fairly short supply.

In order that the Government could expand its building programme and increase social services yet avoid rampant inflation, Fraser deemed it necessary to retain much of the elaborate wartime stabilisation mechanism. The prices of essential goods and services were held down by means of subsidies, and every attempt was made to keep wage rises to a minimum. Yet, largely because of political pressures, the Government found it impossible to keep controls sufficiently stringent to prevent price rises altogether. Bank credit expanded a little as private building increased; food subsidies were gradually lifted, and in preparation for the 1946 general election, Walter Nash, the Minister of Finance, removed sales taxes on building materials, furniture and clothing in the budget of August that year. Price increases were allowed on farm products in 1947 and most fruits and vegetables were released from price control during 1948. Inflation that had been rigidly suppressed by controls during the war now had an opportunity to break free. The retail price index rose ten per cent between the fourth quarter of 1946 and the fourth quarter of 1947.[6] The economic stability of the war years was endangered.

The pressure for relaxation of controls came from all sections of the community. By the middle of 1946 the Chambers of Commerce and the Manufacturers' Federation were clamouring for lower taxes. Their appetites were only whetted by the minor taxation relief in the 1946 Budget. The Road Transport Alliance wanted lower taxes on tyres, motor vehicles and petrol, and was dissatisfied with a budget that gave it nothing. The Federated Builders and Contractors' Association wanted lower sales taxes on building materials but was anxious that the inflationary pressure from an increase in building should not result in a wage rise for workers.[7] Sectional differences which had been kept under wraps during the war were breaking out with renewed intensity.

The Government was well aware of the fact that rising wages would intensify the inflationary pressures within the economy. Yet it would not have been fair, even had it been politically possible, for Fraser's Government completely to resist union demands. Early in 1945 Fraser admitted that railwaymen and dairy-factory workers deserved slight increases in wages, and the Arbitration Court was given power to adjust disparities in wage levels. The wartime wage freeze was over. And once the thaw began it was difficult to stop. In March 1945 the Arbitration Court increased wages by 3½d. an hour and in December 1945 a new Minimum Wage Act was passed, the increases to apply from 1 April 1946. In October 1947 there was a further wage increase. No matter how much the Government might wish to prevent it, the policy of rigid stabilisation was breaking up as various pressure groups demanded relaxation of controls. Union pressure was only one among many forces conspiring to dislocate Labour's delicate system of stabilisation.

The trade union movement found itself in a good bargaining position at the end of the war. Not only were the unions closely tied into the governing Labour Party, but their members were also benefitting from the continual labour shortage which applied despite the demobilisation of the armed forces. During 1945 and 1946 the manpower restrictions which had been in force during the war were progressively relaxed and this further increased workers' bargaining powers by making it easier to move from job to job. All unions, and particularly the strong unions, were eager to utilise this opportunity to secure higher award rates of pay and better conditions. Few were content simply with the considerable amount of overtime that was still available after the war. Just as other sections of the community saw the relaxation of controls moving at too slow a pace, so many unions came to be dissatisfied with the Arbitration Court's cautious response to successive wage claims. In some quarters there was a growing feeling that the Court was simply the mouthpiece for a Labour Government growing cold and insensitive to legitimate workers' demands.

The Watersiders

Leading the campaign for better wages and conditions was the New Zealand Waterside Workers' Union. The waterfront industry with its fluctuating seasonal demand for labour, the complexity of the work involving all types of cargo, and the element of risk in loading and unloading awkward cargoes, has been recognised throughout the world as one where militant unionism thrives.[8] In New Zealand watersiders had always been in the vanguard of the union movement. In an economy peculiarly dependent on exporting and importing they found the strike, and threat of strike, powerful weapons against recalcitrant employers.[9] These were dangerous weapons, however. In 1890 the watersiders had been badly beaten in New Zealand, and elsewhere, by the employers; in 1913 employers, Government and apathy amongst other unions routed the watersiders again.

Nevertheless substantial gains had been made by the New Zealand Waterside Workers' Federation after its formation in

1. Peter Fraser, Labour's Prime Minister 1940-49. *(Auckland Star)*

1906. Special arrangements were negotiated directly with the employers for night work in 1915; certain safety measures were introduced towards the end of World War I; and greater security of labour for permanent workers came slowly as the number of labour calls a day were reduced and preference was given to union members when work was available.[10] When times were good, waterfront labour was in fairly short supply, and the union benefitted. But after 1926 when unemployment increased, the improvements in conditions of work on the waterfront were slower to eventuate, the employers harder to persuade. It was an employers' market.[11] Not until 1937, after many years of discussion and some dubiety on the part of the watersiders, was the bureau system of employment introduced. Under this system watersiders in the main ports were guaranteed a weekly minimum wage and the hours of work were equalised for the men as far as possible. All work was allocated by the bureau which was run by a board of control made up of four representatives from the union and four from the employers.[12] Years of agitation had resulted in the introduction into New Zealand of a system which removed much of the insecurity from waterfront work.

With the election of a Labour Government in November 1935 the watersiders turned their attention more to the political arena. They were quick to register their federation as an industrial union when such was permitted by the Industrial Conciliation and Arbitration Amendment Act of 1936, and the N.Z.W.W.U. warmly supported the introduction of Social Security in 1938. Some £4,000 was contributed to the Labour Party's election fund in 1938.[13] Yet the watersiders' endorsement of political action was never unequivocal. The editor of the *Transport Worker* warned members in May 1938 not to rely too much on political action for all improvements in social and economic welfare. He argued—and most watersiders agreed—that the trade union movement had a specific role to play under a Labour Government. It must act as a pressure group, indeed as the conscience, of the whole labour movement. Without a strong union movement, politicians, even Labour politicians, might grow soft on principles, but hard in their expediency.

Accordingly, the watersiders kept up their pressure for improvements on the waterfront and adopted a somewhat avuncular attitude towards the rest of the trade-union movement. Within their own industry they directed their attention to the Arbitration Court. Never happy with the principle of compulsory arbitration, the watersiders had consistently favoured direct negotiations with the employers. After 1926 when weaker unions rushed for protection to the Arbitration Court, the *Transport Worker* continued to urge its abolition.[14] The court, with its protection for the weak, had always seemed to be the guarantor of second-rate unionism. In the late thirties, as the Labour Government began to see in the court a useful method of controlling wages, the watersiders took up their old cause with renewed vigour.

Given the Government's determination to stabilise wages and prices after war broke out in September 1939 it was impossible for the Labour Government to free the N.Z.W.W.U. from compulsory arbitration. Had the watersiders been able to secure higher wages through direct negotiations with the shipowners other unions would have followed their example. Inflation might soon get out of hand. After much pressure, however, Fraser's Government did give the watersiders their own controlling body in 1940—the Waterfront Control Commission.[15] This body, consisting of three members appointed by the Minister of Labour, maintained the principle of compulsory arbitration; but it also guaranteed speedy action on all disputes between watersiders and their employers.

The union's gain was small, the legacy of discontent considerable. Although the watersiders co-operated in the war effort there was no great enthusiasm for increasing the speed of turn-round of ships, and the practice of "spelling" increased.[16] Clearly the incentives necessary to achieve greater effort on the waterfront were not being provided. They were absent, so the union argued, because the Government placed too much emphasis on economic stabilisation. At first the *Transport Worker* was dubious about stabilisation. It was believed to be "absurd", and impossible to achieve—yet perhaps it was better than nothing.[17] By the end of 1943 earlier doubts were vanishing: "it is safe to say that stabilisation has inflicted greater hardships on . . . workers than they would have suffered otherwise", commented the *Transport Worker*.[18]

Underlying suspicion turned to open hostility as the country began to relax in 1944 and 1945. In 1944 the watersiders elected the thirty-six-year-old Auckland branch president, Harold (Jock) Barnes, to the presidency of the N.Z.W.W.U. Barnes was a large man, and above average in ability. He was also ambitious. He had had a better education than most watersiders, having had several years' secondary schooling at Mount Albert Grammar School. He had also attended some lectures at Auckland University College and was a qualified draughtsman. Moreover, he possessed considerable ability as an orator—his critics preferred to label it demagoguery. What made him dangerous so far as the Labour Government was concerned was the fact that he possessed a personal grievance: his plea for reinstatement to the Public Service after dismissal in 1932 had fallen on deaf ears.[19] In his dealings with members of Cabinet Barnes' language was extreme. He always acted like a man seeking retribution.

The N.Z.W.W.U. was waiting for a militant leader; Barnes was looking for a platform. Before long he was articulating watersiders' grievances with a ferocity that could not be ignored. The Labour Government was his principal target. In October 1944 he stated:

> It is a disgrace to our country that bad conditions and low pay are stabilised by regulations and imprisonment in the manner in which they are today . . . .
> It is not in the workers' interest to continue the Manpower and Stabilisation Regulations . . . . It is the duty of the organised trade-union movement to agitate accordingly.[20]

And in case the Government was not receiving the message, Barnes told his listeners that strikes and go-slows would be used to pressure Fraser's Government into improving workers' conditions.[21]

It would be unfair to Barnes to imply that he was motivated simply by a desire for personal revenge. In fact he had long been a member—albeit a critical one—of the Labour Party. He considered himself a socialist, and he believed that the labour movement had an important role to play in fighting for a socialist New Zealand. Other watersiders' leaders, particularly Toby Hill, the young national secretary of the N.Z.W.W.U. and a loyal supporter of Barnes, shared these beliefs. The unions were to be more than just a ginger group working for better wages and conditions: they were to be the very conscience of the labour movement on domestic and even international affairs. When in July 1946 the Government announced that the export of ten million pounds of butter would be diverted from the United Kingdom to the United States, Hill demanded a full explanation in the name of the watersiders' executive. "If it is not forthcoming," he added, "they [the watersiders] may be compelled to take the action they took at a vital stage in the country's history some years ago when they refused to handle scrap iron for Japan". With no apparent humility Hill added: "The future may shape events in such a way as to throw on to the shoulders of the watersiders the responsibility of determining the destiny of our primary products in this world of chaos."[22] Clearly the watersiders expected that the union movement would be consulted on matters, international as well as domestic.

The N.Z.W.W.U. was much the most vocal union in the post-war years. But it was not without support within the labour movement. The watersiders had friends among the miners, among freezing workers, drivers, carpenters, tramways unions and general labourers. The unions covering these occupations all had fairly militant pasts. One or two, like the New Zealand Carpenters' Union, the Auckland General Labourers' Union, and the miners' unions, were fairly strongly influenced by representatives of the small New Zealand Communist Party. Like the watersiders, all these other unionists were anxious to hear the Labour Government announce bold, new plans for post-war reform.[23] In varying degrees these unions also had misgivings about Fraser's foreign policy which was moving away from pre-war Labour support for independence movements towards a close alliance with the United States.

In effect, a left-wing bloc was emerging within New Zealand's trade union movement. Members of it hoped to capture the Federation of Labour which they saw as having a special role to play in the crusade for a more egalitarian New Zealand. The F.O.L. should be the initiator of radical policy, the brains of the labour movement as well as the final arbiter if Labour politicians failed to carry out instructions.

Domestic considerations rather than foreign policy bulked large in discussions amongst these unions. Like the watersiders, all the left-inclined unions were critical of the Government's policy of stabilisation and of one of the instruments of that policy, the Arbitration Court. They wished to escape from its lengthy and sometimes unsatisfactory deliberations on wages and conditions of work. From direct confrontations with their employers they knew they could wring more substantial concessions. Early in 1947 the Carpenters' Union issued a statement which criticised the Court.[24] Similar criticism was implicit in a statement made by the Ngahauranga Branch of the New Zealand Freezing Workers' Union which talked of the need for "further action" if the Court did not grant the F.O.L.'s current wage claim in full.[25] The Huntly miners were developing a habit of acting first and answering questions later. Just before Easter 1947 they went on strike over a pay claim, thus drawing hostile criticism from the press and public because of the consequent disruption of holiday railway schedules.

While the F.O.L. did make more militant noises because of pressure from the left it was careful not to sanction illegal strike action or threats of strikes. The F.O.L. and the Labour Party, many of whose members had been strong opponents of compulsory arbitration in earlier times, now officially endorsed the system. With a Labour Government in power and watching over workers' interests strikes were held to be unnecessary. Powerful people subscribed to this theory. Fraser, "Bob" Semple (Minister of Works), and Angus McLagan (Minister of Labour), from the political wing of the labour movement were all veterans from the picket lines who believed that direct action was now an outmoded form of protest. They lost no opportunity to propound this theory, and frequently warned that to pursue strike action was to play into the hands of Labour's enemies.

However, it was the support from the industrial wing of the labour movement that gave the Government's policy such strength. During and after World War II the leadership of the two wings of the labour movement co-operated as never before or since. Fraser owed his accession to the Prime Ministership in 1940 at least partly to the support which he had received from F.O.L. leaders such as McLagan, J. Roberts and F.P. Walsh, while Walsh, who dominated the moderates in the F.O.L. after McLagan's entry to Parliament in 1946, owed some of the personal fortune he was acquiring to information gleaned through his close contacts with Labour politicians as well as through his position on the Economic Stabilisation Committee and the committee that fixed prices paid to primary producers.[26]

The political and private fortunes of labour leaders required a continuation of the *status quo*. Walsh argued for this with all the considerable oratorical and manipulative skills at his command. His report presented to the F.O.L. in 1946 advocated a continuation of stabilisation as post-war Government policy. It was endorsed by a majority vote of the F.O.L. and widely praised in the conservative press.

Unions that were more distant from the corridors of power and less satisfied with the *status quo* quickly singled out Walsh as their main target of attack. At the 1947 conference of the F.O.L. they succeeded in defeating him for the vice-presidency of the F.O.L. by one vote, electing W.B. Richards of the Dunedin Tramways Union in his place. Victory was short-lived. With intensive organisation and the scarcely-disguised support of the Government, Walsh turned the tables in 1948. Although only elected to the vice-presidency, (he became president in 1953) the "Old Pro" dominated the F.O.L. His endorsement of the principle of compulsory arbitration remained Federation policy into the 1950s; his lengthy justifications of stabilisation in the late 1940s regularly met with approval in spite of heated criticism from the militants. Walsh's victories, assured as they were by his domination of the Seamen's Union and the Clerical Workers' Union with its massive voting strength, and by his willingness to resort to underhand tactics when lobbying for other votes, did nothing to increase his mana with the militants. They scorned the unionists who provided his power base and detested his tactics. Federation conferences were becoming pitched battles, yet the outcome in favour of moderation was seldom in doubt.

The Government

So long as the watersiders and their allies failed to win within the F.O.L. they made little headway with the Labour Government. As early as 1937 the Government had warned the watersiders not to rock the boat. Their persistence in doing so after the war evoked a firmer response. During 1946, with an election in the offing, Labour Ministers were conciliatory, at least in public. While the principle of compulsory arbitration was stoutly maintained, the Government allowed the Waterfront Control Commission to be reorganised. A new Waterfront Industry Commission with two representatives each from the union and the employers was established under the chairmanship of Judge F.W. Ongley. In August the new commission announced pay increases for watersiders. Holiday pay, meal money and higher rates for Saturday work were also provided.[27] The Government feigned not to hear the watersiders' strong words about the butter deal with the United States. Instead Fraser appealed to all workers to adjust their grievances and to work for a Labour victory.[28]

Once Labour had been returned to power, albeit with a shaky majority of four,[29] the gloves were removed. At the end of November 1946 the watersiders provoked the Government with an overtime ban and a series of tough statements criticising a wages decision and the failure to grant a guaranteed attendance payment to watersiders by the Waterfront Industry Commission.[30] At the root of the trouble was the Government's insistence on the principle of compulsory arbitration for the settlement of workers' grievances. Fraser felt he had no option but to accept the challenge. From the High Commissions in London and Canberra came cables expressing the concern of the Australian and British Governments at the delays while ships were in New Zealand waters, and he was under heavy pressure from the National Party and its supporters among the press and the farming community, who were beginning to assert that government by Labour was tantamount to government by watersider.[31] On 19 December 1946 the new Minister of Labour, Angus McLagan, temporarily assumed control of New Zealand's waterfront, and the following day Fraser informed Barnes that, if normal work were not resumed, the Government would consider abandoning commission control on the waterfront. A series of confrontations between watersiders and Government leaders took place in Wellington.[32] The F.O.L. gave the Government its backing and the watersiders decided, after protracted negotiations with Fraser and McLagan, to return to normal hours of work on 19 January 1947. The question of guaranteed attendance money was re-submitted to the W.I.C., which again rejected it. McLagan then removed Judge Ongley from office as a sop to the watersiders, and lengthy negotiations began over the precise form of a new commission system of control. The Government never wavered from its determination to maintain as chairman a reliable arbitrator with voting powers. In fact the watersiders gained little from the 1946 holdup, while personal animosities between Cabinet and the militants were immeasurably hardened.

Fraser's hostility to militancy grew during 1947. He was conscious of the Labour Party's ebbing strength in the constituencies: branch membership was declining rapidly.[33] The only hope for a continuation of a Labour Government seemed to lie in chasing the support of those middle income groups who were believed to be tiring of Labour. Such support had a price tag: Fraser had to prove that his party was not the plaything of militant unions. This he was increasingly prepared to do.

As 1947 wore on and disputes continued it became clear that the Government's aim was to isolate the watersiders—if possible, just their leaders—from the rest of the trade-union movement. Barnes and Hill were singled out for attack, the Government claiming that they were trying to "wreck" the economy, or in the Prime Minister's words, "threaten the whole fabric of social justice".[34] Semple, the former "Red Fed", and McLagan, the former president of the F.O.L.,[35] were the principal hatchet men. When in April 1947 the watersiders' leaders came again to put their case for reorganisation of the W.I.C. into a body dominated by the union, McLagan refused to entertain the notion. He would not agree that a stenographer be allowed to record the conversation, and showed the watersiders the door after they had denounced the Minister for "Star Chamber" methods.[36] Semple was even more blunt. Never reluctant to speak his mind, he quickly singled out Barnes for attack. At the Labour Party conference in June 1947 he referred to "Mr Barnes and his 'ratbags'", and discussed in some detail his views about the watersiders' leaders.[37] Some days later he issued a lengthy statement:

> Mr Barnes is a wrecker. He is ambitious for personal power. Because of his position as president of a powerful union, because he has adopted the mantle of a protagonist for the worker and of trade unionism, and because he is able to sell his story, he constitutes

a real threat to the industrial peace and general welfare of the people of this country.

Mr Barnes and a small coterie are seeking to dominate not only the Government, but the whole country. They are determining what we shall export and to which countries our exports may go, and their overall authority would doubtless extend to imports. Such a threat would be cause for amusement if it were not so serious.[38]

While many New Zealanders agreed with Semple, giving vent to such opinions only made matters worse. Barnes accused Semple of making slanderous statements, and the Auckland Trades Council passed a resolution requesting that Ministers cease attacking the watersiders, and suggesting that Semple stick to matters of direct concern to his portfolio.[39]

Later in 1947 the Government announced its intention of amending the IC & A Act so as to make the holding of a ballot compulsory before any strike action could be entered upon—a measure which it was hoped would make it more difficult for militant leaders to use the power of their unions.[40] But Government members discovered that the militants possessed more friends than was expected. The National Council of the F.O.L., which was made up of representatives from the district trades councils and which had a more militant bias than the Wellington-dominated national executive of the F.O.L., immediately protested[41] and recommended that all unionists oppose the compulsory strike ballot.[42] Other aspects of the Bill were also criticised by the F.O.L.[43] Clearly the Government's attempt to isolate the watersiders and their leaders had not been an unqualified success. The Labour Government was in danger of falling into disfavour with a number of unions, many of which had little sympathy for the outright belligerence of Barnes and Hill.

However, what Government members had been unable to do on their own in 1947 the deteriorating international situation helped them achieve in 1948 and 1949. As the Cold War grew colder, the rift between moderate labour and the extreme left became deeper, and the N.Z.W.W.U. found that its most vocal support came from the Communist Party which was intent on denouncing Labour Governments whenever they took an anti-

Soviet line in international affairs. The policies of unions which contained a strong Communist element, such as the carpenters, and of the watersiders who were militant for their own reasons, seemed to be running closely together. And it was too much for the Government to refrain from implying that all were treasonous in intent. At the F.O.L. conference in April 1948 and at the Labour Party conference in May, both Fraser and McLagan attacked the Communist Party and the carpenters who had recently been involved in a "go slow", with terms of abuse previously reserved solely for the watersiders. There were few who could doubt that in the attacks on the carpenters the Government was sideswiping all militants. All were depicted as threats to Labour's policy of stabilisation and social welfare.[44]

While such attacks did impress moderate unionists, a strong sense of impending martyrdom seemed only to solidify the rank and file of the watersiders behind Barnes and Hill. There were always a few dissidents within the union led principally by Noel Donaldson, a prominent Auckland watersider. But the overwhelming majority of watersiders backed the leadership. When the *Mountpark* dispute developed in Auckland, first in February and then again in May 1948, the watersiders strongly backed their leaders' actions in the face of hostile statements from Government members. The dispute was over the union's refusal to lift manually the hatches on the "Liberty" class ships.[45] The union demanded that slings be used. On 24 June the W.I.C., with encouragement from McLagan, declared the *Mountpark* to be a "preference" ship, which meant that, since it was declared to be carrying cargo "necessary to the life of the community", no labour was to be engaged for any other ship until the *Mountpark's* requirements were satisfied.

Barnes and Hill immediately took offence. Alleging that the W.I.C. had lost all semblance of independence and had simply become a tool of the Minister of Labour, the union withdrew its representatives from the W.I.C., thus rendering the body inoperable.[46] The shipowners regarded the refusal to lift the hatches as a contravention of the Waterfront Industry Agreement and placed those men concerned on a three-day penalty. As a result the dispute spread beyond the *Mountpark* and by

19 July only one quarter of the watersiders in Auckland were employed. Farmers, Chambers of Commerce and newspapers united in pressing the Government for tough action against the union.[47]

Between the end of May and the early part of July the dispute seemed to drift along. The watersiders consulted their fellow members of the New Zealand Transport Workers' Federation, a loose grouping of unions employed in the transport field, seeking support in case the Government should bow to pressure and take strong action against the union. Some £2,000 was transferred from the N.Z.W.W.U. strike fund to the Auckland union and there was every indication by July that the watersiders were solid, and prepared for any eventuality.

Fraser and McLagan traded abuse with Barnes and Hill. McLagan was labelled a "dictator" by Barnes; Fraser implied that Barnes and Hill were under Communist direction, and appealed for a strong stand by the public against the watersiders' illegal action in refusing to man the *Mountpark*. Early in July one observer reported that "a state of war" existed between the N.Z.W.W.U. and the Government.[48]

While Fraser probably threatened to use the ultimate weapons of union deregistration and emergency powers he was reluctant actually to apply them: the reaction of the labour movement to such measures was incalculable. Instead the Government revived an earlier offer to set up a special tribunal under the Strike and Lockout Emergency Regulations (1939) with a Supreme Court judge to adjudicate on the question of the *Mountpark's* hatches. Finally, after more stormy sessions between Barnes, Hill, McLagan and Fraser, the union's terms of reference for the tribunal were met in large part.[49] By the middle of July work was back to normal again.

The Government made one further attempt to reform procedures on the waterfront. In October 1948 the administrative and judicial functions of the W.I.C. were separated. The W.I.C.'s powers were limited to purely administrative matters and a new judicial body, the Waterfront Industry Authority, which was a final court of appeal and in theory completely independent and subject to no outside influence, was established. By separating administrative and judicial questions the Government hoped to answer the watersiders' complaint that during the *Mountpark* dispute the W.I.C. had been judge in its own case.

Once again peace had been bought at a high price. Barnes and Hill remained at the head of the strongest union in the country and there was no guarantee that further disputes would not develop. Among the watersiders and their allies criticism of the principle of compulsory arbitration of labour disputes remained as strong as ever. The whole future of stabilisation was still in jeopardy. Moreover, Labour's enemies were quick to make capital out of the *Mountpark* dispute and its method of settlement. The National Party lost no opportunity to criticise, and some newspapers savagely denounced the Government. The *Otago Daily Times,* never one of Labour's closer friends, called the settlement "a contemptible exhibition of weakness in [Labour's] often inglorious history".[50]

Smarting from such criticism, Government Ministers were determined that there would be no repeat performance, especially in election year. The police began close surveillance of activities on the nation's waterfronts. Meantime, employers were quick to sense this resolve and increasingly acted as though they welcomed the prospect of confrontation with the militants. When in February 1949 the Auckland branch of the Carpenters' Union decided on a "glow-slow" policy following the award of a minor pay increase by the Arbitration Court and an alteration in carpenters' transport allowances, the Auckland Master Builders' Association, with backing from other employers in the area, dismissed some 2,000 carpenters. The Government was quite hostile to the actions of the carpenters in flouting their promise to abide by the decisions of the Arbitration Court. McLagan refused to set up a tribunal to consider the issue, and when the Carpenters' Union would not hand over the dispute to the national executive of the F.O.L., he announced the deregistration of the Auckland section of the union from under the IC & A Act.[51]

The watersiders were closely involved in the carpenters' dispute. They had recently received a pay rise from the W.I.A.

that was only 20 per cent of what had been demanded, and they felt they had good cause to support their allies whose fight was seen as their fight. By stop-work meetings, and by refusing to handle goods for firms in the Auckland area which were co-operating with the Master Builders, the watersiders did their bit to expand the dispute. The Government was well aware of the watersiders' involvement, and in ministerial statements there were several indications that the Government felt the fight against the carpenters to be a fight against the N.Z.W.W.U. as well. McLagan made references to holdups on the waterfront, and on 1 April he threatened to remove commission control if the watersiders did not abide by their pledge to accept the rulings of the W.I.C. and W.I.A. It was the old story, but with the Government now prepared, if necessary, to see that the denouement was different.

The Labour Government Falls

The carpenters' dispute fizzled out. On 26 May, as soon as 50 per cent of the Auckland members of the old union had joined a new Auckland Carpenters' (fifty-six mile radius) Union set up by moderates who were opposed to their leaders' radicalism, McLagan allowed it to be registered under the IC & A Act.[52] The building industry in Auckland slowly returned to normal. But the dispute broke what friendship might still have existed between the militants and Labour's leaders. It was expected of conservatives that they might use the power of the state against militant unions. For a Labour Government such action seemed unforgivable. What was most galling to the watersiders in particular was the more aggressive attitude which the employers were adopting now that the Government was prepared to hit hard at the unions.[53] In February 1949 not only the employers' representatives (K. A. Belford and T. A. Marchington) on the W.I.A., but also the chairman, Judge D. J. Dalglish, pursued a tougher line with the watersiders. They made it clear to the N.Z.W.W.U. that it could expect from the W.I.A. no greater wage rises than those currently being considered by the Arbitration Court. Since the W.I.A. in theory was meant to be an independent authority, subject to no outside influence, such a statement seemed calculated to bring on a storm of protest from Barnes and Hill. Before the Arbitration Court had made its decision on the F.O.L.'s claim for a wage rise, the watersiders, who had devoted some care to arguing their own case in front of the W.I.A., were being told in effect that they had wasted their time. Barnes reacted in a characteristically extravagant manner. In press statements and in two pamphlets distributed to the watersiders, he alleged that the W.I.A. was meekly submitting to ministerial dictation, and that the employers' representatives were deliberately provoking the union.[54]

On 4 April 1949 the W.I.A. went into recess after a stormy meeting at which the employers' representatives and Judge Dalglish voted together.[55] When the authority met later it was only to indulge in further recriminations. By the end of June, commission control was still not functioning normally, so the union decided to restrict overtime work at Auckland. Immediately McLagan pounced; the powers of the W.I.C. and W.I.A. were officially suspended so far as they applied to Auckland.[56]

The situation rapidly deteriorated. Other major ports became involved in the overtime ban as the union continued to demand not only a return to commission control in Auckland but wage increases as well.[57] McLagan responded accordingly. On 19 July commission control was removed from all those ports where the overtime ban was in operation, and he gave those local ports still not involved in the ban the choice of dissociating themselves from it or losing the benefits of commission control. The dispute lingered on until 10 August when the Auckland Shipping and Stevedores' Association decided to dismiss all workers on the waterfront unless they would agree to work overtime. The union, believing that the Government had encouraged the shipowners to raise the ante,[58] decided to raise its own demands. A ten-point programme including an assurance that there would be no future ministerial interference with the functioning of the W.I.A. was demanded for a settlement. By 13 August the Auckland waterfront was idle and the pickets were out.

With election time approaching, the Government could not

afford a repetition of the *Mountpark* dispute. The shipowners were adamant and refused to negotiate with the watersiders until they withdrew their overtime ban. And when the union's leaders met the Prime Minister on 18 August Fraser told them that the Government was also determined to take no part in any discussion until normal work was resumed.[59] This time, clearly, the Government was going to stand firm. It could not afford the charge of truckling to the militants. Gone were the honeyed words of mid-1946. As a result the N.Z.W.W.U. decided to back down. Normal working hours were resumed on 19 August.[60] For the union it was defeat, one that became more humiliating when McLagan removed Barnes and Hill from the W.I.A. early in September and demanded that the watersiders hold a ballot among themselves to see whether they wished to have commission control continued.

Industrially the watersiders had come to the end of the road with the Labour Party. By the end of 1949 McLagan was determined to destroy Barnes and Hill should they persist with further stoppages. Politically the militants were not much more successful. Barnes played a major part in the campaign of opposition to peacetime conscription which the Government introduced in 1949.[61] In the referendum on 3 August the opponents of conscription were defeated by three to one. But they did have the satisfaction of seeing the largest "no" votes rolled up in Labour Party strongholds. Fraser's victory was a Pyrrhic one; the labour movement was severely shaken by the referendum.[62] By September both the N.Z.W.W.U. and the Northern Drivers' Union were contemplating disaffiliation from the Labour Party. In Auckland, Barnes' disillusionment with Labour was such that he supported B.H. Kingston, the National Candidate for Ponsonby, in the 1949 election.[63] And the most enthusiasm that Toby Hill could muster for Labour was lukewarm endorsement: "Labour is us and the Labour Government with all its imperfections is our Government."[64]

At the end of November 1949 Fraser's Government was edged out of power. Although some Labour stalwarts believed it to be so, it would be an exaggeration to say that the militants were the cause of Labour's defeat. By 1949 dissatisfaction with the Government's administration of controls was widespread, and diverse sectional groups were clamouring for de-control. But unions such as the watersiders' with their continued hold-ups did undoubtedly provide Labour's opponents with a steady target for attack. National Party leaders made ever more frequent references to the problem of industrial unrest as the campaign progressed, finding that promises of toughness met with public approval. Only a few observers seemed to realise what such promises might mean. Miss Mabel Howard, the Minister of Health, was one. She told an election meeting that, in her opinion, the election of a National Government would lead to a strike that would make the upheaval of 1913 "look like a Sunday school picnic".[65]

CHAPTER II

NATIONAL PARTY ATTITUDES

In Opposition the National Party had certainly given vent to some fierce invective against militant unionists. Never kindly disposed towards the trade union movement as a whole, the party showed increasing concern at the rise in the number of serious industrial disputes after the war. Moreover the National Party's close association with the interests of farmers and employers made its members even less sympathetic to rapid increases in wages than was the Labour Government. Since there was an inflationary tendency within the post-war economy the National Party came to place special store by the Arbitration Court which was acting as a brake on unrestricted wage rises. Hostility to the watersiders who posed the most direct threat to the system of arbitration was natural enough; the cries for enforcement of the law against arbitrationist unions that used the strike weapon was no more than could have been expected. But there was more to National's militancy than just wages. In the first place, it was widely claimed in farming and employing circles that there had been a costly deterioration in the standard of work on the waterfront since the war. Practices such as "spelling" seemed to have increased, and the turn-round of ships in New Zealand was often claimed to be amongst the slowest in the world, although proof of this was never forthcoming.

More important for the National Party was the happy coincidence between financial interest and political profit. As the post-war years moved on, members of the National Party increasingly realised that their party had nothing to lose by fastening attention on the actions of militant unionists. Public opinion was turning against the militants, and especially the watersiders. Even fellow trade unionists had good cause to suspect that the watersiders were greatly exaggerating their grievances; wages for waterfront work were, for the most part, every bit as good or better than those operating for the most skilled workers in industry. Moreover, relatively few workers in other industries were prepared to pursue left-wing social and foreign policy goals with the same zeal shown by the N.Z.W.W.U. As in other parts of the world, post-war conditions were breeding an interest in stability rather than rapid social change. The watersiders seemed increasingly out of step with the national trend.

The press was not reluctant to help in the campaign to isolate the militants. No major daily newspaper in the post-war years made more than a passing attempt to understand the peculiar conditions on the waterfront that gave rise to militancy. And all papers were quick to condemn direct action whenever it was used. Feature stories dealing with the waterfront were not uncommon, and they always dealt with the real or imagined iniquities of the union. The affairs of the shipowners, traditionally the toughest employers throughout the world, were never scrutinised. Even cartoonists, notably Minhinnick for the *New Zealand Herald*, played a part in the campaign against the N.Z.W.W.U. and its allies. In seizing on the militants for political ends, the National Party incurred negligible risks.

At first the National Party's statements about industrial problems were confined to generalities—the law must be upheld.[1] But as party leaders began to realise the political potential of the issue there was more talk about the need for tougher penalties against militants who broke pledges and pursued strike action.[2] Moreover, like Fraser, Nationalists were quick to talk about militants and Communists in the same breath. Sidney Holland, their leader, could make it all sound extremely subversive.

Holland was an uneducated man who, unlike Fraser, had taken few steps to remedy the problem. He had risen to the leadership of the National Party at a time when it desperately needed a younger, post-depression image yet possessed none besides Holland who could provide it. Nevertheless, Holland built up a reputation as a most effective leader in opposition.[3]

2. The National Cabinet which assumed office on 13 December 1949. Front row, from *left:* Webb, Broadfoot, Holyoake, Holland, Sullivan, Bowden, Doidge. Back row from *left:* Bodkin, Goosman, Macdonald, Corbett, Algie, Watts.
(Auckland Star)

He spoke bluntly in a harsh voice; what he lacked in profundity he made up for by exaggeration and repetition. Gradually his theme emerged in the late forties: Labour was socialist; socialists and Communists had much in common; ergo, Labour's leaders, despite Fraser's protestations, were soft on Communism. Hadn't Walter Nash once made some approving comments about the Soviet economy?[4] Today's reader would find Holland's speeches crude. But in the cold war environment of the late forties they undoubtedly were effective.

From Holland's utterances on industrial matters it became clear that the problem was more easily stated than solved. His promises while in opposition were seldom more than vague. In the middle of 1949 Holland did say he would "take firm and resolute action against Communism". Echoing his opposite number in Australia, Robert Menzies, he added: "It must be rooted out and swept away, and it will be declared a subversive organisation." In spite of this promise he went on to add that his party would not use a policy of force in solving labour disputes. Instead, the Department of Labour would be given wider powers to deal with disputes.[5] Later, in the course of the election campaign, Holland promised that National would deal with the question of compulsory unionism, so widely believed in party circles to be contributing to the strength of the trade union movement. Special ballots would be held among unionists to find out whether they wished the system of compulsory unionism to remain.[6]

During the election campaign of 1949 other Nationalists were more blunt. William Sullivan, who was to become Minister of Labour in the first National Government, sounded quite menacing when he was quoted as saying that if the penalties against strikes were found to be inadequate, National would increase them:

> We must stop this law breaking and anarchy on the part of the Communists .... We will not put up with any hanky-panky from these gentlemen. If they are not prepared to do their job, it is up to the Government to see they do.[7]

This big, bluff builder from Whakatane, with the deep resonant voice, a man who had been, and was yet to be, a challenger for the leadership of the National Party, commanded respect on the campaign stump. More shrewd than his leader, and better liked by civil servants with whom he was to have dealings, Sullivan was emerging as the National Party's authority on industrial relations. At the end of 1949 it seemed as though there were troubled times ahead.

The Honeymoon 1950

However, the recklessness of the campaign platform quickly gave way to the caution of office. The National Party had good reason to move carefully against the militants. Sober reflection on the outcome of the election indicated that National had won key votes in marginal electorates among workers who were no longer convinced that a conservative government would mean a return to lower living standards. It would be foolish for the National Government immediately to betray this trust by launching an attack on militants that might succeed only in reuniting Labour's badly splintered ranks. Moreover, there was probably a suspicion (misguided, as it turned out) among National leaders that much of the industrial unrest had been due either to personal antagonisms between Barnes and McLagan or simply to ministerial ineptitude. Either way it seemed worthwhile for the genial Sullivan, the new Minister of Labour, to tender the olive branch to the militants.[8]

The watersiders, for their part, had little cause to reject it. Campaign utterances aside, at least some of the personnel in the National Party seemed to Barnes to be moderately sensible on industrial matters. Hadn't Holland promised to review compulsory unionism, which, because of its exploitation by moderate union leaders had long been the bane of the militants? And besides, if it should be possible for Barnes and Hill to work with Sullivan there could be no more effective way of indicating to McLagan and Fraser that they had gone sour on the workers—so much so that even conservative ministers were preferable to them.[9]

However, the union felt it wise to take no risks. There had been a movement underway within the N.Z.W.W.U., partly sponsored by McLagan,[10] to have Barnes and Hill replaced with more moderate leaders. The victory of the National Party made such a move seem both unwise and unnecessary. At the national conference of the union held early in December 1949 all the other nominees for president and secretary withdrew, and Barnes and Hill were re-elected unopposed. A few months later the National Executive of the N.Z.W.W.U. made the national presidency a full-time job. The union was solid—yet inclined to be friendly towards the new Government.[11]

In the middle of January 1950 a deputation from the N.Z.W.W.U. paid a "courtesy call" to Sullivan and there was "a general discussion on waterfront matters".[12] In April the Government decided to resist some strong pressure from the Port Employers for complete abolition of commission control on the waterfront.[13] Sullivan announced that the W.I.A., which had not been operating since Barnes and Hill had been removed from it the previous September, would be restored as soon as

3. William Sullivan, Minister of Labour 1949-57. *(Auckland Star)*

the watersiders had elected their delegates to it by secret ballot. Barnes promptly issued a statement praising the Minister.[14] And on 4 May Sullivan, to whom the watersiders seemed most cordial, made a tour of the Auckland waterfront with Barnes.[15] Relations could be seen to be on a friendly level from Holland's comment (was it a gloat?) at the end of April:

> Industrial relations have been good so far since the Government took office, and I wish to express my appreciation to those including Messrs Baxter, Walsh, Barnes and Hill and to the employers' representatives for helping in the promotion of industrial harmony.[16]

Political expediency was producing—temporarily—some strange allies.[17]

The F.O.L. and the T.U.C.

However, while the watersiders were mending their fences with Government, they were busy tearing them down with the Federation of Labour. Relationships between the F.O.L. and the watersiders had been at a low ebb for some years.

Since the strong criticisms that were thrown at the watersiders by the F.O.L. executive during the waterfront holdup of December 1946–January 1947,[18] and at the special conference of the F.O.L. in February 1947, Barnes and Hill had treated the leadership of the Federation with contempt. The watersiders had continued to lobby for left-wing candidates in Federation elections, but with decreasing success after the narrow victory of 1947,[19] and during 1948 the militants lost control of one of their major power bases, the Auckland Trades Council. The watersiders reacted to these setbacks by stepping up their criticisms of the Federation leaders while at the same time spending less effort lobbying for their removal. So long as compulsory unionism supplied moderate leaders with large paper majorities at Federation conferences the fight by the militants would always be an uneven struggle. Instead, Barnes spent more energy trying to build up the New Zealand Transport Workers' Federation. This organisation, which included not only the watersiders but also railwaymen, drivers and tramway workers, was a loose alliance of militants whose bargaining strength was implicit in the crucial importance to the country of the transport industry.

In the meantime, personal relations between right and left within the Federation became embittered. During 1947 and 1948 the watersiders' leaders made several statements suggesting that men such as Walsh and K.M. Baxter, the secretary of the F.O.L., were employers' men, or Government stooges, capable of the "scurviest tricks" against their fellow workers.[20] The carpenters' disputes in 1949 brought the war out into the open. When the Federation opposed the carpenters' "go slow", the watersiders took a leading part in setting up an "Action Committee" composed mainly of carpenters, drivers and watersiders, to assist the carpenters. This committee was designed to act in place of the F.O.L., which, in the militants' view, was failing to support *bona fide* unionists engaged in a just fight.

The F.O.L. executive strongly resented this challenge to its authority, and demanded that the dispute be handed over to the F.O.L., and published the letter containing this demand

before the carpenters had had time to consider it. The
N.Z.W.W.U. promptly dispatched a letter to the F.O.L. which
said, *inter alia*, that the publication of the letter to the carpenters was "a gross betrayal of the affiliated members of the
Federation of Labour and exposes the national executive of the
Federation of Labour as agents of the employing class".[21]
Such hostility towards the F.O.L. was intensified when at the
1949 conference of the F.O.L. Walsh displayed his cunning by
waiting until some of the militants had left for home before
having re-committed, and defeated, a resolution supporting
the de-registered carpenters.[22] Walsh meantime was on record
as having said that the watersiders were "not fit to associate
with other human beings and should not be allowed to travel
on trams, trains or ships with others."[23]

By the end of 1949 Barnes had ceased to value his union's
formal link with the F.O.L. All the militants' efforts to sway
the Federation had been thwarted by Walsh, and prospects of
victory within that body looked to be more remote than ever.
However, Barnes had no intention of dodging the spotlight
that could always focus on himself as a leader of the militants.
The watersiders and their closest allies would have to go it
alone. This was a decision fraught with danger. But Barnes, the
headstrong, was not the kind who shunned challenges. Nor
were his closest assistants within the N.Z.W.W.U. convinced
of the logic of militancy and of the power of their union to
press for reforms outside the Federation if necessary, the watersiders persistently ignored Federation policy when it differed
from their own. Resolutions of the F.O.L. were accepted only
when they coincided with the watersiders' views; the F.O.L.'s
majority decision to withdraw from the World Federation of
Trade Unions and to ally with its anti-Communist rival was
firmly rebuffed;[24] and to make matters worse, Barnes proclaimed early in the new year that the F.O.L. needed a cleanup: "If
you sleep with pigs you, too, will stink," he added.[25] Clearly
Barnes was getting ready for a parting of the ways.

It seems doubtful whether Barnes realised how eagerly Walsh
and his allies on the F.O.L. executive would accept the challenge.
Walsh was universally regarded at the time as one of the shrewd-

est and most unscrupulous of trade union leaders. Like Barnes, he was ambitious and wished to be the main—even the sole—voice for organised labour. He was anxious, therefore, to see the watersiders' influence within the trade union movement minimised. Once the election campaign was over and there could be no question of hurting the Labour Party, expelling them from the Federation seemed to him to be the best way of formalising the rift within the labour movement. Walsh calculated, no doubt, that the watersiders would, if expelled, carry only a small minority of unions out of the Federation with them. Any rival body set up in opposition to the Federation would therefore be weak, and bidding for support while an unfriendly government watched its every move. Whichever way Walsh and his allies looked at it, they had nothing to lose by pursuing a tough policy against the watersiders.

The initial steps leading to the rupture of 1950 had been taken by members of the Federation executive at the 1949 conference of the F.O.L. when they succeeded in passing a remit stressing the necessity for all sections of the union movement to act on majority decisions of the conference. Member unions were further given to understand that "any violation of majority decisions or disruption of this Federation will in future mean isolation for the disrupters".[26] A pretext for expulsion of the N.Z.W.W.U. was not, therefore, hard to find. On 19 January 1950 letters were sent to the N.Z.W.W.U. suggesting that they disaffiliate from the World Federation of Trade Unions in line with F.O.L. policy, and apologise for the abuse of federation officials at the time of the carpenters' dispute.

When the union refused to comply, a meeting of the National Executive of the F.O.L. on 26 January 1950 decided to issue an ultimatum to the watersiders: apologise for the "disruptive" letter and resign from the W.F.T.U. or they would be expelled from the F.O.L. as from 1 February 1950.[27] In the meantime Walsh was busy checking on Barnes' past, and assembling material to use against him at the F.O.L.'s Annual Conference.[28]

To many unions that were not necessarily close allies of the watersiders this action by the F.O.L.'s National Executive seemed to be not only unwise but also unconstitutional.[29] Baxter, the secretary of the F.O.L., claimed to nearly everyone's disbelief, that the F.O.L. was "actuated solely in the interests of genuine trade unionism". "The watersiders", he added, "are welcome to a place in the F.O.L.—united to carry on the good work—but not while their union pursues a policy of abuse, disruption and failure to conform to the general policy and democratic decisions of the Federation".[30] But the National Council of the F.O.L., meeting on 16 February, could not easily be convinced of the propriety of the executive's motives, and after a stormy session it decided that the matter of the future of the N.Z.W.W.U.'s relationship with the F.O.L. would be held over until the Federation's full conference in April.[31] Nevertheless, battle had been joined; both sides were busy enlisting their troops, and several union leaders who were sympathetic towards the watersiders in this fight, if not to the N.Z.W.W.U.'s general policy, issued a statement asserting that the Federation executive was "completely out of touch with the workers" and "ninety years behind the times".[32]

At the April conference the issue was a forgone conclusion. Walsh had a majority of moderates and could do with the watersiders what he wished. The watersiders found it difficult to get entry to the conference,[33] and were not prepared to wait for ultimate expulsion from the Federation. After gaining admission and testing the feeling of the conference, Hill made a long speech saying that the watersiders now felt they could rely on their own strength and no longer needed the F.O.L. In particular they did not share the F.O.L.'s support for compulsory conciliation and arbitration, and would do nothing to see that the Labour Party was returned to power.[34] On 18 April the N.Z.W.W.U.'s representatives, followed by sixty other delegates representing about 75,000 workers, withdrew from the conference.[35]

On the following day the breakaway group met on the ground floor of the Trades Hall in Wellington while the Federation continued in conference upstairs. A majority of militants wanted reconciliation. A deputation consisting of F. G. Young

4. Jock Barnes and Toby Hill pictured outside the Wellington Trades Hall on 18 April 1950, the day the watersiders walked out of the Federation of Labour.
(Auckland Star)

(New Zealand Hotel Workers' Union), S. Giles (New Zealand Freezing Workers' Federation) and J. Roberts (Canterbury Clothing Workers' Union) waited upon A.W. Croskery, Walsh and other members of the F.O.L.'s National Executive and suggested that, as a basis for unity, the F.O.L. withdraw its threat to the watersiders to expel them unless they apologised for their past behaviour and left the W.F.T.U.[36] But in Walsh and the other leaders of the F.O.L. the desire for unity was not strong. One observer reported that they were confident that the militants would be unable to form an effective organisation and would be forced to return to the F.O.L. on the Federation's terms.[37] They rejected the peace overtures and the militants had no alternative but to get down to the job of establishing the rival Trade Union Congress. This they promptly did. Provisional officers were elected,[38] a committee was established to draw up a constitution which would be submitted to a national conference, and the delegates subscribed £86-5-0 out of their own pockets to help defray initial organisational expenses. A statement was issued by the new body saying that the F.O.L. had "slammed the door on any hope of unity within the trade union movement, and delegates had no alternative but to proceed to set up an organisation that would work towards the principles of unity, freedom from political domination and the right of unions to handle their own business and affairs".[39] The meeting ended on a high note, the delegates returning to their branches with confidence in the future of the T.U.C.

But, as the militant leaders were to find, it was difficult to persuade rank and file unionists that a split in the labour movement was desirable. Walsh's policy of intransigence was soon paying dividends. When the militants began reporting back to their branches the troubles began. As was expected, the rank and file of the N.Z.W.W.U. endorsed their leaders' conduct at the recent conference. But other unions were much less enthusiastic about the split in the labour movement. The F.O.L. moved quickly to minimise the T.U.C.'s opportunities to make propaganda; pamphlets were rapidly circulated which put the Federation's[40] case against the militants; several press statements were made by Walsh and Baxter which warned unionists against allying with Communists;[41] and those militants who had taken office in the T.U.C.'s provisional committee were prevented from arguing their case before the district trades councils.

When the issue of disaffiliation came up for a vote within the unions[42] the militants received only tepid support. West Coast miners, bitter over the F.O.L.'s support for conscription and the Labour Government's hostility to the carpenters, were fairly solid in their endorsement of the new organisation.[43] Several branches of the Carpenters', Drivers' and Tramways Unions also threw in their support. But there were reservations. F. G. Young of the Hotel Workers' Federation was already cooling towards the T.U.C. by the beginning of May, and was critical of the T.U.C.'s pamphlet, "The £ Goes Further Down the Drain".[44] He survived a motion within his organisation to have him removed from office, but his continued survival depended on his having nothing to do with the T.U.C. until his union had voted on whether to disaffiliate from the F.O.L.[45] In due course the Hotel Workers' Union voted to remain in the F.O.L., and T.J. ("Pat") Potter of the Auckland Labourers' Union replaced Young as National Chairman of the T.U.C.[46]

Other unions such as the Auckland, Wellington and Dunedin Tramways Unions, the last in spite of the strong support given the T.U.C. by W.B. Richards, the Dunedin Tramways president, remained critical of the F.O.L., but more sceptical about its rival.[47] Only a handful of unions that had participated in the April walkout from the F.O.L. were active participants in the first full T.U.C. conference called in August 1950.[48] The watersiders and the New Zealand Carpenters' Union were the only national bodies sending delegates, the rest of the delegates representing branches of other national unions. The T.U.C. was beginning to look like an organisation of outcasts.

Ideologically, too, the new body was rather chaotic. To the watersiders, opposition to compulsory unionism and compulsory arbitration was important. Barnes pinned his hopes for victory against the F.O.L.'s leadership on the National Party's promise to remove compulsory unionism—a move which would have slashed away the paper strength that kept Walsh and his allies in command of the Federation—as Walsh and Baxter were uncomfortably aware.[49] But other unions were less clearly opposed to compulsory unionism and compulsory arbitration. Young denied that the T.U.C. wished to break up the arbitration system,[50] and John Roberts stressed that his opposition to the F.O.L. was due to resentment at its "bureaucratic control", and its "one-man, Wellington-inspired decisions".[51]

By the time the T.U.C. got around to formulating its programme in August the fact could no longer be disguised that the new body was little more than an adjunct of the N.Z.W.W.U. In the initial stages after the April walkout the watersiders had kept in the background. But as the early supporters fell by the

5. F.P. Walsh, vice-president of the F.O.L. 1948-53; president 1953-63. *(Auckland Star)*

wayside the watersiders were left in a position of dominance.[52] Nominal leadership of the T.U.C. remained in the hands of T. J. Potter of the Auckland Labourers' Union and A. B. Grant of the Christchurch Rubber Workers' Union. But it was the watersiders who were calling the tune as the August programme showed. The objectives included support for militancy of a "practical type", resisting the "domination by any political party", "socialisation of the means of production, distribution and exchange", and affiliation with "kindred organisations" in other countries.[53] At a moment when it was demonstrably clear that the overwhelming mass of unionists were sceptical about the advantages of militancy, and well aware of its dangers, the T.U.C. was intent on planning something little short of a revolution. By walking out of the F.O.L. the watersiders had isolated themselves more effectively in four months than their opponents combined had succeeded in doing in four years.

Back to a Harsh Reality

The watersiders did more than just isolate themselves from the trade-union movement when they withdrew from the F.O.L. and had a hand in setting up the ill-fated T.U.C. They quickly shattered the rather tenuous friendship which they had with the National Government. In order to prove its attractiveness to workers still within the F.O.L., the T.U.C. had to demonstrate that "practical militancy" produced quick results. Consequently, when the National Government lifted food subsidies on 8 May 1950, increased rail fares and petrol prices, and lifted price control on cakes and groceries—measures which resulted in an immediate rise in the cost of living—the T.U.C.'s unions felt obliged to take the lead in demonstrating hostility to such measures.

In Auckland the watersiders held a stop-work meeting on 9 May and instructed their national leaders to go ahead with a claim for a wage rise of an extra 2/- per hour. A new round of stoppages over wages and conditions on the waterfront began. Work on the *King Neptune* ceased on 9 May over union demands for larger gangs to move its cement cargo. Sullivan acted quickly and set up a special tribunal to hear the case. Work returned to normal.[54] But on 8 June work on the *Myrtlebank* in Wellington ceased when the watersiders demanded additional money and clothing to handle the ship's dirty cargo of lampblack.[55] The W.I.C., on the port employers' application, declared the *Myrtlebank* a preference ship. The watersiders refused to accept this coercion by the W.I.C., and Barnes arrogantly announced that this was the last declaration of preference which the watersiders would tolerate.[56] Despite this threat the men were placed on penalty and by the 19th the Wellington waterfront was at a standstill. The National Government's peaceful few months of industrial relations were over. The watersiders were back to the old game.

The Government was clearly concerned at the serious deterioration of conditions on the waterfront. Sullivan stressed that he expected the decisions of a properly constituted body—in this case the W.I.C., so recently restored to full operation—to be accepted by both employers and employees. However, it was clear that there was some public sympathy for the watersiders in view of the particularly obnoxious cargo they were being expected to handle.[57] Sullivan decided to play safe. He intervened in the dispute and persuaded the W.I.C. to recommend to the W.I.A. that the union's claim for extra money be accepted.[58] Work returned to normal immediately while the W.I.A. considered the matter; militancy seemed to have been rewarded, the object of the exercise attained.

But Sullivan had gone out on a limb in order to retain industrial harmony. It is doubtful whether he could have carried Cabinet with him had he tried such a settlement many more times. The port employers issued a statement deploring the method of settlement of the dispute.[59] This time a Minister from a party which they thought was friendly to employers' interests seemed to be interfering with the W.I.C. on behalf of their opponents. And to cap it all, McLagan decided to make capital out of the dispute:

> The Minister [Sullivan] is running away from an industrial scrap. His own supporters say he is running away. The employers say he is running away. The public say he is running away, and it is idle for him to deny it, because his shoes are still hot; they are still smoking.[60]

A party which had come to power pledged to introduce a new policy for industrial relations could not put up with too much more of this.

The National Government's waterfront worries increased during July 1950. On 5 July the W.I.A. announced that, instead of awarding the watersiders the extra 2/- an hour as requested, it would award only 3d an hour, a rise that was commensurate with the "interim" award to other workers by the Arbitration Court. Militancy which had so recently produced fringe benefits for the watersiders was now shown to be unproductive on the basic issue of hourly rates. There was an immediate outcry from the N.Z.W.W.U. against commission control which had only recently been returned to the waterfront.[61] The system had failed to produce higher wages under a Labour Government, and a change of Government, it seemed, had not improved matters. The union abruptly announced

6. S.G. Holland, National's Prime Minister 1949-57. *(Auckland Star)*

that it wanted the W.I.A. abolished; in its place the men desired a system of direct negotiation between employer and employee.[62] It was the old cry of earlier days; only if the principle of arbitration were removed, if the system which provided a buffer between workers and management were eliminated, could the union effectively use its massive industrial strength. It was unlikely to receive more than a polite hearing from a National Government.

The National Government had done much to encourage inflation during 1950. The removal of subsidies and the lifting of price controls at a time when the international situation—specifically the Korean War—was generating very high demand for wool, meant that prices were rocketing upwards by the middle of the year. To have provided conditions whereby the strongest union in the country could improve its wage rates through direct negotiation would only have added to the inflationary pressures on the economy. And almost certainly other unions would have argued that wage parity with the watersiders should be retained. To have bowed to the watersiders' request for direct bargaining would have opened up a Pandora's box of problems for the Government. More important for the Government was the belief shared by its members that the watersiders were already receiving a more than generous reward for work performed. The Parliamentary debates at this time were peppered with assertions by National Party spokesmen that workers were not working hard enough, and that the forty-hour week was one of the major obstacles to more rapid industrial progress. Even had the danger of inflation not been so great, it is doubtful whether, for ideological reasons, a National Government could have contemplated the watersiders' demands. There were not many aspects of stabilisation that Nationalists believed in implicitly; control of wages, however, was one.

The Government's resolve to enforce the law stiffened during July and August 1950. At the end of July a minor dispute developed on the Auckland waterfront, this time over conditions of work—the provision of "tea breaks" for men working the New Zealand Shipping Company's vessel, the *Rangitoto*. On 2 August the W.I.A. threatened to take action against the Auckland watersiders if they did not resume normal work. The threat was rejected by the union and on 3 August all wharves in New Zealand were idle. It seems likely that the Government was considering strong action against the union. Sullivan announced that he was "greatly concerned",[63] and some of the newspapers, specifically the *New Zealand Herald*, were applying pressure to the Government. In a strong editorial the *Herald* suggested that many people would support the Government in any action it might take against the union. The paper suggested that the union's leaders could be gaoled "for contempt of court", and reminded the Government that it could declare a State of Emergency over the "tea break" crisis. Referring to the Public Safety Conservation Act, 1932, which provided for such a declaration, the editor stated: "it is well that the people should know that the powers are there."[64]

But the Government decided to hold back when the F.O.L.

suddenly became involved in the dispute. Walsh appears to have wanted to associate the F.O.L. with any settlement that might emerge from the dispute because he was aware of the propaganda value which this could have for the Federation on the eve of the first national conference of the T.U.C.[65] A surprise letter was sent by the F.O.L.'s National Executive to the N.Z.W.W.U. offering assistance. Barnes and Hill paid a visit to the F.O.L.'s office on 3 August, and the result was that a large delegation of unionists from all sections of the labour movement met the Prime Minister and the Minister of Labour at 9 o'clock that evening.

Faced with such a massive display of union strength the Government, after threatening strong action, decided to move carefully. At 1 am the following morning a settlement of the dispute was announced. The Government was prepared to appoint a Royal Commission to look into conditions in the waterfront industry, and the watersiders agreed that while the Commission sat there would be no more stoppages.[66] Another serious crisis had passed. Yet there was still no guarantee that peace would be lasting. It would be many months before the Royal Commission could report its findings; Barnes and Hill did not exactly possess an unblemished record of honouring agreements; and the old system of commission control, so troublesome in the past, continued to operate on the waterfront.

Another crisis was not long delayed. Contrary to public belief, the June lampblack dispute had not really been settled; it had simply been put on ice. The watersiders had returned to work when the W.I.C. agreed to recommend that their demands for special rates of pay for handling lampblack be accepted. The union kept demanding that the W.I.A. announce whether it had accepted the W.I.C.'s recommendation.[67] But when the vessel *Ascuncion de Larrinaga* arrived in Wellington and was ready to discharge its lampblack early in September, the W.I.A. had still not formally accepted the W.I.C.'s recommendations on rates of payment. In fact, none of the men who had worked the *Myrtlebank* in June had received any extra money over and above their normal wages.

On 5 September and again on following days representatives from the W.I.A. visited the *Ascuncion de Larrinaga* to view the state of the cargo and to see the conditions under which the watersiders were working. According to the union, the chairman of the W.I.A. at no point saw conditions at their worst. And on one occasion T. A. Marchington, one of the employers' representatives on the authority, instructed the captain of the ship to have his crew sweep the holds before other members of the authority viewed them.[68] As a result of what he saw, Judge Dalglish agreed with the employers' representatives that the W.I.C.'s recommendations for extra money were excessive. On 8 September the W.I.A. announced that, instead of awarding the 2/6 per hour extra for handling lampblack, it was prepared to award only 1/6, except when such cargo was carried in the ship *Myrtlebank*, which had been the subject of the June dispute, and on which "special conditions" applied.[69]

The W.I.A.'s decision placed the union in a difficult position. On the one hand part of the conditions under which commission control had been restored to the waterfront in 1950 was that both union and employers would accept the rulings of the authority. On the other hand, the union had clearly understood in June that the 2/6 was to apply to the handling of lampblack on all ships, and it expected that the W.I.A.'s acceptance of a recommendation from the W.I.C. would be automatic. The watersiders were incensed to find that it was not. There was a feeling among the union's leaders that the system itself was playing them false. Added to this was the contempt which the union leaders had for Judge Dalglish. Relations had been strained since the *Mountpark* dispute two years earlier. Barnes and Hill felt that Dalglish was simply being capricious when he lowered the extra pay rate, especially when he must have known about Marchington's instructions to the captain of the *Ascuncion de Larrinaga*.[70] The union, without any right of appeal, was being expected to acquiesce in a lowering of a rate of pay that it thought it had already obtained, because of the whim of a man it distrusted. Strike action, with all its attendant dangers, seemed the only way in which Barnes and Hill could express adequately their scorn for Dalglish, the employers, and the system under which wages and conditions were fixed.

At Wellington watersiders ceased work on the *Ascuncion de Larrinaga* as soon as the W.I.A.'s decision was known. Two days later Hill announced that if any watersiders were placed on penalty for refusing to handle lampblack work would cease at all ports in New Zealand.[71] The employers rose to the bait, placed the men on penalty, and issued a statement which made it clear that they expected the Government to see that the law was enforced against the watersiders.[72] By 13 September many wharves in New Zealand were ceasing work, and the National Executive of the N.Z.W.W.U. was meeting in Wellington to discuss the next move.

By this time the Government was under heavy pressure from its supporters to apply some drastic remedy to the recurrent disputes. The *Otago Daily Times* asked for "positive action" from the Government that would "prevent the country from being held to ransom by one unruly group of workers".[73] The *Herald*, as always, was more explicit. It tendered some carefully phrased advice:

> The people will look to Mr Holland for firm and decisive action. But they should clearly understand all that may be involved if the Government invokes its wide powers, especially those conferred in the Public Safety Conservation Act. There is in fact no limit to the powers the Government may exercise, or in their impact on the community, the guilty, and the innocent, alike. If however there is no alternative save the power of the State to restore industrial law on the waterfront, the Government must go ahead, confident that it has the support of the vast majority of the people.[74]

Some of the advice was less friendly. The editor of the *New Zealand Observer* criticised Sullivan for his "mealy-mouthed attitude" to the strike leaders, and, changing the metaphor, asked that the gloves be removed. "The Dominion's need," wrote the editor, "is for a man like the late W.F. Massey." In 1913 Massey had not held out olive branches; he had got "stuck in" when faced with strikes. "Immediate, direct and uncompromising action is required."[75]

Such advice, it seems, was unnecessary. At the time of the August dispute the Government had considered using strong action against the union, and in the discussions late at night had given some solemn warnings to the N.Z.W.W.U.[76] The question for the Government was not whether to use force against the watersiders but when would be the best time to do so. It would not easily be persuaded by its friends to take precipitate action. Rather it must watch carefully the reactions of its potential enemies. The F.O.L. obligingly removed itself from the fray when its National Executive, after a meeting on 14 September, dissociated itself from the dispute.[77] This eliminated the prospect of the united labour front against the Government that had haunted Ministers the previous month. But the September dispute did involve lampblack, a cargo which back in June was acknowledged to be particularly obnoxious, and no one could be certain whether the Labour Party might not play on this fact. Parliament was still in session, and it was always possible that Fraser might complicate matters either by trying to enlist public sympathy for men who, in this case did appear to have been shabbily treated on a matter meriting some leniency, or by criticising the Government for not exploring every avenue to a settlement.[78] Not surprisingly, a certain caution still lingered in Government circles.

On 14 September the officials of the N.Z.W.W.U. requested, and were granted, a meeting with the Prime Minister and the Minister of Labour. The meeting began at 4 pm and, after a two-hour break between 7 and 9 pm, lasted till 11 pm. The Government was reluctant to reveal what passed between the two parties; to do so might "prejudice" the chance of a settlement. But Holland did say that the Government had put its case—that it held the union responsible for the trouble and expected the decision of a tribunal such as the W.I.A. to be respected—"with the greatest candour".[79] And it may be assumed that he threatened the watersiders with a declaration of a State of Emergency if the dispute were not quickly settled.

One hope remained, however. And this was that a meeting

between the port employers and the union might bring about a settlement. The Government, therefore, allowed the men time to report back to the union's National Executive and to seek a meeting with the port employers. It was still in no hurry to precipitate a major crisis. On 15 September Barnes and Hill sought a meeting with the port employers. The watersiders were keen to discuss the matter directly with them, a privilege they had long sought. But they found that the employers were prepared to discuss nothing relevant to the dispute. The employers had been deeply aggrieved by the Government's settlement of the June lampblack dispute. They were not this time going to do anything that might facilitate a settlement on the union's terms. Besides, they had probably got wind of the straight talking that had taken place the previous evening. They had nothing to lose by being intransigent, and perhaps a lot to gain.

Consequently, Captain Holm issued a tough statement on the morning of 15 September: the employers would not discuss anything with the union until the union had agreed to accept the recent ruling of the W.I.A. and had returned to work at all ports in the country.[80] By midday on the 15th the union had retaliated in kind. A directive was issued for work to stop at all ports still in service. At 2.15 pm the watersiders again tried to discuss the matter with the employers. But they refused to budge from their earlier stand. The meeting broke up after two minutes. By the evening of Friday 15 September an impasse had been reached. The employers were hoping for strong action by the Government; the union was determined to hold out, and as if to express its contempt for all the authorities connected with the waterfront it withdrew the two watersiders' representatives, J. Flood and A.C. Dellaway, from the W.I.A.[81]

No move for a settlement of the dispute was made over the weekend. But it was clear that the Government was considering action. About 500,000 tons of shipping were idle at New Zealand ports and some foodstuffs, despite the watersiders' offer to handle essential commodities and perishable goods, were in short supply in the cities. Moreover, the dispute was spreading. Drivers in the Wellington area had not been handling goods from the waterfront since the 13th, and the West Coast miners, fellow members of the T.U.C., were about to stop work.[82] On Monday 18 September Cabinet held a lengthy meeting. From the fact that the Commissioner of Police and the Government's law draughtsmen attended the later stages of the meeting[83] it may be assumed that preparations for a declaration of a State of Emergency were being made.[84] On 19 September the port employers were to meet Ministers in a plea for firm action against the union.[85] But the Government had already decided to act. On the morning of the 19th Holland summoned the watersiders' leaders and informed them that unless normal work was resumed on all waterfronts on Wednesday 20 September, "the Government would, under the provisions of the Public Safety Conservation Act, declare a state of emergency to exist".[86]

Having made the decision to implement his earlier threat to the watersiders to declare a State of Emergency—a move which brought instant applause from the press (the *Herald* praised Holland who had "grasped the nettle at last"),[87] Holland proceeded in the House to justify the move on the widest possible grounds. The action of the watersiders was not only holding up work on the waterfront. It indicated an unwillingness on the part of the union to comply with the decisions of lawfully constituted industrial authorities. Worse still, the Government regarded the watersiders' action as bordering on treason. "In the opinion of the Government," Holland told the House, "the present hold-up is part and parcel of the 'cold war' being waged throughout the world and must be treated on that basis."[88] It followed that the watersiders could expect a "no-holds-barred" policy if they chose to reject the Government's ultimatum.

However, one thing remained in doubt—the attitude of the Labour Party. Holland had shown his statement of the 19th to Fraser before making it, and Fraser had immediately decided to take action to see if the dispute could be settled. No doubt he realised that an industrial showdown at this time would divide the Labour movement as much as it would have had Labour still been in office. At 8 pm on the 19th Barnes, Hill, Walsh, Grant and Young met Fraser, Nash, McLagan, Semple, M. Moohan and C.F. Skinner. At 10.30 pm, when the House rose, these men had a meeting with Holland, Sullivan and other Ministers and Fraser suggested that there was one avenue to a settlement not yet tried. The Government should call a compulsory conference of employers and employees, as provided for under the Industrial Relations Act, 1949.[89] Reluctantly Holland agreed to summon the Cabinet to discuss this proposal. With Parliament in session he was not anxious to side-step the law or embark on other action which the Labour Party might oppose in the House. In the industrial relations field Holland was still feeling his way.

The State of Emergency was duly declared on the afternoon of 20 September, and senior officers of the Armed Services met at Devonport to discuss possible repercussions.[90] But the powers conferred on the Government were not put into effect. By this time the employers had been pressured into meeting the union—a meeting much of which was held in the bar at Bellamys, and which ranged over a number of issues, from lampblack to commission control. The meeting continued briefly on the morning of the 21st and was under the chairmanship of an industrial magistrate, Mr J.A. Gilmour. Finally an understanding acceptable to both parties was reached and the Government decided not to put into effect the emergency powers it had taken.[91]

The terms of the settlement were significant. It was clear that both sides had given ground. The employers agreed to discuss directly with the union lampblack rates and other matters, specifically the transfer of men from one ship to another before a job was completed, on condition that the union resumed normal work. The union agreed not to press at that moment other matters that had been raised in the discussions including wage rates and margins for skill. The fact that the men were prepared to return to work without a final settlement having been reached on lampblack rates for the *Ascuncion de Larrinaga* was some comfort to the employers. Finally, the Government had agreed to hurry ahead with its appointment of the Royal Commission promised in August, and in particular to announce its terms of reference.[92] Under threat of serious consequences should they not return to work the watersiders had been prepared to compromise. And, with national attention focussed on their reactions, the shipowners had not dared to appear too recalcitrant. A crisis, incalculable as to its possible repercussions, had been narrowly averted, at least partly because of the efforts of Fraser, who twelve months before would cheerfully have wrung Barnes' neck.[93]

On 22 September the Wellington Port Committee announced that men handling lampblack in the No.5 hold of the *Ascuncion de Larrinaga* would receive 2/6 per hour and not 1/6 as earlier awarded by the W.I.A. On the face of it, the initial cause of the strike had been settled in the union's favour not by the W.I.A., as the union was careful to point out, but as a result of direct negotiations between the union and the employers.[94] By pushing the dispute to the very brink, Barnes and Hill argued that they had won an important precedent. In future the employers would have to meet the union face to face to discuss all outstanding issues. The principle of arbitration, so assiduously preserved in waterfront affairs by successive governments, had been dented. "The union," said the *Transport Worker* optimistically, "has struck off the leg irons of State machinery and legalisms and forced the right to negotiate direct with those who have called the tune all along—the shipowners".[95]

Such statements left little doubt that trouble on the waterfront would continue. At the time of the settlement most newspapers were sceptical. "There will not be any general belief that peaceful conditions have been restored to the waterfront," wrote the editor of the *Otago Daily Times*.[96] The *Herald*'s editor was frankly displeased with the outcome of the dispute and was quite insistent that the watersiders had had their last chance.[97] Such scepticism was justifiable. The harmony on the waterfront was soon shattered. The watersiders announced at the end of September that they had decided not to cooperate with the Royal Commission, claiming that Holland had broken a pledge made to them the previous week that the Commission would enquire into every aspect of the waterfront industry, including the profits of the shipowners, the recent activities of T.A. Marchington and the methods of the waterfront police.[98]

The port employers, too, were not in a conciliatory mood. On 19 October they arbitrarily broke off the discussions which they had been having with officials of the union, stating that they would discuss the issues at stake in the lampblack crisis and no others. They stressed that they were prepared to have the Royal Commission adjudicate on all other matters and chided the union for not cooperating with the commission.[99] The employers were promptly accused by the union of dishonouring their agreement to negotiate directly. Appeals to Sullivan to force the employers to continue negotiating were turned down. All parties were again playing true to form. The industrial harmony achieved in September was beginning to look rather ephemeral. In particular, the Government now seemed quite happy to allow the employers to scuttle back to the safe protection of some independent body, be it the W.I.A. or the Royal Commission.

The intransigence of the employers became clear when at the end of November Barnes and Hill dispatched a stiff letter to the port employers requesting an immediate conference to discuss watersiders' wages.[100] An equally stiff reply came back from Captain Holm. The employers could not see their way clear to raising wages, but the union could, if it wished, appeal to the W.I.A., the Court of Arbitration or the Royal Commission.[101] Direct negotiations to discuss crucial issues such as wages were out of the question. There was some substance to the opinion expressed before the Royal Commission in November by K.A. Belford, a representative of the shipowners. Belford was reported as saying that "like it or not, a showdown is coming on the New Zealand waterfront".[102] Not only the workers, but the employers as well seemed quite prepared to take a hand in facilitating its arrival.

CHAPTER III

THE FEBRUARY DISPUTE

A Showdown?
The danger signs were up by the end of 1950. The watersiders had led a charmed existence during the year. The shipowners had clearly been hoping for some kind of showdown with the union since before the change of government, and some sections of the press, led by the *New Zealand Herald,* had fairly definite ideas about the kind of showdown they wanted. Public opinion, too, was by now quite hostile to the watersiders, having been moulded by those newspapers that wanted to see the union's leaders scalped. During 1950 the *Herald,* the *Auckland Star* and other papers gave prominence to statements and articles about the slow handling of cargo at New Zealand ports, especially when the main cause of this was diagnosed as the attitudes of the watersiders.[1] In retrospect it is clear that a solution to the slow turnround of ships did not lie solely with the union. The shipowners had been in no hurry to introduce new equipment to the waterfront and the harbour boards were slow to start work on new port buildings.[2] The workers' lack of cooperation was not always without cause.

But the press was reluctant to award the watersiders credit for a fair complaint, and quickly slipped into the habit, fostered by others, of associating complaints and stoppages with directions from Moscow. "Not all waterside workers are Communists," the editor of the *Otago Daily Times* generously conceded. "Indeed, it is safe to believe that few of them are. Yet they are jumping to obey the dictates of Marx—and of Moscow—as if the dissolution of the democratic world in misery, violence and turmoil, and the substitution of a totalitarian state was their highest aim in life."[3] Such harsh judgements were seldom supported by factual evidence. But repeated often enough they gained in credibility among a public whose interest in unions was small and whose contact with the waterfront was nil. At the end of October 1950 the editor of the Presbyterian magazine *Outlook* commented:

> If the refusal of the Watersiders' Union executive to take part in the Waterfront Royal Commission Enquiry does not further harden public opinion against them, it will only be because it is already triple-baked.[4]

Clearly, lack of public support was one of the union's greatest problems, and only at a couple of points during the lampblack disputes does the Government appear to have wavered from a conviction that a majority of the people would solidly support whatever action might be taken against the N.Z.W.W.U. What had saved the union during 1950 was an unusual combination of factors. At first the Government had been reluctant, probably for political reasons, to acknowledge that the period of amity was over. Then in the August dispute the F.O.L. had, for its own reasons, intervened. In September Parliament was still in session, and Fraser's intervention in the lampblack dispute had been the crucial factor in bringing about a settlement. But by the end of the year it was unlikely that any of these things would come to the aid of the watersiders in another dispute. The "honeymoon" in industrial relations had most assuredly ended in separation of the parties if not yet divorce.

After the September dispute the F.O.L. issued a warning that in future it would not allow any of its members to become involved in a waterfront dispute unless the dispute had first been placed in the hands of the Federation.[5] Moreover, by the end of 1950 Parliament was no longer sitting, Fraser was dead and Labour members were caught up in a change of leadership in the party;[6] and in the normal course of events Parliament could not be expected to resume until June 1951. The watersiders no longer had "friends" whose intervention could be counted upon.

And yet, a showdown was coming. The Government knew it.[7] The employers knew it.[8] The watersiders knew it.[9] And undoubt-

7. Leaders of the New Zealand Waterside Workers' Union in Auckland, October 1950. From *left:* T. Hill (national secretary); T.G. Wells (national vice-president); H. Barnes (national president) and E.A. Napier (secretary of the Wellington Branch).
(Auckland Star)

edly the F.O.L. also knew it, since the prospect of a collision was common gossip in Wellington.[10]

The Government's attitude is easy to understand. After the series of crises in 1950 it was under such pressure from the press and from its own supporters that any further reluctance to fight the militants in another scrap would have invited charges of spinelessness. Moreover, the political outlook for the National Party was clouding over by the end of 1950. The Korean War had created high demand for wool and skyrocketing prices brought inflationary pressures on the New Zealand economy.[11] Government policy throughout the year had intensified rather than diminished these pressures. Real estate prices were allowed to accelerate; price control was lifted from many items; food subsidies had been removed; and imports were flooding into the country by the end of the year because of a relaxation of import controls.[12] The whole complex body of stabilisation legislation was groggy from the blows it had sustained. The value of the pound which the National Party had promised on the hustings to "make go further" seemed in danger of vanishing altogether.

The local body elections in November 1950, which saw substantial Labour gains throughout the country, were a timely warning to the National Party that its hold on office was by no means assured. Resentment against the Government, as the deputy-leader of the Labour Party, Walter Nash, had pointed out,[13] did seem to be considerable.

For the Government the choices were limited in number. Either some stern economic measures would be necessary, or a way of gaining political kudos by distracting attention from the inflationary state of the economy would have to be devised. The more National members thought about it, the more attractive a battle with the watersiders seemed to be. It offered the prospect of a popular crusade against militant unions, long an object of contempt to National supporters, and it held out the possibility—as yet only dimly perceived—of direct political gain. However they looked at it, National politicians calculated they could not lose by playing tough.

The employers' desire for serious disciplining of the watersiders is even more easily explained. Barnes and Hill were clearly thorns in their flesh. If a Government should assume the responsibility for disciplining the union, perhaps weakening it, and removing its leaders, then the employers stood to gain directly. The pressure for wage increases would diminish and, with their strengthened position *vis à vis* the union, it might be possible to speed up the turn-round of ships in New Zealand ports. And if the Government would assume the responsibility for disciplining the watersiders without directly involving the employers, and if it would do it in the name of protecting public order, so much the better.

Nor is it difficult to understand the F.O.L.'s readiness to dissociate itself from any further waterfront dispute. If all of the things which the employers hoped for should be achieved, including the removal of Barnes and Hill from office, then not only would Walsh's greatest personal rivals be liquidated, but the T.U.C. would be stripped of what relatively small influence it still retained. Clearly the interests of the Government, the employers and of the F.O.L. were running very closely together by the end of 1950.

What does require explanation is the continued militancy of the N.Z.W.W.U. in the face of such opposition. Despite warnings, the union at the end of 1950 seemed determined to press on with the fight. When Holm's refusal to meet the watersiders to discuss wages was received by the union in December 1950 the *Transport Worker* hinted darkly at retaliation when it said: "no watersiders have any illusions as to what steps will be necessary in order to secure a reasonable return for their labour . . . ."[14]

It would be too simple to say that this willingness to fight in the face of grave danger was entirely due to Barnes, whose extraordinary arrogance and belligerence is undoubted. He had certainly earned the nickname "the bull" that had been conferred on him by his subordinates. The important factor, and it was consistently overlooked by his critics, was that Barnes had solid support from the rank and file of the union for most things that he did. The N.Z.W.W.U. was no ordinary union. Its leaders were not elected by a small number of active unionists who manipulated a large paper membership as was true of many other unions at the time. The watersiders were a closely-knit union of men as a whole. They were men with a mission which was to show other workers what could be obtained by efficient organisation and determined use of industrial power. In such a context press hostility to Barnes was a positive advantage. It elevated him in the eyes of his followers. "Every thinking worker will recognise these hymns [of hate] for the praise they are", he told the watersiders.[15] Barnes spoke for his men when he expressed the opinion in December 1950 that the day had gone when workers would argue about wage increases of pennies and halfpennies, and added that unless real and substantial relief was soon given, major industrial trouble was "inevitable".[16] Retreat in the face of danger would be cowardly, the action of a conscript unionist or of a weak-kneed Labour politician. Watersiders were made of sterner stuff.

It was one thing to be able to speak for the N.Z.W.W.U., quite another to be able to speak for the labour movement as a whole. Events were soon to show that while Barnes' union was united in its militancy, few other unions shared the water-

8. Holland in consultation with J.F. Dulles, President Truman's special envoy, in Wellington, 20 February 1951. *(New Zealand Herald)*

siders' desire to take on the Government. The watersiders had isolated themselves from the public and from their fellow workers more than they knew and for reasons that they would never fully comprehend.

The February Dispute

The kind of steady inflation that has been part of modern New Zealand society is bound to cause a certain amount of labour unrest. Wages no sooner catch up with price increases than prices rise again. Wage-earners are inclined to feel that they are operating a treadmill, and that there is a certain futility to their efforts to improve their standards of living. By 1950 New Zealanders had been experiencing the frustrations of fairly rapid price rises for some years. But in that year the problem of inflation grew much more serious and the cries of the unions were insistent as they saw wages beginning to lose ground relatively to other incomes.[17] In May the Arbitration Court had granted an interim increase in wages while it considered the merits of the claims of the F.O.L. and T.U.C. for more substantial wage increases. By the end of the year the F.O.L. was increasingly dissatisfied with the restrictions which limited the Court to one general wage rise per year, and was pressing the Government to alter the stabilisation regulations so as to allow for more frequent wage adjustments.[18]

Some unions were taking the law into their own hands. While unwilling to embark on campaigns of the magnitude of the watersiders' they were nevertheless prepared to try a little direct action in order to impress on the employers the urgency with which they viewed the unsatisfactory level of their wages. The newspapers at the end of 1950 were full of reports of minor industrial unrest. Ships' carpenters, freezing workers, cement workers, and hydro-electric workers all precipitated stoppages of one kind or another, and during the Christmas period there was a national railway strike that lasted ten days, causing considerable inconvenience to would-be holiday makers. This strike was settled only after the Government threatened to use emergency powers, the second time in four months that the big stick had had to be waved.[19] There was, then, a more than usually tense atmosphere amongst all unions as in January 1951 they awaited the judgement of the Arbitration Court on the F.O.L.'s claim for a general wage rise of £2-18-6 per week and the T.U.C.'s claim for £3-10-0.[20]

On 31 January the Arbitration Court announced the result of its deliberations. Instead of increasing wages by a fixed amount the Court awarded a 15 per cent general wage increase. With the exception of the employers and the press, opinions were generally critical of the pronouncement. The National Executive of the F.O.L. stated that the 15 per cent "falls far short of ensuring a decent standard of living on present prices", and stated that it felt the percentage increase rather than the fixed amount applied for would widen the income gap between highly and lowly paid workers.[21] The Secretary of the T.U.C., A.B. Grant, was more hostile: "I am more confirmed in my opinion that the working class has nothing to gain from the Court."[22] Toby Hill's pronouncement was even more ominous: "Those who have made the wages decision are like the Bourbons—they have not heard the sound of marching feet."[23]

It was in this context that the watersiders, who were not automatically covered by the Arbitration Court order, made representations to the port employers for a wage rise. All eyes were fastened on the militants. Would they accept the 15 per cent increase—if it was offered?

The meeting between representatives of the N.Z.W.W.U. and the port employers took place on 8 February. The union asked for an increase in wages from 4/3 per hour to 6/- per hour, a sum that would bring New Zealand watersiders into line with rates currently being paid in Australia. Anticipating that this would be refused, they put forward an alternative proposal for 5/2 per hour. This rate would have ensured that the watersiders retained the traditional margin of 1d per hour over the freezing workers who, it was believed, were now about to receive 5/1 per hour.[24] The minimum amount which the union was prepared to consider was 4/10½ per hour. This was 15 per cent above the 4/3 which they had been receiving since July 1950.

The employers offered 4/7½ per hour which was 15 per cent above the wage rate that had been in force before July 1950, and 9 per cent more than the rate that had applied since that date. The employers argued that since the Arbitration Court's award of 31 January 1951 had incorporated the interim order of June 1950 that had been paid to workers covered by the Court, so the port employers were not bound to give the watersiders more than 15 per cent above the rate in force before the W.I.A. had granted its rise on 5 July 1950. Captain Holm claimed on behalf of the employers that their offer of 4/7½ maintained the "same relative position of the watersiders in comparison with other workers".[25]

He was wrong in one important respect. The W.I.A.'s

award of July 1950 had differed from the Arbitration Court's award in one significant way. Whereas the Arbitration Court's award was stated to be an "interim" award that could at some later date be incorporated into a general wage order, the W.I.A.'s award was "not an interim decision, but a final decision".[26] This meant that it was not seen at the time as an award that could subsequently be withdrawn and replaced by a new one, back-dated to before 5 July 1950. In short, sore as were the watersiders when they received their wage rise in July 1950, they had been awarded one very clear, even if unintended, advantage over other workers. Future wage rises were to be negotiated on the basis of that July pronouncement, a pronouncement which in February 1951 the employers wished the watersiders to overlook. When they offered the union 4/7½ and refused to discuss any higher sum except through some arbitrating body, the employers were asking the watersiders either to accept that their privileged position in relation to other workers had gone, or that they submit the matter to some Government-appointed arbitration body. It was from just such a body that the union mistakenly believed it had emancipated itself at the time of the lampblack dispute in September 1950.

It takes an act of faith to see the port employers' offer of 8 February as anything other than provocative. They could have offered 4/10½ safe in the knowledge that this would neither contravene the law nor put them off-side with other employers. Moreover, with New Zealand ports full of shipping (there were some 600,000 tons in dock or waiting to dock) such an offer might have ensured that the rest of the export season would pass uneventfully. But such considerations seem not to have weighed heavily with the employers. An offer of 4/10½ just might have been accepted by Barnes and Hill; yet there could have been little doubt among the employers that a final offer of 4/7½ would cause the watersiders to resort instantly to direct action in the face of the Government's clear intention to eliminate such extra-legal activity. The moment had arrived, and the employers seemed not about to let it pass.

Barnes and Hill were faced with a direct challenge. The 4/7½ would have seemed miserly at any time; but in the environment

of competition which existed between the F.O.L. and the
militant T.U.C.—an environment in which the T.U.C. had been
attempting to impress upon potential supporters the advantages
that could be achieved through direct action—it was impossible
for them to accept the offer. Moreover, to have accepted the
4/7½ and to have then submitted the higher claim to arbitration
would have involved formal recognition by the N.Z.W.W.U. that
the right to direct bargaining which they believed they had won
at the time of the lampblack dispute had in fact been lost. It
would have meant accepting that the employers had acted
legitimately when they arbitrarily broke off discussions in the
middle of October 1950.

The expected happened. The two-and-a-half hour meeting
with the port employers on 8 February made no progress.
When the watersiders asked for an adjournment to consider
the offer of 4/7½, the employers replied that this was their
"final offer": further discussion would be a "waste of time"
On Friday 9 February, after the wage negotiating committee
had reported back to the men, the Wellington and New Plymouth
branches of the union decided to refuse to accept overtime
until the employers adopted what the watersiders could regard
as a more reasonable attitude.[27] On Tuesday 13 February the
National Executive of the N.Z.W.W.U. met in Wellington to
discuss the situation. Opinion among executive members was
unanimously in favour of a motion that overtime should be
refused at all ports. One member of the executive had earlier
advocated a complete stoppage as a more effective means of
protest against the employers' offer.[28] Before meeting with the
employers later in the day a directive was sent to all branches
of the N.Z.W.W.U. to cease accepting overtime.

By choosing to operate a ban on overtime rather than a complete strike the union was being careful. A strike would paralyse
the country and very quickly force the Government to take
emergency measures to see that the necessities of life were
available to the population. The union calculated, however, that
an overtime ban would be enough to put pressure on the
employers but not enough to warrant a State of Emergency.
Sufficient work could be done in forty hours to keep the popu-

lation supplied with the necessities of life.

However, the employers had the legal power to turn an overtime ban operated by the union into a sixteen-hour week, and were prepared to use it in the hope that the Government would quickly step into the dispute. Section 47(b) of the *Order of the Waterfront Industry Commission* read as follows:

> If overtime to 10 pm or special overtime 11 pm to midnight is required by the employer, the foreman or clerk in charge shall in all cases notify the men not later than 4 pm Mondays to Fridays, both inclusive, and not later than 11 am for overtime on Saturday afternoon. Any individual man or men who desire to knock off work when the vessel is working in overtime or special overtime hours shall, immediately on such notification by the foreman or clerk in charge, state whether they intend to work overtime or special overtime or not. Such men, however, are to be permitted to return to the same job if still unfinished the following morning if the foreman has been so notified.
>
> This sub-clause is intended solely to cover special individual cases, and does not entitle men to refuse overtime collectively.[29]

If the union should decide not to work overtime the employers could place all men on a two-day penalty. This would mean that for every day when the men collectively refused to accept overtime no work would be offered at all for the next two days.

At a brief meeting[30] between the union's representatives and the port employers at 2.30 pm on 13 February the employers warned the watersiders that these sanctions would be invoked if overtime work were stopped.[31] The National Executive of the N.Z.W.W.U., continuing its meeting in Wellington, decided that it would stick to its overtime ban. On Wednesday 14 February at most ports no overtime was worked. The employers promptly backed up their threat with action. V.P. Blakeley for the port employers announced that experience had shown that the waterfront could not possibly operate on a 40-hour basis, and the watersiders at all ports where the overtime ban was in force were placed on penalty.[32] By 16 February scarcely any work was being performed anywhere on New Zealand's waterfront.

At this point it is possible that both employers and the union hoped that the Government would step in on their respective sides and force some quick negotiations. By slowing the rate of waterfront work to sixteen hours a week the employers clearly assumed that the Government would have to step in, and once in, would almost certainly side with them. But Barnes seems also to have hoped that public opinion would side with the watersiders, recognising that it was the employers who had slowed work to a crawl. The employers would be forced to act more reasonably. Barnes was quoted as saying in Napier, where he had gone for the watersiders' annual cricket tournament, that the watersiders had pursued "entirely constitutional action.[33] Our membership was, and still is, prepared to work a forty-hour week. The employers have chosen to institute the equivalent of a sixteen-hour week. That is their responsibility."[34] In Dunedin the Secretary of the union's branch stated that in his opinion the men had been "locked out". "The bosses sacked the men when they reported for work this morning."[35]

But the union's bid for the support of public opinion was being made without the support of the press. As of 15 February no newspaper in the country had bothered to print a careful analysis of the complex issues involved in the watersiders' wage claim or the overtime ban. Like the employers, newspaper editors could sniff the wind and knew that action was coming. They did not wish to prejudice the employers' case against the union.

The Government Intervenes

Cabinet met under the chairmanship of K.J. Holyoake, the Acting Prime Minister,[36] late in the afternoon of Thursday 15 February. It decided to call both parties to the dispute for meetings on the Friday morning. The meetings had to be delayed until late on Friday afternoon since the union's leaders had to travel back from Napier.[37] At a meeting of Cabinet representatives, employers and union leaders, the employers stated emphatically that they were not prepared to depart from their offer of 4/7½ per hour, but they were quite prepared to allow the dispute to be settled by the W.I.A., or the Court of Arbitration or the Royal Commission. The union replied that the 4/7½ was quite unacceptable. Barnes reduced his wage claim

THE FEBRUARY DISPUTE   73

from 6/- per hour to 5/2 per hour, and there was also some discussion on the basis of a 15 per cent increase on the 4/3 rate which would have resulted in a new wage rate of 4/10½. Below this, however, the union would not go.[38] To the employers' suggestions for arbitration of the dispute Barnes was quite adamant. The W.I.A., he said, had not been operating since the September lampblack dispute; the Court of Arbitration had not adjudicated on waterfront affairs since 1940; and the Royal Commission was never designed to act as an arbitrating body, and its terms of reference had never been satisfactory to the union.[39]

At this point in the discussions Holyoake asked the union whether it would accept the ruling of an independent chairman appointed by the Government to adjudicate on the issues involved in the dispute, should a compulsory conference of the parties be convened by the Government. Barnes replied "most emphatically" that the union would not agree to accept the findings of a Government-appointed arbitrator. After the employers had withdrawn at Holyoake's request, Barnes stated that the Government must allow direct bargaining of the type that had taken place between 20 September and 18 October 1950 under the chairmanship of Mr Gilmour. The Government insisted on arbitration. After a brief consultation with the employers and another round with the union's leaders, Holyoake called Cabinet together, the members of which had been waiting in Wellington pending the outcome of the meetings with the disputants.[40]

This special Cabinet meeting was held about 8 pm on the Friday evening. There is no reason to believe that any one present dissented from Holyoake's and Sullivan's statements made earlier to the union's leaders about the need to uphold the principle of arbitration. Indeed it was at this meeting that Cabinet formally endorsed the decision to force the watersiders to abide by arbitration. About 10 pm Cabinet's decision was conveyed to the union's leaders in yet another meeting in Parliament Buildings.

Later in the evening a letter was delivered outlining the Government's case to Toby Hill, the Secretary of the N.Z.W.W.U. The letter stated that the Government viewed with "serious concern" the action of the union in refusing to carry out normal hours of work "in accordance with the long-accepted conditions of employment on the waterfront". The union was reminded that it had agreed in June 1950 to accept the W.I.C.'s decision, subject to the right of appeal to the W.I.A., and that the cessation of overtime was a breach of the Commission's Main Order. "It goes without saying," the letter continued, "that if your Union is not prepared to abide by the conditions of employment it cannot expect to retain the benefits which have accrued to your members under Commission control." The letter concluded with an ultimatum: if normal hours of work were not resumed on Monday 19 February, the powers of the W.I.C. and W.I.A.[41] would be suspended. The final sentence contained an ominous warning to the effect that if the union allowed the present situation to continue it would "result in inflicting serious hardship on all sections of the community".[42]

This letter is significant for it is the first statement of Government policy on the February dispute. It is significant mainly for what it did not say. In the first place the Government made no comment as to the reasonableness of the employers' wage offer. In fact, Sullivan claimed later that Cabinet had carefully avoided passing comment on the fairness or otherwise of the shipowners' offer.[43] Perhaps some Cabinet members, or even the public, might regard the offer as provocative. Instead, the Government took a firm stand on the high ground of defending the principle of compulsory arbitration, and in its desire to hold the N.Z.W.W.U. to the promise it had given the previous year to abide by the directions of the W.I.C. It was a stand in the defence of "law and order". The letter was quite free of emotional utterances that subsequently found their way into ministerial statements. There was no mention of the lampblack dispute, or about the dispute being "part and parcel of the Cold War". The letter was couched in reasonable language, and it represented the Government's case at its strongest.

It is not easy to tell whether, had there been no other developments between Friday 16 February and the following Monday, the watersiders would have backed down in the face of the Government's threat. Certainly it seems unlikely; a showdown had been anticipated for some time. The watersiders knew that at some stage they would have to face a combination of Government and employer.

It seems reasonable to assume, then, that Barnes and Hill had decided as early as Friday evening to recommend to their branches that they reject the Government's ultimatum. One thing, however, diminished the possibility that they would have second thoughts. This was the Prime Minister's rather sudden and clumsy appearance on centre stage. Arriving home on the Friday from a trip to London and Washington, Holland was guest at a reception in Auckland that evening. At the time he arrived home he had little knowledge of the delicate manoeuvrings currently under way in Wellington. But this did not prevent him from making statements that were undoubtedly to raise, rather than lower, the temperature of the negotiations. The *Herald* quoted him the following morning as having issued a grave warning to anyone who stood in the way of the Government in marshalling its defence resources. He added:

> Any individual or group of individuals who stands in the way of the country's preparations for defence to ensure peace ... by limiting the handling of goods is a traitor, and should be treated accordingly.[44]

This threat was clearly aimed at the watersiders. Holland had made similar statements off the cuff before, and there were many more to come. But at a moment when the industrial situation called for restraint on all sides, it was a distinctly unhelpful contribution. What was so significant about the statement was the implication contained in it that industrial hold-ups were more than domestic problems: they were part of a conspiracy against the "free" nations of the world.

For the watersiders and other militants such assertions touched raw nerves. Holland had recently made a series of adulatory declarations about American foreign policy. On leaving Washington he had pledged that he would "lend every fibre of his being" to the promotion of good relations between the United States and the Commonwealth, and had been quoted as adding "tell me what else I can do, and I will do it".[45] Such a willingness to associate himself with the wave of militant anti-communism currently sweeping across the United States seemed dubious enough to the watersiders and others on the left who found themselves critical of aspects of American foreign policy. But the further implication—that industrial holdups in allied countries, whatever their real origin, would have to be crushed in the name of a united foreign policy—gave a more sinister twist to Holland's utterance on the evening of the 16th.

Watersiders sensed a direct connection between Holland's promise in Washington and the threat issued in Auckland. The N.Z.W.W.U. was being singled out as public enemy number one. Resistance stiffened immediately. Barnes, and many a watersider as well, sensed that Holland had not only opted for America "right or wrong"; he had received orders while away to tame the militant unions. To Barnes the Prime Minister of New Zealand had become the "Senator from Fendalton",[46] a spokesman for those vested interests seeking an intensification of the Cold War. Inadvertently Holland had convinced the watersiders that they were among the few authentic voices of New Zealand nationalism. A fight against the Government and the employers would be more than a fight over wages. It would be an assertion of national independence.[47]

Holland helped stiffen the watersiders' resolve to see the fight through, and the telegram sent by the union's leaders to the branches acquainting them of the Government's ultimatum suggested that the men reject it.[48] The question as to whether the dispute would continue beyond the Monday deadline was over now to the rank and file. Most of them probably trusted their leaders to handle this ultimatum as they had so many before it. But if there were any doubters among the rank and file the port employers silenced them by their actions on the morning of Monday 19 February. When watersiders reported to work at all ports they were greeted by notices telling them that work was being offered "subject to the acceptance of normal hours of work including overtime if required".[49]

This notice, as most watersiders realised, subtly altered their legal position *vis à vis* the Order of the Waterfront Industry Commission. It may have been a contravention of the Order when the National Executive of the union directed a cessation of overtime as from the 14 February. Only individuals, and not the union as a whole, could opt to cease work at 5 pm after the 4 pm call for overtime was made, although there had always been some doubt about where the line could be drawn between individual and concerted action. But the notice which greeted the men on the morning of the 19th clearly placed the responsibility for accepting overtime on to each man individually before he would be allowed to work even an eight-hour day. Normal work meant overtime if the employer chose to offer it. It was highly likely under these circumstances that a large body, if not all of the watersiders, would see this new stipulation—compulsory overtime in effect—as a contravention of the forty-hour week, and as an arbitrary interference with the W.I.C.'s regulations. Before the men had had a chance to meet to vote on whether to accept the Government's ultimatum the employers at all ports seemed to have changed conditions of work to such an extent that the men saw themselves as "locked out".[50] The head office of the N.Z.W.W.U. in Wellington was promptly flooded by the telegrams of branches reporting their votes to refuse acceptance of the ultimatum.[51] Speaking for the Wellington branch, J.E. Napier said: "The men consider this to be a lockout. They will be in attendance each morning, ready to perform their normal work on an eight-hour day basis." Barnes added that the decision reached was "that of the membership". The employers and the Government would learn, he said, "that this is not a two-man union, but that it is solid."[52] Later in the day Hill wrote Sullivan as follows:

> This is to advise that the Government's ultimatum was presented this morning. We have been advised by all branches that they have rejected same.[53]

The Government Declares War

The watersiders had slowed the time worked on the waterfront to forty hours per week with their decision of 13 February. The employers slowed it still further to sixteen hours per week with their penalties which began two days later. Then on 19 February the employers set conditions for work that made a complete stoppage likely. At most ports no work was done on the 19th although the watersiders made it clear then, and on subsequent mornings, that they were still prepared to work a forty-hour week. But the employers were not prepared to employ men even for sixteen hours a week if they did not agree, in advance, to accept overtime. At Lyttelton, where some of the men had not lifted their discs on the 19th but simply returned to the ships they had been working the previous week, as was the custom when a job from a previous work day was unfinished, the employers quickly rounded them up. These watersiders were told to finish work at noon unless they were prepared to accept work again for the same ships under the new conditions— namely that they accept overtime if it was offered. The men refused, and the union quickly pointed out that the employers' action in this case was also contrary to the usual custom which allowed men to finish work on a ship for which they had been signed up before being asked to contract for further work.[54] Whether the employers intended it or not, (and it is difficult to give them the benefit of the doubt) their new requirements for work had very quickly created a situation where the Government would be forced to declare a State of Emergency. At the height of the export season the nation's waterfront was virtually at a standstill.

By the time Cabinet met on the afternoon of the 19th to consider the official reply from the N.Z.W.W.U. the issues had become very complex. Both the union and the employers had now taken actions which contravened, or went somewhat beyond the rights conferred in the Order of the Waterfront Industry Commission. But the members of Cabinet decided that there could be no turning back at this point, and Sullivan was told to go ahead with suspension of commission control from the waterfront.

Cabinet's decision was scarcely surprising. Eight of the fifteen members of Cabinet were employers and/or farmers.[55] The employers in Cabinet no doubt felt leniently inclined towards their fellow employers if they were aware that they had transgressed. The farmers were almost certainly more concerned about the necessity for speeding up the shipment of primary produce than with the welfare of urban trade unionists.

The other seven members of Cabinet (six of whom were lawyers)[56] represented farming electorates or city districts where employers and white collar workers, rather than unionists, made up the voting strength of the National Party. The trade unions had no voice at all in the Cabinet which on 19 February 1951 decided to press ahead against the N.Z.W.W.U. It seems unlikely that the recent actions of the shipowners were discussed.[57] Sullivan was prevailed upon to issue a statement disagreeing with the union's claim that the watersiders had been "locked out",[58] and his statement was repeated the following day by V.P. Blakely on behalf of the port employers. But both men neglected to take up the questions which the union had raised about the employers' activities on the morning of the 19th.[59]

The watersiders were informed by letter on 20 February that the powers of the W.I.C. and the W.I.A. had been suspended,[60] the announcement having been made to the press on the evening of the 19th. The text of the letter made it clear that it was the Government's opinion that only the union had failed to observe the Order of the W.I.C., and hence deserved penalising.

For the next twenty-four hours the union was not quite certain what would happen next. At most ports the men reported for work prepared to work an eight hour day, but were not hired. The removal of commission control meant that they were no longer eligible for the guaranteed daily attendance money or the guaranteed weekly minimum wage of £5-10-0, or any bonus.[61] The men waited about for a while and then drifted away. On the evening of the 20th Barnes and Hill issued a lengthy statement setting out the watersiders' case. Its tone was clearly designed to impress other trade unionists.

> In fighting for an equitable wage rate to meet the soaring cost of living the union is fighting the battle of every wage-earner in New Zealand.
> The employers' refusal to permit the 40 hour week to be worked on the waterfront can be taken as the opening barrage of the Holland Government's offensive on the 40 hour week. This is a calculated attack on the part of the shipowners, with the connivance of the Government, to smash trade unionism.

The statement filled eighteen column inches in the Labour-owned *Southern Cross*. But other newspapers were no longer anxious to provide the watersiders with a forum for debate. The *Evening Post* published only two column inches of the statement,[62] and the *Herald* nothing at all. Those people who wished to know more about the watersiders' case were finding it increasingly difficult to read the facts.

While the watersiders were wondering what would come next, the Government was busy planning. Between the 19th and the 21st it had come under massive pressure from farmers, employers,[63] harbour boards,[64] and particularly from the press. They were unanimous in their desire to see the Government show some muscle.

In this dispute, as during the years leading up to it, the press played an important part. No chance was missed by an editor to darken the already blackish public image of the watersiders. Yet, in the early stages of the dispute there was no uniformity in the arguments presented for an attack on the N.Z.W.W.U. As early as 15 February the editor of the Dunedin *Evening Star* was prepared to endorse what seemed to him to be the employers' view—that it was "time . . . for a showdown".[65] However, fellow editors of evening papers were more cautious. The *Auckland Star* was inclined to feel in the first days of the dispute that industrial unrest was scarcely surprising given the rampant inflation that existed. Strikes, however, would have "most serious consequences if continued".[66] The *Evening Post*, too, was mild at first.[67] By the 20th, however, the *Post* had warmed to the fight. The editor announced that further "appeasement" of the watersiders was "out of the question". The Government's duty to "take further measures" was "crystal clear".[68]

Meanwhile, the other major evening paper, the Christchurch *Star-Sun*, was brooding in silence, preparing an editorial which none of its fellow evening papers was ready yet to match for extravagance of utterance. On 22 February the editor burst forth with a charge that he did not feel called upon to substantiate—that the watersiders were "being used as tools of the Cominform, the external arm of Communism that is preparing the way for Soviet world domination". It followed from such an analysis that any punishment the Government cared to mete out to the watersiders would be quite acceptable to the editor of the *Star-Sun*.[69]

The morning papers, on the whole, took a shorter time to resort to hyperbole, and some felt little obligation to examine the specific issues at stake in this dispute. The *Herald* in an editorial on 16 February saw the watersiders as dealing a "wicked blow at their country and the British Commonwealth" by holding up shipping. Working only forty hours per week would also "be detrimental to the defence effort". Yet the defence effort was not of such high priority for the editor to feel that the employers should have paused before reducing wharf work to sixteen hours per week. The overtime ban, the editor told his readers, was "a piece of tyranny to which the employers cannot submit". The two-day penalty was quite in order. The editor was quick to point out, however, that if the dispute was not settled swiftly the Government would have to step in. Indeed, such would be essential; for whether the watersiders were aware of the fact or not, the dispute was "serving the purpose of World Communism".[70]

The *Otago Daily Times* was similarly impressed by the theory that the dispute was serving to "further the Communistic policy of creating disorder".[71] Only the *Dominion* and the *Press* were reluctant to cast the mantle of traitor over the watersiders in the early stages. Both papers in their first editorials on the dispute did make some attempt to discuss the specific issues at stake, although the *Press* got off to a bad start by assuming that the watersiders' award of July 1950 had been an interim award, and the *Dominion* made little attempt to understand the watersiders' criticism of the employers' activities on the morning of the 19th.[72]

The *Press*, however, was the only paper which seemed to be in some state of dubiety over whether the dispute had become a lockout. The editor felt that it was not, but provided himself with an escape: "Anyone who sees nothing wrong in a strike if he believes in its objective should not complain if others take the same view of a lockout".[73] Looking over the newspapers it becomes quite clear that, however varied were the reasons they provided, they were unanimous in their desire for a fight. None would have disagreed with the editor of the *Auckland Star* who, on 22 February, urged the Government to "make this the last waterfront holdup":

> The Government now has an opportunity to teach the leaders of the waterside workers' union and all who follow them so submissively a lesson that is more than overdue.[74]

In the editorial rooms of the country the battle posts were being manned with all the excitement and anticipation of soldiers about to embark on a crusade for king, country—and employer.

It seems unlikely that all this beating of drums was the critical factor in deciding the Government to declare a State of Emergency. The probability that emergency powers would be taken had been discussed with the watersiders as early as the 16th, and Cabinet that evening had almost certainly made contingency plans. The immediate effect of the pressure from friends was simply to stiffen the resolve of National Ministers and to hasten the declaration of a State of Emergency. The encouragement from the press had another effect as well. It was responsible for the more wide-ranging assault that was to be launched on the militants and for a certain self-righteourness that began to creep into ministerial letters and utterances after 20 February. The reasoned tone of the letter to Hill on the 16th gave way to the temptation to red-bait. Holland's incautious comments of the 16th soon degenerated into a frenzied bellow. By the 23rd, even the usually imperturbable Sullivan was claiming that the tactics used by certain union leaders "were just part of a world-wide movement to sprag [sic] and wreck the democratic system".[75] As Walter Brookes was later to comment, the "good honest New Zealand lack of concern about fine academic distinctions" was taking the upper hand when a point was to be gained.[76]

What counted for more with Cabinet when it was deciding its next moves on 20-21 February was the total absence of any opposition to the taking of emergency powers. The F.O.L., true to its promise after the lampblack dispute, was hoping to

THE FEBRUARY DISPUTE

keep clear of the waterfront dispute except in the unlikely event that the watersiders would place the matter in its hands. The Labour Party, too, was in no position to do much for the watersiders even had its members wished to. Parliament was not sitting, and the Parliamentary Labour Party was yet to assemble in Wellington for its first major caucus meeting since Walter Nash had been chosen as leader. Cabinet ruled without opposition.

Cabinet met on the afternoon of 21 February, and late in the day a Proclamation was issued under the Public Safety Conservation Act 1932, declaring that a State of Emergency existed. On the following day the Waterfront Strike Emergency Regulations were gazetted and a notice was issued under the Regulations giving the N.Z.W.W.U. until 8 am on Monday 26 February to end the dispute, otherwise the Regulations would be put into force.

The Public Safety Conservation Act had been enacted in the week following the April riots in Auckland in 1932. The Act gave the Governor-General the power to declare that a State of Emergency existed if either the "public safety" or "public order" was imperilled, or if the provision of the necessities of life for the community was in danger.[77] Once a State of Emergency had been declared, the Governor was entitled to make by Order in Council such regulations "as he thinks necessary for the prohibition of any acts which in his opinion would be injurious to the public safety".[78] Traditional liberties such as the right of trial by jury could be curtailed by any regulations issued under the Act, and any existing Acts of Parliament could be suspended. There was no right of appeal.

The legislation had been intended for use in any further depression disturbance. But it had not been invoked. The Labour Government did take emergency powers at the beginning of the war, and these were kept in force while Labour remained in office against the wishes of Holland, the then Leader of the Opposition. In 1947 Holland had accused the Labour Government of keeping in force regulations which had "all the elements of a Communist system, of totalitarianism and dictatorship".[79]

Once in power, the National Party had come to realise that a declaration of a State of Emergency might be useful in a time of industrial trouble. The Strike and Lockout Emergency Regulations, 1939, were not repealed. The Waterfront Strike Emergency Regulations, 1951, based as they were on a set of Regulations used by the Queensland Government in 1948, gave the Government unlimited powers to deal with the watersiders. What is more, there was no provision within the Public Safety Conservation Act necessitating that Parliament be called. Any Government, once it took emergency powers, armed itself with a blank cheque; the funds were limitless.

The Regulations announced on 22 February 1951 gave the Government the widest possible powers to deal with a strike. Since there was doubt in some quarters whether this particular dispute was a strike or lockout, the Regulations first set about defining a strike in such a manner that the overtime ban and subsequent actions by the union came within the scope of the definition. A "strike" was defined *inter alia* as the act of any number of workers who discontinued their employment "whether wholly or partially, and whether by refusing or failing to work overtime or otherwise" or the "refusing or failing to accept engagement for any work in which they are usually employed".[80]

Having defined a strike, the Regulations went on to declare that it was an offence for any person to be "a party to a declared strike", or to encourage a strike, or to publish anything that is "intended or likely to encourage, procure, incite, aid or abet a declared strike". A member of a union that was a party to a strike was deemed to have encouraged it unless he could prove otherwise. It was declared to be an offence for anyone to make any payment or contribution to any union or person that was a party to a strike. The rest of the Regulations conferred special powers on the Minister of Labour and the police. The Minister could suspend any award of a striking union and appoint a Receiver of its funds. The police could arrest people for picketing, displaying signs, or holding processions, and any member of the police force who was above the rank of Sergeant had unlimited power of entry into or upon any land, premises or place for the purpose of enforcing the Regulations. The Regulations also gave the Government the power to order the armed forces to undertake "any kind of work".[81]

If these Regulations were put into effect they would cut off completely all the traditional methods used in the prosecution of a strike. Picketing, poster displays, processions and public meetings would be impossible, and the newspapers would have strong reason to cease publishing what they had already begun to curtail: any expression of opinion by the watersiders. The press was quite right when it pointed out that, with such regulations in force, the only way in which a union that came within the scope of the Regulations could win, would be by toppling the Government.

By the 22nd the ball was back in the watersiders' court. They had three full days to reconsider their position, three days in which the editor of the *Herald*, who was shocked at the period of time they had been allowed, believed they would "plot further mischief".[82]

Meantime, all leave for Cabinet members had been cancelled,[83] and there was considerable press speculation and not a few suggestions from editors, as to what should be done in the likely event that the N.Z.W.W.U. would defy this new ultimatum.[84]

CHAPTER IV

SUMMONING UP SUPPORT

The Situation in Late February

The port employers had good reason to be pleased with the trend of events during the third week of February. There was never much likelihood that the Government would side with their enemies; but there had been a danger that at least some Government members and/or some newspapers might have regarded the employers' demand of the 19th—that a guarantee of overtime be given before normal work would be allowed— as provocative. But none had openly done so. Neither the press nor members of the Government were very familiar with the Order of the Waterfront Industry Commission. And besides, both were by this time disposed to ignore any complaint from the union. The result was that the employers had survived the first days of the week with few questions being asked and much support being proffered.

By 22 February when they saw the Waterfront Strike Emergency Regulations the port employers must have scented victory. After several false starts during the previous year, the Government, without whose support they could never succeed, had finally leapt into action. What had started as a confrontation between employers and workers over wages was now a matter of State. The employers could relax more, confident that at worst they could not lose. The only issue that remained for them was the question of how much ground the N.Z.W.W.U. would have to give before a settlement was reached. Would the waterfront be allowed to operate again with the old union intact? Or could there be a complete reorganisation along lines more satisfactory to the employers' interests? From the last week in February the employers began directing their efforts to this end.

At the same time life was becoming more difficult for the watersiders. By the weekend of 24-25 February they were undeniably in a weakening position. Not only had the Government openly sided with the employers during the previous week. It was also, with the help of the press, opening up a veritable barrage of abuse against the N.Z.W.W.U. On 22 February the Prime Minister once again issued a statement which would do little towards settling the dispute and much towards stiffening the watersiders' resistance. As with his statement on the 16th, Holland did not actually mention the watersiders by name. But few people, least of all the watersiders, can have been in any doubt about who was being referred to. New Zealand, Holland began by saying, was "actually at war":

> There is the enemy within, which is just as unscrupulous, poisonous, treacherous and unyielding as the enemy without. He works day and night; he never lets up. He gnaws away at the very vitals of our economy just as the codlin moth enters and gnaws away at the "innards" of an apple while everything on the outside looks shiny and rosy. This Government is alive to the danger that besets us and is determined to ensure that he does not succeed.[1]

Such statements by Ministers were warmly endorsed by the press,[2] and it is clear that a sizable number of people were already convinced that the struggle with the watersiders was a battle against the omnipresent Communist menace.

At first sight the surprising thing is that so little evidence was ever produced to substantiate such serious charges against the watersiders. The first piece of evidence that was proffered was the fact that the N.Z.W.W.U. belonged as a matter of choice to the maritime section of the World Federation of Trade Unions, an organisation that was controlled by Communists. Yet the records of the union provide no evidence that the watersiders were acting upon any directions from the W.F.T.U., either when they began the overtime ban in 1951 or on any previous occasion. Correspondence from the W.F.T.U. was rare, and never contained more than rather heavy doses of anti-American propaganda. The connection between the N.Z.W.W.U. and the W.F.T.U. really had nothing to do with any interest in

A. IT'S THE SAME WAR

the policies of international Communism among the overwhelming majority of New Zealand's watersiders. In the light of what is known of Barnes' temperament, and taking into account the very vague justification which he offered for belonging to the W.F.T.U.,[3] it seems more likely that the watersiders' connection with this international body was nothing more than a characteristic gesture of defiance towards the F.O.L., which had withdrawn from the body in 1949. There is no evidence that the association was a portent of disaster for New Zealand as Sullivan and several newspapers were to allege.[4]

The second line of attack against the N.Z.W.W.U. was that some of its leaders were active members of the Communist Party. This was undeniable. The most prominent Communist was Alex Drennan, formerly vice-president of the N.Z.W.W.U. and president of the Auckland branch in 1951. He had been until 1948 the president of the Auckland Trades Council. The only other prominent member of the Communist Party on the

B. "HANDS UP ALL THOSE WHO VOTE FOR A STRIKE!"

National Executive of the union, however, was J. Mitchell of Auckland. Neither Barnes nor Hill are known to have had any association with the Communist Party.

Probably the most commonly used "evidence" that the N.Z.W.W.U. was an agent of the Cominform was of the guilt-by-association variety. Many critics pointed out that the union's policy throughout the post-war period had enjoyed fairly consistent support from the small New Zealand Communist Party[5] This, too, was true; the watersiders were seen by the Communist Party as being perhaps the only really united industrial union in the country, moreover one that was radical in its views on foreign as well as domestic affairs. But it was one thing for the Communist Party to show friendship for the watersiders, quite another to dominate them. By the early part of March 1951 some prominent members of the Communist Party were harbouring serious doubts about Barnes' wisdom in pursuing the dispute. Aware that the watersiders could not win, yet anxious that the union's strength should be preserved so that they could fight another day, they sought to encourage wiser counsels within the N.Z.W.W.U.[6] But it was no good. The Communists had few members in high places within the union, and these were loyal to Barnes and Hill who were able to go their own way. Sid Scott, who in 1951 was General Secretary of the Communist Party, was to write some years later of Barnes that he was "a man of very strong personality—too strong to be the tool of any organisation or any other man".[7]

The fact that the N.Z.W.W.U. and the Communist Party agreed less and less with one another would seem also to take care of the more cautious accusations that were levelled at the watersiders by papers such as the *Press*—that they were unwittingly tools in Moscow's hands.[8] At this time the loyalty of the New Zealand Communist Party to Moscow was never in doubt. It is inconceivable that the policy which prominent New Zealand Communists were following during the dispute was at variance with any words of advice that might have been tendered by the Kremlin.

It does not seem possible that the National Government was ignorant of the fact that the 1951 waterfront dispute had virtually nothing to do with either the W.F.T.U. or Moscow. Nor can Ministers have failed to realise that the dispute was concerned first and foremost with the questions of wages, conditions and the principle of arbitration. And yet smearing the watersiders' leaders with the Communist label became a favourite ministerial rhetorical device, the most striking example of which was Sullivan's statement of 26 February 1951:

> The present strike is an extension of the Cold War to New Zealand. The Government's patience ... is exhausted. The leadership of the watersiders has led its members up the Cominform garden path .... Can we tolerate law-breaking by an organization dominated by Communist international instructions, or do we stand firm in our belief in genuine differences of opinion under our democratic way of life?[9]

Such fierce attacks on the watersiders did have an obvious purpose. They assisted the Government in its fight against the union, the more so because no one was given a chance by the press to refute the charges. However, as the dispute wore on, more came to be at stake than a simple victory over the watersiders. The dispute came to assume a symbolic importance for the Government. In its own way the 1951 waterfront dispute became a struggle by conservatives to reassert complete political and economic dominance after a lengthy period of Labour rule.

In the United States 1950-51 was the peak year for McCarthyism while in Australia R.G. Menzies was embroiled in a fierce fight over the ill-starred Communist Party Dissolution Act. In both countries the abiding concern about Communists in high places was a front for deeply-seated frustrations among political conservatives. In the United States the Republican Party had felt cheated of victory in 1948 and many Republicans vented their frustrations against the Democratic Party by attacking some of the architects of its foreign policy such as Owen Lattimore and Dean Acheson.[10] In Australia the Liberals' initial frustration at the seeming permanence of the welfare state was vented through attacks on those institutions which appeared to be its most frightening innovations—the industrial unions.

New Zealand in 1951 was also experiencing this symbolic ritual. The previous year had not been a good one politically for the new Government. Every move that was taken to reduce the number of controls had only resulted in increasing inflation. And inflation carried with it a threat of political defeat for the Government which tolerated it. Both the local body elections in 1950 and the Brooklyn by-election in February 1951[11] pointed to the fact that National's hold on power was tenuous. The waterfront dispute offered the prospect of a crusade that was only partly to do with the issue of militant unionism. Such a crusade would also mark the full resumption of power by those conservative groups—employers, farmers, and the press—that had been forced to suffer fourteen years of rule by a Labour Government, a Government which had elevated to positions of national status unionists and erstwhile employees.

For New Zealand's conservatives the waterfront dispute became a struggle to restore "decency" to national life, to restore a "true harmony" of interest groups which Government and employers could once again direct to their ends. When Holland stated on 22 February 1951 that New Zealand was "actually at war", he meant it. He did not seriously mean that the battle was against the agents of a foreign power. Had the watersiders in fact been traitors in this sense Holland would have been extraordinarily negligent had he not imprisoned them forthwith. Rather he meant that it was a battle against a whole left-wing ethos that was foreign to conservatives and to himself as an ex-organiser of that depression aberration, the New Zealand Legion. An explicit statement of this view was made in July 1951 by Sir Wilfred Sim, the President of the National Party. Defending the Emergency Regulations he claimed that the country was "locked in war with the Communist-Socialist cause". The *Evening Post* reported him as saying to the National Party conference:

> The greatest rebuff of all would be suffered if New Zealand could, by a mighty effort unite itself into some kind of remarkable co-operative effort by all classes to live together for a period of industrial peace, produce as never before without stint, and so provide for the people of New Zealand, without any more delay, the clothes, houses and other essentials which were so desperately needed.
>
> New Zealand led the Empire in the rejection of the Socialists in 1949, recognising them as a menace to stability and orderly progress. It now remained to revise objectives and, with new drive, reject from the precincts of Parliament Communists and all allied or associated with them.
>
> We may thus begin a true reconstruction of New Zealand life, freed, let us hope, from the hubbub and pandemonium which the Socialists have introduced into Parliamentary affairs, and aim to end the whole sickening confusion that besets us at present in economic, educational, social and even moral life.[12]

When members of the National Party saw the danger as so omnipresent they were likely to feel that no weapon to combat it could be too outrageous.

The Watersiders Lobby Their Friends

It is clear from the lengthy statement made by Barnes and Hill on 20 February that they saw the dispute essentially as a battle for higher wages and conditions that would be resisted by employers with the aid of a conservative Government. Had they realised by the weekend of 23-24 February that so much more was at stake they might have followed a more conciliatory policy. Instead, they were feverishly at work among their fellow unionists, drumming up support for a firm stand against the Government and the Emergency Regulations. And first indications were that that support would be considerable.

Over the weekend of 17-18 February Barnes and Hill began discussions with officials of other unions. The T.U.C. had already made a statement supporting the watersiders, but this was not considered very significant. That organisation was even weaker than it had been six months earlier at the time of the national conference; its membership was now little more than 20,000. More important for the watersiders was the assumption which they made, and which some press commentators seem to have felt justified,[13] that they would have the support of New Zealand's railway unions as the *quid pro quo* for the watersiders' efforts on behalf of the railwaymen during the Christmas strike. On the support of the railwaymen rested much of the union's chance of making a holdup effective. With the wharves stopped and no trains running the transport system would be paralysed.

There were other unions also which showed some early interest in the watersiders' case. Barnes and Hill were asked to address the National Council of the Hotel Workers' Federation, and on 21 February after hearing their speeches, F.G. Young announced that the hotelworkers were endorsing the watersiders' actions and would pledge their support.[14] Two days later most freezing workers at Ngahauranga ceased work after the Emergency Regulations had been gazetted. But as of the 22nd, the watersiders had made no general appeal for assistance, and neither had they been offered much. The press statement issued on the 21st had been a propaganda exercise directed at other unions, rather than an S.O.S.

The F.O.L., meantime, had been holding fast to its resolution of September 1950 not to get involved in waterfront disputes unless called upon to do so by its member unions. The National

Executive meeting on the morning of the 19th did not discuss the current crisis.[15] However, by the 22nd one of the F.O.L.'s larger affiliates, the New Zealand Harbour Board Employees' Union, had become caught up in the cessation of work on the waterfront, and on 23rd it wrote to the F.O.L. requesting that it convene a meeting of representatives directly involved in the dispute.[16] Such a gathering was summoned immediately, and met at 2 pm on the same afternoon at the Trades Hall in Wellington.[17]

The meeting gave Walsh and his supporters on the National Executive a chance to assess the likely repercussions within the trade union movement should the Government put the Emergency Regulations into force. It was soon clear that a majority of these unions wanted nothing more than a swift return to work. It was decided, finally, that the F.O.L. should "make an attempt to open up negotiations with the authorities with the object of arriving at a settlement". After the meeting members of the National Executive waited on the Prime Minister, and were admitted for a discussion with him at 6 pm.[18] Holland was asked to explore every avenue before putting the Emergency Regulations into force. He replied very firmly to the deputation that the Government "was going to see that the food of this country be not destroyed, that Great Britain be not starved and that the national security and defence was assured". The watersiders, he said, knew what was in front of them; it was up to them to back down before 8 am on Monday 26 February.[19] In spite of the very severe Regulations that were threatened there is no evidence that the F.O.L. did more than request the Prime Minister to think carefully about all that was involved. Certainly no threats were made. Had any Government members been afraid that serious objections would be raised by the labour movement if the Regulations were put into effect, this meeting must have reassured them.

The National Executive of the F.O.L. had kept faith with the resolution which had been passed on the 23rd. It had waited on the Prime Minister and in the evening it sent urgent telegrams to Barnes and Hill mentioning that the F.O.L. was about to enter the dispute.[20] But no word was passed on to the watersiders about the tone of the conversation with the Prime Minister. There is no reason to believe that Walsh was anxious that the watersiders should back down. Indeed, he may have been hoping that they would not.

Over the weekend of 24-25 February the Government and the watersiders were carefully counting their friends. The Government, following the meeting with the F.O.L., had little cause for alarm. The watersiders did not know much about the meeting and would probably not have been deterred if they had. Barnes and Hill were in close touch with several industrial unions, whose leaders were carefully reading the lengthy Waterfront Strike Emergency Regulations. And A.B. Grant, the secretary of the T.U.C., was active on the watersiders' behalf issuing a lengthy statement attacking the *Press* for an editorial, and suggesting that the Government was about to launch a "frontal attack" on the wages and conditions of all workers.[21] In Christchurch on the 25th an open-air meeting in Latimer Square was attended by 1500 people who heard the watersiders' case. But everybody was really waiting to see what would happen on the Monday morning, although the odds were lengthening against the watersiders accepting the Government's ultimatum. From Auckland came a report that the union was removing all its property from its headquarters in Quay Street, and that it appeared to be preparing to go underground.[22] It was beginning to look as though a lengthy struggle lay ahead.

At 8 am on the morning of Monday 26 February watersiders gathered at all ports to consider the Government's ultimatum — return to normal hours including overtime, or the Emergency Regulations would be put into effect. Representatives from the press were invited to listen to any discussion and to witness the voting. In Wellington, T.G. Wells, the branch president, opened the meeting by telling the men that the law required them to resume work immediately. A motion was then moved that Wellington watersiders reaffirm the decision of the previous Monday to offer themselves for work on the basis of an eight-hour day, Monday to Friday. There was no discussion on the motion and when the motion was put it was carried unanimously

9. Servicemen loading meat into the *Port Lyttelton*, Queen's Wharf, Auckland, March 1951. *(Auckland Star)*

10. Servicemen unloading coal from the *Kaitangata* at Western Wharf, Auckland, under the watchful eye of a police constable, March 1951.

on a show of hands. The same procedure was followed with the same result elsewhere in the country. A further motion condemning the Government for its action in not allowing the watersiders to work a forty-hour week was moved at most ports. In Wellington the branch secretary, E.A. Napier, stated that none of the present leaders of the union had ever been parties to any agreement which involved compulsory overtime. Compulsory overtime, he said, had operated only during the war and the Order of the Waterfront Industry Commission which had applied prior to 20 February 1951 did not make overtime mandatory. It was, said Napier, quite reasonable that the watersiders should refuse to accept the employers' conditions imposed on the previous Monday. Again the motion was carried without dissent, as was a third motion calling on the Government to summon Parliament to discuss the State of Emergency. After a brief address from Hill (Barnes was addressing the Auckland watersiders at the same hour) the men left the wharves. Many removed gear from their lockers and took it with them. Later in the morning pickets were posted at all gates along the Auckland waterfront, and the following day they appeared in Wellington as well.[23] The defiance of the Government's ultimatum was complete.

It is clear from these actions that the watersiders believed they had a watertight case. They were prepared to work a forty-hour week and were being prevented from doing so. Therefore the responsibility for any shortages of food or supplies which might warrant putting the Emergency Regulations into force lay elsewhere. Moreover, the union pointed out that in the settlement of the wages issue it wanted nothing more than that the precedent established at the time of the lampblack dispute be maintained. Napier told an *Evening Post* reporter that the union was quite willing to accept a tribunal similar to the one which had produced a settlement in September 1950—a conference of employers' and workers' representatives presided over by an industrial magistrate without voting powers. In short, the watersiders still insisted that the principle of direct negotiation which they believed they had won had to be maintained.[24]

Fearing that a major battle lay ahead, P.M. Butler, who was

a member of the F.O.L.'s National Executive, made a private approach to the watersiders on the morning of the 26th. He urged the N.Z.W.W.U. to adopt a more conciliatory attitude. From this meeting (Barnes was not present) he emerged with the impression that the union would in the last resort accept that a chairman should have voting powers if the parties to the dispute were called together. He made this point to Holland and Sullivan when the National Executive of the F.O.L. met the Government later in the day. Holland was "not impressed" at first, but, as the delegation left the Prime Minister's office at 4 pm, Holland stated that, if Butler could get an assurance from the watersiders in writing by 5 pm that a chairman's ruling would be accepted, then the Government would consider setting up a "special committee".[25]

Butler and Croskery were then sent by the F.O.L. to the watersiders' national office to inform them of the Prime Minister's message. Somewhat to his surprise, Butler discovered that he had earlier misunderstood the watersiders. Barnes (who had arrived from Auckland), Hill, Napier and Wells made it clear to him that under no circumstances would the watersiders risk an adverse decision by a chairman of any committee set up by the Government. Croskery and Butler argued until 5.25 pm that such a policy was unreasonable, and that it played right into the Government's and the employers' hands. Barnes, however, stated that the Tory Government would have to be "taken on" sometime. The wharfies were determined to take them on. If they were big enough the wharfies would win. If the Government was good enough it would win. Barnes added that "it is a gamble"; the F.O.L. "could take a short price on the result".[26] He was confident the wharfies would win out. Butler's personal diplomacy had failed. This was to be the N.Z.W.W.U.'s last chance to save itself, and the watersiders (Barnes's domination of his colleagues was the critical factor) had rejected it. The battle was on.

The Last Days of February

The watersiders' gamble, however, was bound not to pay off. After they had rejected the Government's ultimatum and nothing had come of Butler's mission, the Government swiftly put the Emergency Regulations into force. From this time onwards it was an offence for anyone to be a party to this waterfront dispute which was now declared to be a strike. The Government was armed with unlimited powers.

Once it possessed these powers the Government's bargaining position *vis à vis* the union was immeasurably stronger. Signs quickly emerged which suggested that Holland and Sullivan were preparing to fight on a wider front than the simple maintenance of the principle of arbitration. In a press statement issued on the afternoon of the 26th Sullivan stated:

> The Government's patience with the Waterside Workers' Union is exhausted and it is now compelled to take decisive action. When people not only break the law but defy it, the time for negotiation has passed. That situation has been reached on the waterfront.

The Minister went on to say that the Government understood the difference between "honest trade unionists and those people who insidiously undermine the trade union movement". The "brow-beating, Communist-serving agitator will be crushed".[27]

The following morning the Government began to reveal what it had been planning the previous week. In Auckland and Wellington servicemen were brought on to the wharves to handle perishable cargoes. In Auckland some 200 servicemen from the three services unloaded 6,400 boxes of butter, and took over the Auckland Farmers' Freezing Company cool stores when the shed hands refused to accept the butter and walked out. The watersiders watching from the port building jeered as the men, many of them new to such work, dropped some boxes. In Wellington an Air Force detachment moved on to Pipitea Wharf and unloaded two coastal vessels. The wharves, meantime, were being closely guarded by a strong force of policemen.

At the same time the Government, which had been in contact with the mayors at the four main centres the previous week,[28] announced the establishment of Emergency Supplies Committees. These were given the power to allocate service labour to vessels according to an order of priority determined with

the help of an advisory committee made up of representatives
of the shipping companies, harbour boards, armed services,
police, Master Carriers' Association, Transport Department and
the W.I.C. They were also to assist in the formation of new port
unions, should the Government require it.[29]

On Wednesday 28 February the Minister of Labour announced
that the N.Z.W.W.U. had been deregistered under the powers
given him by the Industrial Conciliation and Arbitration Amendment Act, 1939. Since they were not registered under any other
Act of Parliament, this meant that the watersiders were no longer
recognised as belonging to a union or possessing democratically-
elected leaders.[30] Any representations by Barnes and Hill on
behalf of the watersiders who were out of work could be ignored
if the Government so wished. On the following Tuesday
Sullivan made it clear that he intended to have no further
direct dealings with Barnes and Hill when he had them ejected
from his office. "We are not prepared to carry on any discussion
with the waterside workers' representatives, Mr Barnes and
Mr Hill. That is a decision of the Prime Minister and myself . . . .
In future, discussions with the watersiders must be with responsible men, representative of the industry."[31] It was becoming
clear that if the watersiders wished to see the dispute settled
they would have to do more than accept the principle of arbitration and give a guarantee that they would abide permanently
by any decision handed down by an arbitrator; they would
also have to find themselves some leaders acceptable to the
National Government.

The act of deregistering the union on 28 February provided
the Government with even wider powers to affect the future
shape of the waterfront industry. It could in one blow destroy
the idea of a national union on New Zealand's waterfront. This
Sullivan and Holland appeared to be aiming at. Hoping that
some of the South Island branches of the N.Z.W.W.U., which
were known on occasions to have disagreed with national
policy, might use the opportunity to form separate units,
Sullivan announced:

> I will be prepared to give favourable consideration to the registration
> of unions at the various ports when I am satisfied that the workers

at these ports are prepared to conduct their affairs in a proper manner and faithfully carry out their conditions of employment.[32] The national union, carefully constructed by the workers over many years, was now legally dead. In its place there could be a local union at each of the twenty-six ports. Moreover, the fact that there was now no union and the Order of the Waterfront Industry Commission had been suspended a week earlier, meant that the employers would have the freedom to employ on the waterfront whoever they could get. They would not have to give preference to unionists; employment would be open to all comers.[33] There could be, if the employers could only find the men, a clean sweep on all the waterfronts in New Zealand. It was a wonderful prospect for the harassed port employers.

For the watersiders it became even more a "do-or-die" struggle. Not only their national union and their leaders, but also their future employment on the waterfront were at stake. On the 29th their funds were also placed in jeopardy when the Public Trustee was appointed as Receiver of the union's funds, and action was taken to seize records as well. Little wonder that the watersiders' resolve to see the fight through was strong by the end of February; the option was humiliation. The Auckland branch of the deregistered union unanimously carried the motion on 1 March:

> That the Government's action in deregistering the Union inspires the membership of this branch to greater effort to win the victory for trade unionism. We therefore reaffirm our solidarity with the National Union and supporting trade unions. We also recommend [that] National and Local Organizations be set up embracing all Unions involved in the dispute.[34]

Once the old union was placed outside the law and was unable to hold public meetings or distribute propaganda its statements and activities ceased to draw attention from the press. Before the Emergency Regulations had been announced on 22 February the press had already shown a tendency to cut down on the amount of space given to statements by Barnes and Hill. After the 26th, when it became an offence under the Regulations to print or publish any statement that was intended to, or likely to, aid a declared strike, or to report such a statement, newspapers had the perfect excuse to do officially what they had begun to do voluntarily—carefully censor any material that might be in any way helpful to the watersiders' case.[35] With every day that passed the odds against success for the watersiders grew steadily longer.

The Labour Movement Splits

Once the Government had armed itself with such extensive powers to deal with the waterfront dispute it was impossible to visualise the watersiders winning much more than some token victory on one of the points at issue. And to achieve even as much as this they would need hefty support from all sections of the trade union movement. Little short of major civil upheaval would have been necessary to shake the determination of Holland who, in a national broadcast on the evening of 27 February, drew up the battle lines:

We could give in to the strikers—but we won't.
We could capitulate to direct action—but we won't.
We could let tyranny replace democratic government—but we won't.
We could let down every other worker who abides by the law—but we won't.
We could let direct action pay better dividends than democratic methods—but we won't.
We could shirk our plain public duty—but we won't.[36]

The watersiders' friends, however, were diminishing. When the crunch came, past quarrels and old enmities began to tell against them.

As soon as the Emergency Regulations went into force on 26 February there were some repercussions within the trade union movement. The T.U.C., which was holding a national conference in Wellington to discuss wages, reaffirmed its full support for the watersiders until the Regulations were lifted and stated that it regarded them as an attack on all trade unionists. Most militants agreed. Waikato miners had met the previous week and the men were clearly disturbed at the prospect of the Emergency Regulations going into force. On the 26th meetings were held at most of the pitheads in the country and work ceased as those unions affiliated with the T.U.C. expressed their opposition to continuing work while the Emergency Regulations were operating. By 1 March almost all the West Coast, King Country and Waikato mines were idle.[37] Only Kamo, the Runanga and Buller mines in Westland, and the Canterbury, Otago and Southland mines were still working.

On that date the National Council of the United Mine Workers of New Zealand, which over the previous six months had been trying to steer the miners along a more moderate path than that being followed by the T.U.C., capitulated and decided to instruct all its branches to cease work immediately.[38] By the weekend of 3-4 March most had obeyed and more than 4,000 miners at twenty-one pits were out on strike in protest at the Emergency Regulations. Coal supplies dwindled rapidly, and railway schedules and gas supplies were soon affected.

Many freezing workers were also alarmed at the severity of the Emergency Regulations. Some work had ceased at the Ngahauranga works on 23 February. On the 26th further meetings were held and all work ceased at Ngahauranga, at the Gear Freezing Works in Petone, and at the Wellington City Abattoirs. On the following day the men at Borthwick's at Belfast and at the Longburn and Patea Freezing Works as well as at the Levin Abattoirs also walked off the job. By 15 March the only work being performed in the area covered by the Wellington District Freezing Workers' Union was at Waitara and Tomoana; the previous day the Auckland works had also ceased activities. In all cases the men objected to the Emergency Regulations and to the presence of Services' personnel on the wharves.[39] At the height of the waterfront dispute nearly 7,000 freezing workers at twenty-one works were on strike.

The Wellington area was most seriously affected by the stoppages at the freezing works. The *Evening Post* reported on 27 February that demand for meat in most Wellington butchers' shops was heavy and on the following day some suburban butchers closed altogether, one leaving a notice in his window reading "BACK IN THE SPRING". Other shops carried little more than sausages and other small goods. Hotels were feeling the impact, and there was a heavy demand for poultry. By 8 March even the lions at the zoo were on short rations.[40]

The existence of the Emergency Regulations also brought about a cessation of construction work on the Waikato hydroelectric chain. On the 27th, after a short meeting of the men at Mangakino, work stopped at Maraetai and Whakamaru. About 1,000 members of the New Zealand Workers' Union engaged on these sites were affected. A.E. Clarke, the project engineer, told the press that the men would not work because of the Government's actions over the waterfront.[41]

In spite of these events it was clear by the first week in March that the Emergency Regulations and the presence of servicemen on the wharves had not led to the complete paralysis of the transport system that the watersiders had hoped for. Those unions whose men were directly involved with work on the waterfront had ceased work. Besides the watersiders, the Harbour Boards Employees' Union was on strike, refusing to handle goods loaded or unloaded from ships by servicemen; seamen, cooks and stewards also refused to work with servicemen, despite the fact that F.P. Walsh was president of the Seamen's Union and was not anxious to aid the watersiders.[42]

However, the actions of the drivers' unions and the railwaymen fell somewhat short of what the watersiders had hoped for. The National Councils of both the Amalgamated Society of Railway Servants (A.S.R.S.) and the Railway Tradesmen's Association (R.T.A.) announced that they opposed the Regulations and would not handle goods unloaded by non-union labour. But other goods and passenger services were continued, though on restricted timetables as the shortage of coal became more serious. Drivers in Auckland and Wellington similarly announced that they would not cart goods to and from the wharves, a decision which hampered the activities of the servicemen and necessitated the use of Army trucks for handling cargo to and from the Wellington waterfront. But other deliveries were maintained; at no point was the nation completely without public transport.

If the holdup was to be effective, more support for the watersiders or opposition to the Emergency Regulations would have to be forthcoming. On 27 February the T.U.C. decided to try political pressure. Grant approached the Parliamentary

Labour Party and the National Executive of the F.O.L. and
asked them to send representatives to join a delegation to wait
on the Prime Minister for the purposes of protesting against the
Emergency Regulations. The Labour Party, however, declined
to join the delegation, Nash telling Grant that "no good purpose
could be achieved" by a combined approach to the Government.[43]
The following day Nash issued a statement on behalf of the
Labour Party that placed the party in a somewhat equivocal
position. Nash stated that he believed that a compulsory conference of the disputants should have been called as provided for
under the Industrial Relations Act 1949 and as promised by
the National Party in its 1949 manifesto. Emergency powers,
he said, should be used only as a last resort when "all normal
methods had . . . failed". Nash also emphasised that the Labour
Party firmly supported conciliation and arbitration as methods
of solving industrial disputes,[44] and it seems fairly likely that
it was this firm belief in arbitration that made him reluctant
to have anything to do with the militant T.U.C.

The F.O.L.'s position was much less equivocal. Croskery,
Walsh and Baxter were not prepared to do anything towards
a settlement of the dispute unless they had complete control
of negotiations and had a promise from the watersiders that
arbitration would be agreed to and that any decision arrived at
by this process would be fully accepted. The F.O.L. was happy
to participate in a conference of sixty-three delegates from
unions affected by the dispute on the afternoon of the 27th.
And it was satisfied with the resolution obtained from it.
This called for a compulsory conference between watersiders
and employers with an independent chairman and the right of
appeal from the conference to a tribunal whose decision would
be final.[45] But the National Executive ignored the invitation to
join the T.U.C.'s delegation to the Prime Minister protesting
against the Regulations.[46] Subsequently it claimed that the
F.O.L.'s reservations about the Regulations had been adequately
conveyed to Holland during the meeting of the 26th, and that
there was doubt "whether any good purpose could be achieved"
by further protest.[47] Above all, Walsh seems to have been
anxious that the dispute not get side-tracked from the central

11. Members of the Auckland Branch of the N.Z.W.W.U. (deregistered) meet for the first of their daily meetings at the Trades Hall, Hobson Street, 1 March 1951.

issue of arbitration. This was the watersiders' most vulnerable point.

On 1 March the watersiders still refused to place the dispute in the Federation's hands and would not accept the idea of a conference with the ultimate right of appeal to a tribunal whose decision would be final. The F.O.L. now retired temporarily from the centre of the stage. Baxter announced that the Federation "at the moment contemplates no further action in the national waterfront dispute". It had "done everything it could be expected to do within reason", he claimed, and added:

> The Waterside Workers' Union can blame only itself for its present position. The 1950 conference of the Federation laid it down very clearly that it would never allow itself to be diverted by individuals or factions who endeavour to use the trade union movement to forward their own policies, whether they originate in this country or overseas. In refusing to submit what appeared to be a good case to a tribunal and accepting the decision with the right of appeal the officials

of the Waterside Workers' Union were making every effort
to drag trade unionists into a conflict with the state.[48]
Labour solidarity in the face of the Emergency Regulations was
now publicly non-existent. The press cheered, most newspapers
trying to drive the wedge deeper by suggesting what was to
become a familiar plea, that the Labour Party should climb off
the fence and join the Federation.[49]

Meantime the T.U.C.'s delegation had been received by
Holland, Sullivan and other Ministers on the evening of the 27th.
The meeting lasted fifteen minutes. What the delegation lacked
in numbers it made up for with threatening language. Grant
and T.J. ("Pat") Potter, the President of the T.U.C., demanded
that the Government revoke the Emergency Regulations which,
they claimed, were aimed not only at the watersiders but at the
freedom of all New Zealanders. The delegation told Holland
that no government in a democracy had introduced such measures
and survived. If he kept the Regulations in force, Holland would
be committing political suicide. Unless the Regulations were
lifted there would be no negotiations.[50]

There was nothing about these statements likely to frighten
the Government. To Holland and Sullivan it must have been a
pleasure to see how unrepresentative of the labour movement
this delegation was. What was more, Sullivan probably knew by
this time that the F.O.L. was about to bow out, for contacts
between Walsh and the Minister were growing more frequent.
For the meantime the Government's cause and the Federation's
were one and the same—the defeat of the militants.

By the first week in March, the watersiders' self-imposed
isolationism was really telling against them. Barnes was booed
and howled down by a vociferous minority when he attempted
to address a meeting of the Wellington Drivers' Union on
1 March,[51] and at a further meeting of unions involved in the
dispute on Saturday 3 March it was clear that personal hostility
between Barnes and Walsh was considerable.[52] By the 5th Walsh
was getting the upper hand. Most unions affected by the holdup
seemed to be drifting towards a conviction that the watersiders
would have to accept some form of arbitration or the dispute
might continue for months.[53]

Realising that the tide was now going their way the National Executive of the F.O.L. decided on the afternoon of 5 March to summon a special conference of the Federation for later in the week.[54] This would, it was calculated, endorse the actions of the National Executive and strengthen Walsh's hand in his attempts to isolate the watersiders and the T.U.C.

It was at this point that the watersiders who were anxious not to suffer a complete loss of face, decided themselves to make a desperate effort to negotiate a settlement to the dispute. Barnes and Hill met representatives from the New Zealand Freezing Workers' Association and the United Mine Workers on the 5th, and the following day a deputation waited on Sullivan. Sullivan refused to discuss the dispute with Barnes and Hill but did confer with the freezing workers and miners, who requested that a compulsory conference of the disputants be convened. But it was clear that the watersiders still refused to allow the chairman of any such conference to make a decision.[55] After reporting the discussion to a meeting of Cabinet Sullivan wrote to S. Giles, National Secretary of the Freezing Workers' Association, that the Government was "not prepared to consider any proposal for the settlement of this dispute which departs from the principle of conciliation and arbitration".[56]

If a settlement of the dispute were to be reached before the F.O.L.'s special conference on 8 March had decided to isolate the watersiders, the watersiders would have to compromise. Consequently Giles and A.V. Prendiville of the United Mine Workers' Union, spent many hours with Barnes and Hill on the 7th, trying to persuade them that their future was doomed if they did not accept arbitration. They succeeded. The following morning they delivered a letter to Sullivan on behalf of the deregistered N.Z.W.W.U. This letter stated[57] that the watersiders would go to conciliation "and, if necessary, Arbitration for settlement". The letter concluded that the watersiders were prepared to recommend resumption of normal work on the waterfront so long as the Emergency Regulations were lifted, and the *status quo* was to operate on the waterfront as before the dispute had arisen.

The letter shows that some very considerable soul-searching had been done by the watersiders, undoubtedly because of pressure from Giles and Prendiville, who were most unenthusiastic at the prospect of the F.O.L. Conference recommending their combined isolation. The result of this soul-searching was that the watersiders were prepared to make a package deal with the Government. They would jettison their demand for direct negotiation with the employers and would, if necessary, allow an arbitrator to make a decision, though Prendiville and Giles in conversation with the Minister made it clear that the union wished to be consulted about, and have the power of veto over, whoever the Minister suggested as the arbitrator.[58] For the watersiders this was clearly a surrender on the major point that had been at issue since the middle of February. Barnes and Hill wanted to retain some face with the labour movement. They hoped that the Government would be sufficiently anxious to settle the dispute to agree to reregistering the union, and recognising them for what they were—the democratically-elected leaders of the N.Z.W.W.U.

This was the first occasion on which it became clear that the Government was not interested in a quick solution to the waterfront dispute. Nothing less than complete submission by the watersiders was now demanded. In fact the request by the watersiders that they have some say in who was to be the arbitrator was not an unreasonable one. Successive governments since the principle of compulsory arbitration was first introduced in 1894 had usually made efforts to see that both Arbitration Court judges and *ad hoc* arbitrators of labour disputes were acceptable to both workers and management. Yet Sullivan seized on the watersiders' demands, as he understood them, as grounds for not accepting the proposals submitted in the letter by Giles and Prendiville. Prendiville, however, did not give up hope. He felt that Sullivan had been unnecessarily abrupt in terminating the discussions; when he encountered H.L. Bockett, the Secretary of Labour, at the Trentham races on Saturday 10 March, he informed Bockett that it was his understanding that Barnes and Hill would be prepared, if necessary, to have Sullivan appoint an arbitrator who might not have the prior approval of the union.[59] Giles, however, was unable to convince Bockett that this was the case when he rang him on the following day. But when in frustration, the President of the United Mine Workers issued a press statement on the matter[60] Sullivan's reply belittled the genuine efforts which the miners and freezing workers had been making to get a settlement. The Minister claimed:

> They did not agree that the Government should appoint an arbitrator if the parties could not agree on one. Now they say they are prepared to accept such a proposal.
>
> What form of arbitration? The form they set down, wiping their own Authority, and requesting a set-up to suit themselves? Such a preposterous proposal could not be entertained for one minute.
>
> The ludicrous position is that both these organisations associated with the watersiders, have partially withheld their services from the public, and then come along asking that they negotiate a basis of settlement for an organisation that is wholly on strike. Looks like a committee of strikers to settle a strike.[61]

This statement is interesting on two counts. In the first place Sullivan had left no doubt in the minds of Giles and Prendiville during their meetings of 6-8 March that, while he would prefer the watersiders to go back to the W.I.A., he would be prepared to consider a compulsory conference if he could get complete agreement from the watersiders that he, and he alone, would appoint the arbitrator. This had been what all the discussion with Giles and Prendiville had been about. Yet, on the 13th, any discussions outside the W.I.A. had become a "preposterous" idea. The second thing of interest is that Sullivan seemed, by his statement, to be ruling out as negotiators the very men with whom he had been dealing during the previous few days. By the 13th, Giles and Prendiville had earned a degree of ministerial opprobrium almost equal to that of Barnes and Hill.

At first sight one might be tempted to conclude that Sullivan had been shamming all along, and that he had never intended seriously to discuss negotiations. Yet this was not the impression he gave to Giles or Prendiville. They would not have expended so much effort had they seen negotiation as a hopeless quest from the start. A closer look at ministerial statements between 1 and 13 March suggests that Sullivan had in fact been participating in two sets of activities that were really mutually contradictory. On the one hand he had been talking about negotiated settlements and a belief in the principle of arbitration. On the other hand he had also been talking since early in the month about the need for a new deal on the waterfront. When he had announced the deregistration of the old union he had looked forward to the prospect of a series of new port unions on the waterfront, and by the end of the first week in March there were some reports—premature as they turned out— that Sir John Allum in Auckland had had some success with his efforts to find men ready to participate in the formation of a new union there.[62] Moreover, in an idle moment on 8 March, Sullivan had himself said that any solution to the dispute would not be satisfactory to the Government "if it merely meant a return to work under the old order of things".[63] Holland had followed suit on the 9th with a statement that "the evils of the present system must be corrected once and for all", and that the Government did not intend just to "patch things up temporarily".[64]

All this kind of talk was really quite incompatible with a negotiated settlement of the dispute in question between the employers and the watersiders. The Government had set in motion a train of events which would have to be halted if a settlement were to be made at this point. It would have had many questions to answer publicly, not least those that would be asked by the press which had, since the old union had been deregistered, set up a truly fearsome racket demanding a vast series of changes on the waterfront. The *Herald* had been only one amongst many when it had demanded "a clean sweep . . . of arrogant leaders, of broken engagements, of bad faith, of community blackmail", and had appealed to "honest workers" to come forward and make "a fresh and clean start".[65]

The full realisation that a settlement with the old union on the basis of arbitration would require a display of statesmanship may have come when the Prime Minister and the Minister of Labour paid a flying visit to Auckland on 12 March and had discussions with the Mayor's Emergency Committee.[66] Sir John Allum, an extreme conservative of long standing, (Ben Chifley called him "that rank old Tory")[67] probably encouraged the Government to be firm, and promised to do everything within his power to find the men necessary to form a new union in Auckland quickly. Such assurances probably convinced Holland and Sullivan that it was worth pressing ahead. Negotiations would have to be put off, and this was easily accomplished in the statement of the 13th. Giles and Prendiville retired hurt, the victims of two conflicting policies being pushed by a Minister who was probably pleased now to find that they were incompatible. The watersiders' position grew weaker daily.

CHAPTER V

DESERTED BY THE UNION MOVEMENT

Walsh Whips the F.O.L. into Line
   The Government decided to prolong the dispute after the second week in March because it wanted to achieve more than formal acceptance of the principle of compulsory arbitration. Government members, like their many supporters among farmers, employers and the newspapers wanted blood. For many reasons they wanted not just a moral, but an actual victory over leftwing labour. Such could be seen to have been achieved if the national union of the watersiders was broken and Barnes and Hill were driven from the waterfront. From the time when Holland and Sullivan sensed that this prize was within their grasp they pursued it with single-minded devotion.
   But the pursuit led them across some dangerous ground. Clearly, the whole system of compulsory arbitration meant that it was the State's responsibility in the last analysis to see that unions registered under the I.C. & A. Act respected its procedures and did not resort to direct action. There were many precedents for the National Government's demand in February 1951 that compulsory arbitration be adhered to. There were no New Zealand precedents, however, for the Government's decision in March to go ahead with the smashing of a national union of workers, nor for the many further conditions which were to be imposed by the Government before it would entertain a settlement of the waterfront crisis. The dispute was entering a new stage by the second week of March. Intent on its aim, the Government was preparing to use the power of the State in what some came to feel was a dictatorial manner.
   In retrospect it is clear that the Government was able to act as it did only because there existed at the time a unique set of circumstances. The support of farmers, employers and the press

was to be expected. Why should they complain about Government actions which would directly benefit themselves? But much more important to the Government's calculations was the unprecedented absence of any strong arguments against continuing the dispute.

Under normal circumstances there would have been strong economic arguments against prolonging a waterfront stoppage. Even with servicemen at work on the wharves New Zealand's export trade would in all probability be severely affected and overseas reserves run down.[1] But 1951 was not a time of "normal circumstances". Export receipts for the previous year were at a record level due to the high demand caused by the Korean War. Reserves were high and so also was the Government's flexibility. If the cost of prolonging the dispute should be considerable, the country could probably afford it. As the *Evening Post* was later to say, it was buoyant economic conditions which enabled this dispute to become by far the longest, most widespread and most costly industrial struggle in New Zealand's history.[2]

In addition to this factor, the Government was not suffering any serious harassment. The newspapers had clamped down on discussion of the crisis; almost no letters defending the watersiders appeared in papers after 26 February. Moreover, with broadcasting in the hands of the Government it was possible to ensure that only committed supporters of the official line could express an opinion over the radio or in the correspondence columns of the *New Zealand Listener*.[3] In addition to these factors, the Government's usual political opponents were either silent or compliant. Apart from the statement of Nash's at the end of February the Labour Party had made no move in the dispute; some members of the Parliamentary Labour Party were known to be enjoying, vicariously, Sullivan's battle with the militants.

But the most important single factor in the Government's calculations was the attitude of the Federation of Labour. The destruction of the old N.Z.W.W.U. was not to be achieved single-handed. If it was the Government that erected the scaffold and placed the rope round the watersiders' necks it was the F.O.L. which released the trap.[4]

On the afternoon of 5 March the National Executive of the F.O.L. made its decision to summon a special conference of its affiliates. The declared purpose of the conference was the consideration of recent activities of the National Executive and affiliated unions, and the determining of a policy in relation to the waterfront stoppage. But the National Executive did not intend to approach its affiliates with an open mind, waiting to find out the opinions of the rank and file. At a meeting of the National Executive on the afternoon of 7 March elaborate preparations were made for the conference scheduled to begin the following morning. No visitors were to be allowed and the services of some hefty doorkeepers were sought. Walsh was to be the principal speaker on the first day and was to present the National Executive's version of the waterfront dispute to the conference. Baxter was to supplement. After much deliberation it was agreed that Barnes, but only Barnes, was to be invited "to state the case for the watersiders".[5]

The Special Conference duly opened at 11 am on Thursday 8 March, with Croskery in the chair. One hundred and fifty-seven delegates with a total card vote strength of 245 were present. The only incident had been the presence of Potter and other members of the T.U.C. who had handed out leaflets at the door to the delegates as they assembled in the Wellington Town Hall.[6]

The morning session belonged to F.P. Walsh, the vice-president. At great length he summarised the activities of the National Executive, ending with a declaration to the effect that the National Executive supported compulsory arbitration, upheld its concept of democracy against totalitarianism, believed that direct action would "lead to a kind of civil warfare", and wanted the watersiders to cooperate with the F.O.L. to achieve "bread and butter gains" rather than "indulge in a disastrous political action under directions from the Communist-controlled W.F.T.U. in Warsaw and Moscow". It was an extravagant speech.[7]

The afternoon session was mostly taken up with speeches by delegates. But the discussion was carefully controlled from the stage. A militant speech from a delegate would be followed by one from a member of the National Executive who would return the discussion to the sins of the watersiders and the need to keep the principle of compulsory arbitration firmly in mind. At no point did the National Executive look as though it would lose control of the conference. Nevertheless, as a prophylactic measure, Walsh assumed the chair on Friday morning, Croskery being absent "owing to illness in his family". Walsh proceeded to move that his report of the previous day be adopted by the conference, and the minutes record that only nine delegates voted against the motion. This was the test, and Walsh was on the winning side. In quick succession his allies moved a series of resolutions calling upon the National Executive to enter negotiations with the Government "with a view to protecting the interests of our affiliations and other workers who are likely to be affected by any continuation of the present dispute".

A meeting with the Prime Minister was arranged for 12.30 pm the same day. At this meeting Walsh informed Holland that the National Executive of the F.O.L. had been instructed to begin negotiations, and Holland replied that the Government was ready to negotiate with them, but not with Barnes or Hill or Drennan, or "any known communist". Walsh proposed that the Government should be prepared to accept "normal work" on the waterfront, and that after a resumption of work the issues would be negotiated between the Government and the Federation and any unions the F.O.L. liked to call in. But Holland refused. In due course he would negotiate with the Federation only on the question of the terms for a resumption of work; he was not concerned by the prospect that the crisis might continue for another week or more.[8]

This new turn of events posed a problem for the National Executive of the F.O.L., which had hoped to have matters firmly settled on the Friday afternoon. It was now clear that Holland was not prepared to accept a quick solution to the waterfront crisis. Nor was he prepared, as yet, to begin negotiations with the F.O.L. about the terms for a resumption of work. Walsh knew that the unions gathered in Wellington wanted a quick settlement. But he could not at this point give a guarantee to the Prime Minister that they would accept unconditionally whatever terms the Government and the Federation's National Executive at some future date might agree to for a resumption of work. But in reporting back to the final session of the F.O.L. conference, Walsh did ask that the negotiation of terms for a resumption of work be left to the National Executive of the F.O.L. and the organisations immediately affected by the waterfront holdup, who would meet with the Government the following week. With a masterly display of chairmanship Walsh knocked back resolutions, one from the right wing of the Federation, another from the left wing,[9] that would have tied the hands of the National Executive in its negotiations with the Government. Instead, his own motion was put and carried. This stated that in all negotiations there would be no departure from the policy of compulsory arbitration, and that any representatives of the watersiders, miners and freezing workers, or any other unions not affiliated to the F.O.L., would have to state in writing that they accepted compulsory arbitration before they could take part in the negotiations. "Failing such assurance by the watersiders", the motion continued, "this Conference has no option but to inform our affiliations that we cannot and will not lend any further support to this dispute."[10]

Walsh, clearly, had swept the conference delegates off their feet. For the most part they were representatives of the more moderate unions, none of the T.U.C. unions being eligible to attend. And the moderates were looking for strong leadership. They mistrusted the watersiders and there was a certain resentment at the substantial wages and conditions they had won over the years. Walsh was able to convey this impatience with the watersiders. He seemed to the delegates to be alternately tough and principled. He had a hand in a press release on the Thursday calling on the watersiders "to abandon their Communist-dominated misleaders";[11] but on the following day as things went his way, he seemed more avuncular, more concerned with the fate of the men involved in the dispute. The watersiders, he told the conference, must be "saved" along with the rest of the trade union movement.[12]

The result was that the National Executive emerged from the two-day meeting without any embarrassing resolutions on the books. No protest against the Emergency Regulations had been moved, as one irate delegate discovered too late in the closing stages of the conference. But the National Executive did emerge with all that was necessary to isolate the watersiders. And, what was more, Walsh intended to do just this, as the *Herald* suspected, when it headlined its final reports of the Conference: F.O.L. ISOLATES WATERSIDERS.[13]

After most of the delegates had returned home the Federation's National Executive got down to work. A letter was dispatched to the watersiders, freezing workers and miners asking them to refer the dispute to the Federation and to give a written guarantee that they would accept compulsory arbitration.[14] The freezing workers replied that all parties were prepared to agree to arbitration, and upbraided the Federation for not having lent assistance to the efforts of the miners and freezing workers to bring about a settlement over the previous week. None of the three unions was prepared to give unconditional support to any efforts that the Federation and its affiliates were about to make to negotiate the terms for a return to work, though the miners and the freezing workers who continued to hold a brief for the watersiders did agree to join in the discussions which the Federation held with the Government on 13 and 14 March.[15]

These discussions were brief, and at first nothing was forthcoming because the Government would not reveal to the unions concerned the terms on which it was prepared to consider a return to work. In fact, on neither day did Holland or Sullivan give much thought to a settlement of the dispute. They were both busy buttressing the Government's position. A number of measures were announced which together suggested that the Government was planning an extended fight with the watersiders. On the 13th compulsory military training was suspended for the duration of the dispute in order that 4,000 eighteen-year-olds could be put back into civilian life. This meant that more members of the regular forces could be released for emergency work on the waterfront. Cabinet also issued instructions for a recall of the cruiser *Bellona* and the frigate *Taupo* from Commonwealth naval manoeuvres in Australian waters. In

Auckland it was also announced that eighteen Wrens from HMNZS *Philomel* would be posted to supply duties on the Auckland waterfront as from the 14th.[16]

From Whakatane, the home of the Minister of Labour, came news that was more ominous for the watersiders' already slim chances of a reasonable settlement. The registration of a new port union was announced, and it was said that the Government had been receiving many inquiries about the formation of new unions at other ports.[17] The following morning it looked as though Tauranga might follow suit; a group of Judea Maoris applied to work on the waterfront there.[18]

This news was particularly significant. Allum was trying hard in Auckland, but it was Sullivan, himself, who had finally succeeded in getting a new port union underway. Once a new union had been established at Whakatane the Government had good reason not to agree to any settlement that might allow former watersiders there to return to their old positions. Moreover, success at one port raised the prospect that it could be repeated throughout the country.[19] Holland and Sullivan could see a day, which they hoped was not far off, when there would be no further problem on the waterfront. The wharves would be being worked by a new set of men and the old troublemakers would be completely outmanoeuvred. There would be no jobs for them to return to.

Flushed with the prospect of victory, Holland, after "considerable discussion", finally placed before the waiting unionists on the 15th a list of points which the watersiders would have to accept before there could be any negotiations for a permanent settlement. The "Seven Points", as they were known, were the work of Holland alone.[20] They had been discussed briefly with representatives of the port employers on the morning of the 15th and they were described as preliminary "aims" which all parties were expected to strive for during further negotiations. They were:

    1. The basis of all negotiations shall be that agreements and obligations are honourably observed by all parties.

2. To devise ways and means for a quick and just investigation and settlement of disputes within the framework of conciliation and arbitration.
3. To devise ways and means of increasing substantially efficiency in the industry, and of speeding up the turnround of ships.
4. To ensure that secret ballots are always taken on strike issues.
5. To make the waterfront industry one in which any worker may enter in the same manner as in other industries.
6. To place the industry as far as is practicable, on a basis of fulltime permanent employment, as in other industries.
7. To establish a system that will ensure to waterside workers a just reward for their labours comparable with that obtained in other industries.[21]

The most interesting thing about the "Seven Points" is that they were no more than a set of general aims. Holland probably hoped that they would be sufficiently high-sounding to seem reasonable to the Federation's supporters inadvertently involved in the dispute, while at the same time not specific enough to draw from the watersiders an instant, hostile denunciation. The "Seven Points" made no mention at all of the three things which the Government had already decided to enforce—an end to the national union, no place for Barnes and Hill within the new port unions, and the careful screening of men who might wish to join the new unions. These things the Government had already hinted at; it intended to delay stressing them until it was sure that the Federation's unions would resume normal work, thus isolating the watersiders. To announce them at this point might have deterred some of the Federation's affiliates from recommending a resumption of normal work. And at this point the Government's most important aim was isolation of the watersiders.

The Government's ploy worked perfectly, because Holland had the active support of Walsh. The delegates from the seven Federation affiliates that had been parties to the discussions with the Government[22] met on the 16th, and under Walsh's guidance they agreed that Holland's "Seven Points" were "a reasonable basis for a settlement".[23] And having endorsed the Government's aims, and demanded that the watersiders accept them, the delegates went back to their branches to encourage their rank and file to do likewise by voting "yes" in the ballots that were to be held for a return to normal work.

Meantime the freezing workers and miners had been discussing the "Seven Points" with Barnes and Hill. The discussions were anything but amicable. After the Federation's meeting on the 16th, Prendiville, Crook and Kilpatrick sensed that their unions would quickly be isolated along with the watersiders if the latter did not make a quick and unqualified acceptance of the "Seven Points". Barnes, however, still cherished unreasonable hopes of a victory, and he refused to endorse the "Seven Points" unequivocally. Indeed, when he first saw them he told the miners and freezing workers "to stick them up their . . .".[24]

After some tempestuous scenes, Prendiville conveyed to Sullivan the watersiders' reply on the 17th.[25] Three points (1, 6 and 7) the watersiders accepted without qualification; to point 3 about the need for arbitration the union, after agreeing, added simply that it was to be understood that the watersiders did not want to be tied specifically to the Arbitration Court.[26] To the second point, that there should be an investigation of ways and means to speed up the turn round of ships, the watersiders also agreed, adding that they expected equal importance to be given to the provision of improved facilities for workers on the waterfront. Of points 4 and 5 about secret strike ballots and easier entry to employment on the waterfront, the watersiders were chary. Point 4 was bypassed with the statement that, since workers did not have the legal right to strike, the questions of the ballot was scarcely relevant. Point 5 was acceptable only if an adequate guaranteed wage such as had previously been paid only to "A" class watersiders was given to "B" class men as well.[27]

Prendiville found the Government in no mood to accept quibbling. A week before Sullivan had demanded nothing less than total surrender and by 17 March the Government's position *vis à vis* the watersiders was even stronger. Sullivan fastened on the watersiders' answer to point 5, which was the main problem and said that in future the port employers must have the fullest powers to hire and fire watersiders. Prendiville replied that since the Government and the watersiders were not too far apart on the other point negotiations should begin for a return to work and point 5 could be submitted to conciliation and arbitration at a later date.[28] The watersiders were not prepared to accept Prendiville's suggestion and neither was Sullivan anxious to settle on such a basis. The talks collapsed, the Government maintaining that lack of progress was due to the watersiders' intransigence.[29] Once again the miners and freezing workers' efforts at diplomacy had failed. Prendiville this time vented his wrath on Barnes and Hill who, it was suggested, should place point 5 to a vote of all watersiders.[30] This was not done, and after 23 March Prendiville ceased to have any further contact with the watersiders. Yet Government and watersiders were still deadlocked.

From the Government's point of view the collapse of the talks was no disaster. Cabinet had been preparing for a long fight for some days now, and on 20 March Sullivan stated that he could see little prospect of an early settlement. All the indications were, he said, that the dispute would continue for "some weeks". For the first time he stated publicly—almost as an aside—what the Government had intended to bring up at the negotiation stage with the watersiders. Under no circumstances would the old union be reregistered. Nor would Barnes and Hill be recognised in any way. The old waterfront regime "must be swept away".[31] And just to emphasize the Government's intention to secure complete capitulation from the watersiders on all points they might raise, Sullivan applied more pressure to the union. He announced that some £70,000 back pay accumulated as bonuses for work performed before February 1951 would not be paid out.[32] In addition a further proclamation of a State of Emergency was issued on the evening of 20 March and the Post and Telegraph Department was given special powers under the regulations to open mail containing, "or suspected to contain" any material in support of the watersiders.[33] On the 19th the police were specially requested by

Sullivan to apprehend any people who contributed to benefits for watersiders, and on the following day the police stepped in and banned a public meeting of watersiders being planned in Christchurch. In Auckland the T.U.C. was prevented by Allum from booking the Town Hall for a public meeting to discuss "prices, living standards and civil liberties".[34]

The Government was going to go ahead with its plans for new unions throughout the country, waiting in the meantime till the watersiders out of sheer exhaustion decided to capitulate. In a national broadcast on the evening of 23 March, Holland appealed for people to come forward to join the new unions at each port. He stated that work would be offered at the basic rate of 4/7½ an hour which, he claimed, included "the full fifteen per cent" awarded by the Arbitration Court.[35] The broadcast ended on a tough note. "There will be no retreat, no appeasement and no surrender in the Government's solution of the waterfront crisis". To the watersiders he added: "Outside your own ranks, and a few extremists in other industries, you have scarcely a friend in New Zealand today. The ones hardest hit by your tactics are not the Government but your fellow workers and their families".[36]

With the aggressive pronouncements after 20 March the Government had at last clearly revealed its ultimate objectives. But it would have been slower to do so had it not been confident that the watersiders were being deserted by the rest of the union movement. Most gas workers in Auckland and Wellington had voted to return to work on 9 March after the F.O.L. had appealed to its affiliates to maintain essential supplies.[37] The harbour board employees' unions considered returning to work even before their representatives had heard the Government's "Seven Points", and the Auckland Harbour Board's staff voted to work alongside servicemen for the first time on 12 March.[38] At the Westfield freezing works a secret ballot revealed a desire to return to work including the handling of goods ultimately to be shipped by servicemen, although a substantial minority refused to fall in with the majority's decision. At the Ocean Beach and Mataura freezing works in Southland the men voted overwhelmingly on 12 March to return to normal work. Cool store workers were divided; in Auckland strikers still outnumbered those who would resume normal work by a small margin, but in New Plymouth cool store workers were back on the job on 13 March.[39] In a secret ballot conducted by the Labour Department, Dunedin drivers decided by 77 to 39 to go on with normal work.[40]

Clearly the desertion rate was accelerating, but a bitter blow for the watersiders was the split that developed between them and their closest allies. On 17 March, after the abortive meeting between Prendiville and Sullivan, Prendiville, Crook and Kilpatrick resigned from the negotiating committees of their unions, the miners and the freezing workers, and rejected the watersiders' brief. At its best the watersiders' cause had never been particularly popular; to be associated with it now seemed to be a distinct liability.

The F.O.L.'s National Executive was also busily encouraging this desertion of its enemies. On 21 March it tightened up the pressure by calling on all workers to resume work. In the statement that was issued it was clear that this directive "carried with it the obligation to handle goods at present being loaded and discharged on the waterfronts". The statement continued:

> The [watersiders'] stubborn policy of persisting in this dispute which is contrary to the wishes of the majority of unionists, and the scornful rejection of the assistance of the Federation towards reaching a settlement, leave the Federation with no other course but to give effect to the unanimous decision of the Special Conference.[41]

There were immediate results. Many unions had been waiting for the green light for a return to work. The southern harbour board employees' unions voted during the next few days to return to work and on the 23rd the Auckland Sugar Workers' Union agreed to handle goods loaded and unloaded by servicemen. The Auckland Drivers' Union also voted overwhelmingly to resume servicing the waterfront, and Hastings drivers voted 70:18 to handle all goods as requested.[42] As the *Herald* had predicted, the F.O.L.'s directive had "strengthened the Government's hand tremendously".[43]

For the watersiders, worse was to follow. On 29 March the

1,000 Mangakino workers who had been on strike in protest against the Emergency Regulations voted to return to work. The greatest blow of all was the return to normal work at the end of the month by the railwaymen; the secret ballots throughout the country showed a majority of 3,152 for normal duties.[44] The watersiders had placed much faith in the railwaymen whose cause they had espoused during the Christmas rail strike. Drennan had been out to Otahuhu to appeal to the railwaymen on 18 March, telling them that if the watersiders were subdued there was not much chance of the railwaymen making a success of their wage claims.[45] But it was no good; hopes of a national transport strike had crashed. While at Otahuhu, Woburn and Addington there were narrow majorities for assisting the watersiders, the vote at the smaller workshops was overwhelmingly in favour of normal work.[46]

By the beginning of April the only unions still on strike in protest at the Emergency Regulations were the Wellington District Freezing Workers, the Wellington Drivers, the cement workers at Portland and Golden Bay, and most branches of the United Mine Workers' Union. The Seamen's Union was in a state of disorder; Lyttelton and Auckland produced majorities in favour of a return to work, while Wellington (where Walsh, the Seamen's president, presided) and Dunedin favoured a national strike.[47] There was some substance to the *Herald*'s gloat of 30 March:
> In early March, servicemen were isolated by other unions. Now almost all other unions are back to work. The watersiders are isolated.

In most cases the decisions that were made to return to work were not achieved without considerable acrimony being stirred up within the unions concerned. In all the unions there was a hard core of men who objected to the idea of a secret ballot which provided an escape route for the unionist who was not sufficiently strong-willed to state his opinion openly. Moreover, while many of these hard-core unionists had little love personally for the watersiders, they were resentful of the Emergency Regulations and the use of servicemen on the waterfront. For these men, 1951 was a battle in part for the retention of old, accepted trade union principles. Consequently, serious splits revealed themselves within most unions. Older men with longer trade-union experience tended to resist the call for a return to normal work; younger men, frequently pressured by the needs of their families, were more easily convinced that the F.O.L.'s directives were right and proper.

Within the Auckland Gas Workers' Union there was a group of about twenty workers who felt they could not submit to their branch's decision on 9 March. Their employers dismissed them on the 12th.[48] At the Auckland freezing works several hundred men refused to load frozen carcases into railway wagons as their union had agreed to do. They were also dismissed.[49] A similar problem revealed itself within the harbour board unions. Conscience was costly.

In fact, 1951 demonstrated that the fight went deeper than between groups of unions; it went down to the foundations of unions themselves, to the individuals who comprised them. But as the weeks went by it became increasingly apparent that the spirit of old-style unionism predominated within few unions, and had complete control in only a handful. Where it did dominate, the union was probably already in the T.U.C. Within the F.O.L., Walsh could claim to speak for the majority of men in almost all of its affiliates.

There can be little doubt that the F.O.L.'s actions during March 1951 delivered slashing blows at whatever chances the watersiders might still have had of salvaging anything from their fight.[50] Federation decisions encouraged the Government to be more ruthless, and they diminished whatever sympathy might still have lingered within the union movement for the watersiders' cause. Throughout the weeks that followed the special conference of the F.O.L., its National Executive found itself in substantial agreement with each new condition that was put forward by the Government as a basis for a settlement. On occasions, the National Executive would even urge the Government on; at the Annual Conference of the F.O.L. held at the end of April the executive proffered several pieces of advice to the Government,[51] and during May Walsh appeared to feel that

Holland was not moving fast enough in his attempt to purge New Zealand of the "wreckers".[52]

At the time, the press was unanimous in its praise of the actions of the F.O.L. The *Dominion*, which, like many newspapers, claimed to speak for "the people", said that the actions of the Federation would "receive the warm endorsement of the great majority of the people".[53] The *Taranaki Daily News* had called Walsh's advice to the watersiders "logical, right-minded, courageous".[54] Members of the National Party, too, were fulsome in their praise of the Federation. Some years later in Parliament, K.J. Holyoake stated:

> The National Party . . . was fortunate in that the Federation of Labour, the responsible workers' leaders, stood firmly with the Government. The task would have been impossible without the Federation's aid.[55]

The Federation's opponents within the labour movement were not quite so enthusiastic about Walsh's activities. One of the illegal pamphlets circulated during the dispute was entitled "If it's Treachery, Get Tuohy".[56] It read in part:

> TREACHERY is a hard word. For Walsh's sabotage of workers struggling to defend their conditions—not only watersiders now, but all workers—it's not hard enough.
> The scab is the outcast of society, the lowest, most despicable living creature. The sooler-on of scabs is lower and filthier than that.
> Walsh has been a sooler-on of scabs for over 20 years.

Mopping Up Round the Edges

By the end of March the Federation of Labour had whipped almost all of its affiliates back into line. Those that were beyond its reach, such as the Wellington freezing workers and drivers, as well as the miners, had to be manhandled by the Government.

By the last week in March the only substantial body of freezing workers still on strike in protest against the Emergency Regulations was in the area stretching from Taranaki to Nelson and covered by the Wellington District Freezing Workers' Union. Meat supplies had been inadequate in the Wellington area in the early stages of the dispute, although the shortage was eased a little when sixty master butchers began working at the Wellington City Abattoirs at the end of the second week in March. They worked again over the weekend of 17-18 March[57] but meat remained a scarce commodity in the capital city.

Once most F.O.L. unionists had returned to work in significant numbers and the strikers' ranks were thinning, the Government felt emboldened to attack those who remained recalcitrant. In the third week of March it was demanded of the freezing workers in the Wellington area that they hold a secret strike ballot to see whether or not a majority of the men wished to return to normal work. At Waitara, when the branch received a request on 15 March from the Wellington District Freezing Workers' Union to join all the other branches that were on strike, the men decided to hold a ballot which resulted in a 352:64 vote in favour of continuing normal work.[58] At all the other branches, however, no work was being performed, and when the Government's request for a secret ballot was discussed openly at meetings it was rejected on a show of hands.

Under the provisions of the Industrial Conciliation and Arbitration Amendment Act (1947) it was an offence for a union to take strike action before holding a secret strike ballot. Sullivan accordingly felt justified in deregistering the Wellington District Freezing Workers' Union on 26 March. A few weeks later the Public Trustee was appointed as Receiver of Funds of the deregistered union. Sullivan went further than this, however. He announced that he would consider registering twelve local unions in place of the one big union he had deregistered.[59] Clearly he was going to avail himself of the opportunity to disperse this group of militants as well as those on the waterfront.

On 30 March new unions were registered for the Nelson Freezing Works and the Wellington Abattoirs. By 13 April the police and officials of the Labour Department had rounded up enough men to form new unions with skeleton membership at the other works in the Wellington area. For the most part the members of the deregistered union eventually agreed to join the smaller units when they saw that their union had been effectively smashed, although it was some weeks before the number of men at work approached adequacy. At Nelson in particular the employers took the opportunity to refuse to re-engage some members of the old union. Twenty-five former employees were told on Monday 2 April that there was no work for them. The *Herald* reported that among them were slaughtermen who had been employed at the Stoke works for periods ranging from fourteen to twenty-eight years. Eleven of those excluded were ex-servicemen.[60]

The case of the Wellington Drivers' Union, members of which were still refusing to handle goods unloaded or loaded by servicemen, was a more difficult one for the Government. Early in March a strike ballot had been conducted by the Labour Department in the Wellington city area.[61] This ballot resulted in a 283:185 decision to refuse carrying goods handled by servicemen.[62] The Master Carriers' Association pressed the Government[63] to deregister the Wellington Drivers' Union so that new, smaller units could be formed in its place. For the most part the drivers had been employed on other carrying work, but a few companies that did a lot of the carrying to and from the waterfront were feeling the financial strain. Late in the month some drivers requested the union to hold another ballot in the Wellington area. The secretary, T.M. Magee, agreed: on 2 April the drivers reversed their position by a vote of 200:184. Magee, however, insisted that a similar ballot be held in other areas such as Petone, Masterton, Martinborough and Palmerston North that were also under the jurisdiction of the Wellington Drivers' Union. In these areas the Labour Department did not supervise the balloting. The final vote, when totalled, was 274:257 in favour of the initial stand taken by the union. On 9 April Magee announced that the union stood firm in its intention not to handle goods to or from the waterfront if servicemen were involved in handling them.[64]

In spite of the fact that a majority of the drivers had decided in secret ballots not to cooperate, Sullivan went ahead and deregistered the Wellington Drivers' Union on 10 April, and thirteen days later the Public Trustee was appointed Receiver of Funds. A new union, the Wellington (thirty-mile radius) Drivers' Union was formed with the assistance of the employers.[65]

and registered by the Minister on the 12th. Another five small unions were soon registered within the area formerly covered by the Wellington Drivers' Union.[66]

Not to be outdone, Magee registered a new union (it was really the old) on the 13th under the Trade Unions Act 1908. Magee's union covered the wider area. Sullivan thereupon announced that any man wanting to be employed as a driver in the Wellington area would have to be a member of the union registered on the 12th as soon as that union had obtained an award from the Arbitration Court.[67] He added, not without a touch of glee, that he doubted whether drivers if they remained in Magee's union would be quite so enthusiastic when they knew that they would have to pay two union subscriptions. Just to be on the safe side, on 4 May Sullivan cancelled the old union's registration from under the Trade Union Act 1908. New regulations were gazetted empowering him to prevent other registrations under that Act.[68]

Using these powers the Government was able to foil Magee's attempts to keep the old union in existence. About fifty drivers who refused to join the new union, regarded as a "scab" organisation, were in due course dismissed by their employers.[69] Small unions replaced the one big union in the Wellington carrying business as well as at the freezing works, and Magee's union never succeeded in retaining more than token strength.[70] The militancy of the drivers was slowly sapped, just as it had been from the freezing workers.[71]

The cement workers, whose strike had caused some fairly serious delays in the building industry, were more easily dealt with. The Portland Cement Workers' Union, which had been affiliated with the N.Z.W.W.U., had been on strike since the end of January 1951 because of a wages dispute with its employers. The Golden Bay Cement Workers' Union, also affiliated with the N.Z.W.W.U., struck on the day when the Emergency Regulations were put into force (26 February). The Government moved against both unions on 3 April. They were deregistered and the Public Trustee was appointed Receiver of Funds on the 23rd. A new union formed mostly from members of the old began work at Portland on 10 April but it took longer before the required fifteen men would come forward at Golden Bay and apply for registration as a new union. Twenty-one finally applied on 1 May and the company re-engaged them, the new union being registered on 8 May.[72]

The Government never completely broke the seamen's strike against the Emergency Regulations. Part of the difficulty was the F.O.L. For the Federation the seamen's strike was a difficult proposition; F.P. Walsh was the president of the National Council of the Seamen's Union. Walsh wanted the watersiders isolated and was anxious that seamen at all ports vote to return to normal work. However, he also wanted to retain his position of power within his union. And with the seamen fairly evenly divided (Auckland and Lyttelton favoured a return to work; Wellington and Dunedin opposed it) it was necessary for Walsh to adopt what Dick Scott later called a Jekyll and Hyde posture.[73] On the one hand Walsh cooperated with the Government in most matters and gave assistance to the Civil Emergency Organisation that was responsible for maintaining essential supplies in Wellington during the dispute. On the other hand the seamen's office issued no publicity for or against the strike, and Walsh occasionally issued to the press statements from meetings of seamen which protested at police harassment. As president he also helped raise money for relief for seamen on strike.[74]

Walsh retained his position as president of the National Council mainly because the Government was not prepared to deregister a union led by its closest ally. Moreover, so long as it was clear that the prospect of getting non-union labour to man coastal vessels was small—and the oil companies discovered this when they tried to round up some free labour in April— the Government would gain little by deregistering the Seamen's Union. Coal was the only commodity which could be carried no other way than by ship, and by April the Navy was manning the necessary colliers.

The miners were a different proposition. The Government tried very hard to break their strike against the Emergency Regulations, as did, after 17 March, Prendiville and Crook, the president and secretary of the United Mine Workers of New

Zealand. But all had to be content with a few minor successes. Most workers at the open-cast mines in Huntly and Waitewhena resumed normal work early in April after secret ballots had been held there. The majority of underground miners in the Huntly, King Country and West Coast areas, on the other hand, remained on strike; meetings of workers refused on a show of hands the request from their national office that secret ballots be held on the strike issue.[75] At Huntly it was necessary for the police to provide protection for those open-cast miners who resumed work. More than twenty policemen were stationed there instead of the normal three, and a watch was kept at the open-cast mines day and night. A policeman rode on the engine of every train bringing in coal from the mines.[76]

When it became clear early in April that most of the underground miners were going to refuse to hold a secret ballot, Crook criticised the men for not adhering to the union's strike rules.[77] After Crook and Prendiville refused demands that they resign from the National Council of the U.M.W., representatives of those underground miners still on strike met in Wellington to set up a national strike committee. G. Harrington (Runanga) and R. Ross (Wallsend) were elected president and secretary, and five members of Prendiville's and Crook's National Council were elected to the new strike committee. The miners' national organisation was split wide open, though there was no doubt that Harrington and Ross now spoke for the majority of miners.[78]

With the underground miners holding out, and the supplies coming from the open-cast mines being inadequate for the country's needs, the Government turned its attention to the quite large stockpiles of coal on the West Coast. Army personnel moved to Denniston, Seddonville and Ngakawa early in April to transport available coal to Westport.[79] There the ship's company of HMNZS *Taupo* discharged and loaded the colliers, sending away an average of three ships a week, each with 2,700 tons of coal.[80] The stockpiles of coal quickly diminished and soldiers were then put to work mining coal at the few open-cast mines on the West Coast such as Denniston and Stockton. By the end of June the output of coal at these mines was nearly up to pre-strike figures.[81] The strike in fact gave a very considerable boost to open-cast mining in New Zealand as a whole. Sullivan told the National Party conference in July that the Government had stimulated action at open-cast mines hoping to lessen the country's dependence on underground mining, and the power of underground miners to paralyse the country. The open-cast men, he said, were "sane, solid trade unionists".[82]

The servicemen who helped with coal supplies received liberal praise from the Government. For those who loaded the colliers and manned them, Sullivan said that no praise could be too great.[83] They worked efficiently, and they enjoyed themselves. Yet, as time wore on, their presence on the West Coast coal fields actually delayed a return to normal work. By June the financial pinch was being felt by the miners; many were prepared to waive their objections to the Emergency Regulations. But individual branches of the U.M.W. could not contemplate returning to work if servicemen were in the vicinity. The Buller Gorge Miners' Union was a case in point. In the third week in June the men voted to return to work if the Government would guarantee that all servicemen would be removed from their mines. This guarantee was not given; naval men, Captain Bourke of the *Taupo* was reported as saying, would remain in order to assist in maintaining as high production as possible. The foreseeable occurred. The miners decided to remain on strike.[84] Sometimes it seemed to the men that the Government really did not want to see the strike ended.

Although the Government's main success was with the open-cast mines, it certainly made a determined attempt during April to break the solidarity of the underground miners. The Government fastened its attention on the small, isolated King Country mine at Ohura, seventy miles inland from Mount Messenger.[85] The Ohura miners had struck against the Emergency Regulations. At the end of March they complied with the order from Prendiville and Crook to hold a strike ballot, and voted to remain on strike. After receiving a confusing telegram from Crook which they interpreted to mean that all miners elsewhere were returning to work, and knowing no better because of their isolation, the men at Ohura decided early in April to break their resolution of the previous week and return to work. But when Benneydale members of the King Country Council (made up of delegates from Ohura and Benneydale mines) arrived at Ohura to apprise the men of the true state of affairs, the police prevented any meeting from taking place. Moreover, the local president was forbidden to address his men, other than to read them a telegram from Prendiville. The opposite result to that intended by the Government immediately occurred. Miners who had been prepared to work now stayed out. Moreover, when reports of the police activity in Ohura reached Kamo in Northland, that union also came out on strike for a month.[86] The Government's zeal was sometimes self-defeating.

Some work was done at the Ohura mine-face. But of the thirty-one who worked in April, eighteen were Polish immigrants who, just having arrived in New Zealand, were under bond to work where directed by the Government.[87] The contingent of police in the town seemed to spend more time harassing the strikers than on their principal task of protecting the strike breakers. Meetings were regularly broken up, homes were entered by the police, cars were tailed and T.W. Calcott, the Ohura miners' president, was arrested when he attempted to speak to some of the men at work.[88] At Ohura the Emergency Regulations were used to the limit by the police with the Government's encouragement. But all this activity did not have the desired result. The men's determination to hold out increased in direct proportion to the extent of police activity. Finally in May the pressure was eased. The Government had failed to break the solidarity of the union, while the determination of the men at Ohura, in the face of something approaching a police terror, was becoming a kind of *cause célèbre* among less beleaguered strikers elsewhere.

The miners generally suffered more than other workers caught up in the waterfront dispute. In collecting relief, getting other employment and even in receiving reports on the steadily bleaker prospects in the national holdup, they were disadvantaged. Single men tended to drift away, especially after the Government threw many of them out of miners' hostels when they fell behind with their rent.[89] But those with families and homes—and diminishing savings—had no option but to stay, trying to eke out an existence on the allowances made available by their relief committees which were organising hunting and fishing parties to collect food.

For Holland and many National members the fight with the miners had a particular symbolic significance. Deprived of the necessary power to punish the striking miners during the hot war of the forties[90] they were now savouring their cold-war opportunity to the full. Victory was sweet.

CHAPTER VI

THE LATER STAGES OF THE DISPUTE

The Routine
   By the end of March the waterfront dispute was a standoff. The Government was determined on complete victory; the watersiders were equally determined to "continue to fight to a successful and honourable conclusion".[1] Neither side was making rapid progress towards its goal, and the dispute drifted into April with no sign of negotiations, let alone a settlement. The Government went ahead with its schemes to complete the isolation of the watersiders and in due course it embarked on a new crusade—the registration of new unions at every port in New Zealand. The watersiders, for their part, struggled to retain friends and to keep up morale.
   Meantime the country adjusted fairly quickly to the challenge of the 20,000 men who in the first weeks of April were still on strike. Most transport services were operating by the first week of April. The railways were on limited schedules and were using diesel locomotives as much as possible so as to conserve the limited supplies of coal. The inter-island ferries after some hold-ups when seamen refused to man them early in April, were back in service with voluntary labour by the 11th.[2] The main ports had been worked with servicemen since early in the dispute, and the Emergency Supplies Committees at all main ports, and the Overseas and Coastal Shipping Priority Committees in Wellington, worked in close cooperation on the business of shipping essentials.[3]
   For the 3,200 servicemen employed on the waterfront by the end of March it was a pleasant change from the normal routine. The work for which they had no training was performed with zest, though not always with the greatest care. There were two fatalities during the twenty weeks

that servicemen were on the waterfront, and a number of injuries.[4] The Government and the press gave much praise to the rate of work of the services personnel, claiming it was an example of what should be able to be expected from watersiders. And it was true that, with the elimination of "spelling", the services' rates of work did seem to be somewhat better than those applying before the dispute.[5] However, it has to be remembered that the men were especially well treated throughout the dispute. All servicemen in New Zealand received a 2/- per day bonus for the duration of the dispute; those employed as transport drivers, cool store workers, mine workers and merchant seamen crews received an additional 5/- per day bonus. Supplies of beer were occasionally provided by the employers in the early stages, thus helping add to the carnival spirit on the wharves.[6]

The Government also went to some effort to provide reasonable accommodation for the servicemen while they worked the waterfronts. At Wellington the early air force contingents were housed at the Trentham camp. But as numbers grew, other accommodation had to be provided. Various ships were commandeered for the purpose and provided floating hotels for several hundred men.[7] The *Bellona* which was in Wellington in March, New Plymouth in April, Auckland in May, and Wellington again in June, also provided a regular contingent of eighty men for waterfront work.[8]

The Government sought payment from the port employers for the work done by the servicemen. This money was handed over to the respective Services Boards. The principle laid down was that the employers would pay for the work at the same tonnage or unit cost as was paid for civilian labour prior to the dispute. In the specific case of waterfront work the employers paid a surcharge to cover the increase in wages from 4/3 to 4/7½ per hour.[9] Acceptance of the controversial rate of 4/7½ which had been rejected by the N.Z.W.W.U. in February became one of the Government's conditions for a return to normal work on the waterfront. Having said in February that it was not presuming to pass judgement on the pay dispute, the Government had found that in specifying conditions for a return to normal work it had no option but to accept the controversially low rate offered by the employers. To have enforced any higher rate of pay would have lent credence to the union's claim that the employers' offer had been unduly parsimonious.

Meantime the lives of the watersiders fell into a routine.[10] The men would report regularly to appointed meeting places to hear progress reports from their officials. In Auckland the men gathered at the Trades Hall in Hobson Street until in April the police told the Auckland Trades Council to forbid them to use it.[11] At Lyttelton the Coronation Hall was used until the Lyttelton Harbour Board came under pressure from the police.[12] When deprived of halls the men would gather in the streets where the police during the month of April reluctantly allowed the meetings to continue.[13] Not until 1 May did the Government gazette more stringent regulations against meetings of "strikers" and police harassment increase in the cities—in Auckland in particular.

Organising relief for the watersiders and their families was a major problem for the branches of the N.Z.W.W.U. Considerable sums of money were withdrawn from the union's bank accounts before the Public Trustee was appointed Receiver of the union's funds early in March, although £27,000 which had been placed in a special strike fund was not able to be reached in time.[14] Some canvassing for extra financial assistance was engaged in, despite the Emergency Regulations, and there were several quite large donations and loans to the relief fund, not the least of which was the sum of £30,000 sent across by Australian watersiders.[15] Several food depots were set up in Auckland; in Wellington there was one in Newtown and another at Lower Hutt. The relief committees purchased food in bulk, finding that co-operatives such as the Hutt Valley Consumers' Cooperative would usually provide groceries despite the Regulations.[16] The countryside was scoured for vegetables, and beef and mutton were bought on the hoof,[17] killed on farms and brought to depots for distribution. In Auckland, bread was purchased in bulk from Buchanan's Bakery. Fishing and shooting parties helped augment the depots' supplies at irregular intervals.[18] The police, for the most part, had to turn a blind eye. Occasionally they threatened retailers with prosecution if they sold to watersiders,[19] but there were no actual prosecutions. Confrontations with large numbers of watersiders and their wives could have led to some ugly scenes.

One factor worked in the watersiders' favour. Jobs were plentiful in most of the main ports,[20] and quite large numbers of watersiders took full or part-time work.[21] Wives, too, went out to work in large numbers, their incomes helping to tide families over the lean period. But many families with rent, mortgage and time payment commitments found it difficult to keep up with instalments. Some firms treated these cases ruthlessly, arguing that the men were responsible for their own predicament.[22] But a few were tolerant. In Auckland the Farmers' Trading Company, which in normal times handled a fair proportion of the watersiders' purchases on time payment, was particularly understanding. In Wellington the Maple Furnishing Company was similarly disposed, while several restaurants provided free meals for men involved in the dispute if they could produce a union card.[23]

In the first weeks of the dispute morale was high. Barnes' confidence was contagious, and most watersiders succumbed to the belief that Holland had gone further than was safe for his Ministry. On 14 March Barnes told a special meeting of members in Auckland that, in spite of the fact that the N.Z.W.W.U. was in effect supported only by the miners, the Wellington freezing workers, the Mangakino workers, some drivers and the railwaymen, the "forces of sound trade unionism would win". The actions of Walsh and the Government in trying to isolate the watersiders had all failed, he told the men. The miners' action in refusing to mine coal was now being felt by the country, and he was sure that the struggle would be won. His report was adopted unanimously; he was telling the men what they wanted to hear.[24] Two weeks later he claimed that 25,000 men were on strike and that the Government's position was "shaky".[25]

There was, nevertheless, a certain uneasiness amongst the men about the dilemma which faced the smaller branches. On 14 March one member of Auckland's executive was of the

E. "The Country is right behind the Government."

opinion that the National Office had failed to forward sufficient information to the smaller branches which accounted for the news that Whakatane had "cracked". On the 20th, Drennan, the Auckland president, moved at an executive meeting that the National Executive be called together.[26] The news that a new port union had been formed in Whakatane was particularly troublesome to men at the main ports where loyalty was almost one hundred per cent; it seemed to indicate that there was a certain "yellowness" within the ranks. And while they appreciated the fact that it was difficult to get relief money to the men at the smaller ports—the police had trailed delegates from Auckland when they had visited Whakatane with money early in March—the watersiders at the main ports expected the men to hold out, come what may.

Nothing fostered morale in the cities so much as the feeling that unionists were being persecuted by a ruthless Government in association with a reactionary press and unreliable union leaders. When the press ceased to publish any statements issued by the watersiders' leaders, refused to print any letters supporting them, and gave no publicity to the fact that early in March almost the entire Auckland branch donated blood to the Blood Bank, the men saw their world closing in on them. When they resorted to distributing pamphlets to other workers setting out their case and were arrested for infringements of the Emergency Regulations,[27] the feeling of persecution intensified. The news that friendly unions were being prevented from holding special meetings[28] further heightened their determination to fight. Sullivan's refusal to discuss the crisis with their elected leaders, Barnes and Hill, was regarded by the watersiders as an outrage;[29] any potential criticism of the leaders from amongst the ranks subsided. Sullivan's further statement on 20 March that Barnes and Hill would have to go, the national union along with them, was the final straw. The Prime Minister's broadcasts and those of selected trade union leaders beginning in April fell on deaf ears. If anything the militancy of the men was stronger by the beginning of April than it had been a month earlier; and it increased with time. Differences of opinion were sunk in the face of omnipresent danger. If the actions of Government, press and F.O.L. were designed to undermine the watersiders' morale, the results were the opposite of what was intended.

In fact the union became a kind of embattled enclave within the community. The press treated the strikers viciously, Minhinnick of the *Herald* picturing them on one occasion as rats.[30] Fellow unionists, torn by conflicting loyalties between old union practices and F.O.L. policies, were wary. And the general public, knowing little of the watersiders' case and even less about what the men were going through, tended to measure social status according to their degree of remoteness from the struggle. "Wharfie" had long been a term of abuse.

The watersiders experienced little difficulty keeping up their *esprit de corps* in the extra-legal atmosphere. Maintaining their press and distributing their literature developed into a deadly serious game of cops and robbers. Armed with their emergency powers the police searched many watersiders' homes for illegal printing presses. In the later stages of the dispute cyclostyling machines were kept in cars, the actual production of pamphlets being performed while the cars were in motion. Even today many an old watersider treasures a collection of illegal pamphlets, many of them alternately savage and witty, as a memory of the grim excitement of 1951.[31]

The Labour Party Enters the Dispute

As March dragged on into April and no solution to the waterfront dispute seemed in sight, the Labour Party decided to use its good offices to see if a solution could be reached that would allow the men to resume normal work. Labour entered the dispute cautiously; most of its front bench spokesmen had at some time or other experienced difficulties with Barnes and Hill. Moreover, many of the steps being taken by Holland in this crisis were in accord with legislation passed by a Labour Government. Labour had introduced and kept in force the Strike and Lockout Emergency Regulations; the power to deregister a striking union had been added to the I.C. and A. Act in 1939; the introduction of secret ballots came in 1947. The Labour Government had used the power of ministerial deregistration on more than one occasion, the most notable being in the case of the Auckland carpenters in 1949. What was more, the Labour Government on that occasion had also insisted that one of the carpenters' leaders (R. Stanley) not be associated with the new union.[32] Emergency powers had also been threatened on several occasions even if they had not actually been used during any of Labour's confrontations with the watersiders.

Moreover, when the dispute began, Walter Nash had been leader of the Labour Party for only a few weeks. Industrial relations was one of the few fields which Nash had left to his colleagues during his fourteen years as Minister of Finance. And now, when he needed their assistance most, a number of the Labour Party's senior members (including McLagan) were sick and unable to help.[33] Nash made frantic efforts to get up to date with developments in the dispute during the last days of February,[34] but all these difficulties contributed to the rather equivocal statement on the dispute which the Labour caucus issued at the end of the month. In the statement Nash counselled caution over the use of emergency powers and he urged that a compulsory conference of the disputants be called. No mention was made of any prior necessity for the watersiders to accept arbitration, although the statement made it clear that the Labour Party believed in compulsory arbitration. Finally, Nash stressed what many people had been saying: industrial trouble was inevitable if the Government continued to allow runaway inflation.

The only thing new about Nash's statement was Labour's advocacy of cooperative contracting, something which the Labour Government had previously rejected.[35] As a policy utterance the statement satisfied no one. Those who were one hundred per cent behind the Government found Nash's comments quite unacceptable. At best they were regarded as "unhelpful";[36] at worst he was "making common cause with the T.U.C.[37]". Acting true to form, the editor of the *Otago Daily Times* suggested that the Labour Party was "lacking in political morality".[38] The watersiders and their allies also took little comfort from Nash's statement. To them his comments on the Regulations conceding the Government's right to use them, but counselling caution, looked like equivocation.

Nevertheless, the caucus of the Labour Party had established a special committee to look into the waterfront dispute and during the month of March Labour members' attitudes became somewhat clearer. As Holland and Sullivan grew bolder and the dispute remained unresolved, the committee sensed that the Labour Party could not in good conscience remain on the sidelines. First the Government had rejected, on what seemed rather tenuous grounds, the approaches made on the watersiders' behalf by the miners and freezing workers. And then when the watersiders agreed to most of the "Seven Points" and were prepared to discuss the others, Holland still refused to do business. Rather than there being any substantial issues at stake, it seemed to Labour leaders by the end of March that the Government was holding out until the watersiders publicly admitted defeat. They could see that the cost of such a humiliation would be considerable. It would take a long time to achieve, would benefit few except employers, F.O.L., and National Party leaders, and would almost certainly leave such a legacy of bitterness amongst the men that necessary reforms on the waterfront[39] might never be attained.

What made the matter more serious for the Labour Party was that various sections of the party were calling for a clearer definition of policy. The Otago Labour Representation Committee wanted a special Labour conference aimed at hammering out a united policy against Holland. Other sections of the party were asking for guidance from the central office as to what their official attitudes to unions involved in the dispute should be.[40] Clearly, the longer the dispute continued the more confusion it was creating in Labour's ranks.

Consequently, on 29 March Nash used a public meeting at Hamilton organised by the Waikato Trades Council to make a major statement on the current crisis. He suggested that since disagreement remained substantial on only one (point 5) of the Government's "Seven Points", the matter could be cleared up by a compulsory conference on the question of an open union. This conference would have an independent chairman, and the watersiders would have to agree in advance to accept the chairman's decision. "If the watersiders hope to have any future in this country," Nash added, "they will have to agree to arbitration and will have to honour their obligations and agreements. If the Government cannot get the assurance of the watersiders that they will agree to the decision, Parliament should be called together."[41]

On the question of the Emergency Regulations, Nash made his position somewhat clearer than he had done on 28 February. While he admitted that a Labour Government would have used emergency powers "to ensure that essential supplies were delivered to hospitals and to homes," he could not agree with some of the powers which Holland had taken. He did not like to see freedom of speech curtailed or the right given to officials to open private correspondence. Another thing Nash did not agree with was the clause in the Regulations that made it an offence to give food to assist a watersider's wife and children.[42]

Statements of this kind were anything but popular with the press. The comment by the *Evening Post* was typical of most newspapers. The editor suggested that Nash was having difficulty in "getting off the fence," that his suggestion of a compulsory conference was "unrealistic", and that there was no purpose in summoning Parliament. "A patched up peace," said the *Post*, "is emphatically not wanted."[43] The Labour Party's attitude was even less popular with the F.O.L. When Nash extended an invitation to the Federation's National Executive on 2 April to attend the Labour caucus two days later, he mentioned that he had been thinking of inviting Barnes and Hill. The Federation immediately declined the invitation. Baxter made it clear that, like the Government, the F.O.L. did not recognise Barnes and Hill, and it chided the Labour Party for contemplating doing so.[44]

Yet criticism of this kind did not deter the Labour Party. After caucus had met on 4 April, and had heard reports from its committee (Barnes and Hill were not actually invited), Nash told the press that Labour Members were concerned at the apparent willingness of the Government to allow the waterfront position to drift until shortage of food brought deprivation to the homes of some of the workers concerned. He added that there would be serious economic consequences if the struggle became protracted, and said that the Labour Party was prepared to do all that it could to assist in bringing about an early and satisfactory settlement.[45] Similar points were contained in a letter which Nash sent to the Prime Minister on the 5th, and in this letter he also asked why the Government had not made any formal reply to the letter that had been sent on 8 March by the miners and freezing workers. He added that the Labour Party had "thoroughly examined" the Emergency Regulations and that it regretted that the Government had not seen fit to repeal "those portions of the regulations which all liberal minded people regard as an unnecessary infringement of civil liberties".[46]

Nash's statement and his letter showed that the Labour Party's concept of how emergency powers should be used was rather different from that of the Government. To Nash they were a last resort, to be used to enforce a return to the principle of compulsory arbitration. They were not to be utilised to throttle discussion while a Government proceeded to indulge in far-reaching reorganisation of an industry and of labour relations in general at the expense of the country's economy and of workers' homes and families.

With the wraps on the press, however, no one was able to defend Nash's view. Editors tore into him, suggesting that he was insincere and indulging in cheap politics.[47] And Holland was quick to exploit his opponent's weaker tactical position. He censured the Labour Party for "fence-sitting", and added:

> Surely we have got enough problems on our plate already without Mr Nash adding to our difficulties by making pointless suggestions about holding conferences with law breakers, and those who have done their best to starve the people and paralyse our trade, those who have deliberately caused the destruction of hundreds and thousands of cases of fruit, those who have tried to hold up food for Britain, those who have done their best to intimidate others who are prepared to work?

Holland went on to suggest that there was no room for a middle position on the waterfront dispute:

> If [Labour Members] believe in law and order they should range themselves alongside constituted authority and the Government....
> Those who are not with us in this crisis are against us. Those who do not back up the Government are backing up law breakers....
> The Government is not making mistakes. It is doing the job, and doing it well.[48]

It was a savage piece of rhetoric and it answered none of the points which Nash had raised. Along with the press criticism it hurt Nash deeply, for he had been at great pains to dissociate himself from the specifics of the watersiders' case. He was more determined to fight on. Another press statement was issued, this one more explicit in its criticism of the Regulations than the statement of 5 April.[49]

A week later Nash decided to see what could be done to bring about a meeting of the parties to the dispute with an eye to a settlement. To A.G. Osborne MP, who had written cautioning Nash against appearing to assist the watersiders, he wrote:

> To me, the necessity to get back to work on the waterfront is so great that I would take any reasonable step to find out a method by which it could be done. It would be wrong to condemn the waterside workers without ever having heard them, and we are taking some steps whilst we can to find out under what conditions they will go back to work in the normal way.... I hope at the same time to remove some of the bad practices that have been in existence, in Auckland and other places, for some years.

Nash went on to say that none of his colleagues thought that by doing so he was agreeing with Barnes and Hill:

> I know what has happened over the years. I have experienced quite a lot of the effects of it, but I do not think, at the moment, that there is anything more important than to have normal work restored, and this cannot be done except by understanding what the watersiders do want. I am certainly not in any way "flirting with Barnes".[50]

Between 12 and 19 April Nash was in close touch with the watersiders. On the 12th along with his deputy, C.F. Skinner, and A.H. Nordmeyer and M. Moohan, Nash held discussions with Barnes, Hill, T.G. Wells (Wellington Branch of the N.Z.W.W.U.) and F.G. Young (Hotel Workers). Barnes was stubborn, but the Labour Members worked hard to persuade him to adopt a position that would be acceptable to the Government. At the end of the meeting Barnes agreed to send a letter to Nash which accepted fully Holland's "Seven Points" and the principle of compulsory arbitration.[51]

However, the letter which Barnes did send to Nash the following day was written in a haughty manner and made it clear that, as yet, the watersiders were not prepared to accept unconditional surrender. In Nash's opinion the letter was "not worth presenting" to the Prime Minister and "would only extend the trouble".

On 16 April Nash again made an attempt to get a settlement. He drafted a letter of the kind which, in his opinion, the Prime Minister might consider as a basis for settlement. The letter was handed to Young who forwarded it to the watersiders. The watersiders amended it and returned it the same day. The letter stated that the union would accept a settlement of the wages dispute by a chairman if a compulsory conference of the parties to the dispute were called. The union would accept the "Seven Points" so long as those objectives were sought "by negotiation under terms acceptable to both the workers' and employers' organisations". The letter stipulated, however, that any reforms necessary to implement these "Seven Points" should not be settled "by an unfair or one-sided interpretation arbitrarily enforced on the parties by a chairman acting as arbitrator".[52]

Again Nash told the watersiders that their letter contained "too many qualifications," and that it would require "more unqualified acceptance" before he would feel justified in submitting it to Holland. Nevertheless, Nash did go ahead with a meeting that he had requested with Holland for the morning of the 17th. He spent two hours with the Prime Minister and told him of his discussions with the watersiders' leaders. He stated the reason why the union had reservations about point 5 of the "Seven Points" which had stressed the need for an open union, and he told Holland of the watersiders' opinion that membership of the N.Z.W.W.U. could be "opened up" if an

adequate guaranteed wage was promised to all members of the
union. Holland replied that he could accept a public endorsement of the "Seven Points" and acceptance of compulsory
arbitration as bases for discussions. But there would have to be
an end to the watersiders' national union. Nash, according to
Holland, "expressed doubts as to the practicability or advisability of this course".[53]

The Leader of the Opposition reported back to the watersiders' leaders on the 18th, and the union decided to advance
its position one step further towards a settlement. In a letter
to Nash which Nash conveyed to Holland on the 19th, Barnes,
Hill and T.G. Wells of the National Executive accepted both the
principle of arbitration by an independent chairman and the
"Seven Points" without any qualifications. But they did make
it clear that they expected the national union to be reregistered.[54]
A somewhat fuller letter making the same points was taken
from the union to Holland by F.G. Young on 19 April. This
letter ended: "We take it that a re-registration of all Unions now
deregistered and the return to work of all workers on the basis
of no victimisation and the abolition of the Regulations would
automatically follow a negotiated settlement of the waterfront
dispute." [55]

Nash felt some sense of achievement when he saw these
letters. After many hours of discussion with the watersiders'
leaders he had persuaded them to make two major concessions.
The principle of arbitration, the failure to accept which had
initially involved the Government in the waterfront dispute,
had now been accepted publicly and unequivocally by the
watersiders themselves in a letter to the Prime Minister. And
the "Seven Points" which were set down on 15 March as a
necessary basis for negotiations had also been accepted without
qualification. Both Nash and the union's leaders now felt that
it was over to the Government. Holland should be prepared to
concede a point in return by not enforcing separate port
unions. Indeed Nash could see no easy way whereby the
Government could enforce separate port unions. Since this
was a national waterfront holdup being conducted by nationally-
elected leaders of a national union he could not see how nego-

tiations for a return to work could be conducted other than on a national level. The Government, he felt, should concede that the demand for separate unions was unrealistic.

First indications were that the Prime Minister might agree. He had already prepared a radio broadcast for the evening of 19 April when he received the watersiders' letter late in the day. He changed the text of his talk and sounded quite conciliatory:

> I do not regard the condition they [the watersiders] have imposed, or the understanding they have given themselves as finally barring the way to an honourable settlement of the trouble.[56]

There was an immediate surge of hope amongst the thousands of men out of work. Nash, it seemed, had been largely instrumental in achieving a breakthrough. But it was not to be. Within twenty-four hours a very different Holland, this time harsh and uncompromising, announced that the watersiders' proposal of the 19th was "entirely unacceptable" to the Government because the condition contained within the letter—namely the reregistration of the watersiders' national union—"cut right across the Government's publicly announced policy". An "irrevocable condition" for a resumption of work, he said, was that separate unions would have to be formed at all ports in New Zealand. The deadline for deregistered men to join the new unions on a priority basis was generously extended until Monday 23 April.[57]

It is worth pondering about this apparent *volte face* by the Prime Minister. The conciliatory statement of the 19th is the hardest part to explain. On the face of it this moderate statement ran counter to all the hard talking and occasional bombast that the Prime Minister had uttered during recent weeks. Yet, a careful examination of the Government's actions during April suggests that there may have been good reason to sound cautious on the 19th. There was almost certainly some doubt amongst Cabinet members about whether they could proceed much further with the dispute. While Sullivan had hoped for separate port unions since the beginning, the Bockett twins who were responsible for much of the effort involved were dubious about whether enough men could be found at a time when labour was in such short supply.[58]

Try as they might, a month's efforts to get new unions into operation at the main ports had come to nothing. As of 19 April only five unions at the minor ports of Whakatane, Tauranga, Tokomaru Bay, Motueka and Opotiki were operating. At least some members of Cabinet probably thought that circumstances might force the Government to make a concession in favour of the national union.

The Government first indicated that it would like to see an end to the national union on 28 February. On 21 March Sullivan insisted that it would have to go, and in a broadcast on the 23rd Holland appealed for men to come forward to establish the new unions. But the number of volunteers was small. The watersiders remained solid; Holland's opinion that a majority of the men would really like to return to work on the Government's conditions proved baseless. Moreover there were very few people outside the union who were interested in taking employment on the waterfront. The same boom conditions that had made it possible for the Government to contemplate a long dispute in the first place, made it possible for watersiders to obtain part or full-time jobs elsewhere, thus increasing their ability to endure the stoppage on the waterfront. And the adverse publicity which the waterfront industry had received in recent years, plus the fact that 4/7½ per hour was not very generous, acted as disincentives to potential strike-breakers.

Nevertheless, Sullivan tried hard to make some progress at the major ports. Mayors and their Emergency Supplies Committees were encouraged to take a leading role in calling on local watersiders to come forward and form new unions. But few reported success. The failure at Nelson on 7 March was repeated on 2 April when only three of Nelson's eighty-five watersiders attended a meeting to which they had all been invited by the Mayor.[59] And the calls of Auckland's Allum and Wellington's Macalister [60] for watersiders to come forward continued to go unheeded. Nor did the Labour Department have much success in New Plymouth. By the end of the first

12. Walter Nash, Leader of the Opposition, 1951-57.

week in April it was necessary, therefore, to try new methods if separate port unions were to be established. Sullivan discussed his plans with the Government caucus on 6 April,[61] and two days later he revealed in a national broadcast that every watersider in the country[62] had been sent a personal letter inviting him to register with the Labour Department if he was prepared to return to work under the basic conditions which were set out by the Government in the letter. A card for registration purposes was enclosed. First consideration for positions in the new unions would be given to deregistered watersiders, Sullivan added.[63] The newspapers joined in, urging the watersiders to form new unions at each port. It was an offer that "every ex-watersider who takes pride in his citizenship and realises his obligations should be ready to accept," said the editor of the *Herald*.[64]

Scarcely anything happened. The Labour Department claimed it had received some cards back, hoping to cause some uneasiness amongst the men. Nearly all watersiders, however, had simply turned their cards over to their leaders. Not even the pleas by leaders of the Returned Servicemen's Association,[65] nor the broadcast appeals by several union leaders, nor even the promises by Holland and Sullivan to be tough with anyone who might intimidate strike breakers,[66] encouraged more than a handful of watersiders to break ranks. On the 12th, hoping to undermine the watersiders' morale, Sullivan made it clear that the alternative to accepting the Government's offer was a much longer holdup;[67] the port employers agreed with this in a statement on the 13th;[68] while the press did its bit in the campaign of psychological warfare by pointing out how much the watersiders had forfeited in wages by ceasing work.[69]

Still there was no progress. On the evening of 17 April Sullivan announced that in addition to former watersiders, non-unionists who had worked on the wharves in the past ("seagulls"), or any other men wanting to take up waterfront work as a full-time occupation, could now register with the Labour Department.[70] It was a "logical move", claimed the editor of the *Herald*, since "intimidation" had "prevented" watersiders from replying to their letters.[71] Yet again this move did not bring any spectacular results. As of 25 April registrations in Auckland were still considered to be quite inadequate for a new union to be formed.[72]

It seems likely that by 19 April not only Holland, but several of his colleagues, were beginning to doubt Sullivan's chances of success. They were becoming painfully aware that they had been the victims of their own propaganda. For years not only National's leaders but Labour's, too, had suggested that the bulk of the N.Z.W.W.U. were not really supporters of the militant policies of Barnes and Hill. It was disturbing to discover that the union was solid and would not be cowed easily. So when the letter came from the watersiders on the 19th and Holland was without the strong arm of Sullivan—the latter was away in New Plymouth with the Bocketts "showing the flag" to Navy personnel working the port as well as consulting with Labour Department officials about the possibility of a new union—the Prime Minister felt justified in replying to it cautiously, keeping all the Government's options open including the possibility of retreat on the question of the national union. It was quite possible that Sullivan would have no progress to report on the formation of a new union in New Plymouth.

Two things brought about a stiffening of the Government's nerve. One was Sullivan's arrival back from New Plymouth. Increasingly emerging as the strongman in the crisis, Sullivan was appalled when he heard the Prime Minister's conciliatory broadcast and told Holland as much in blunt terms.[73] What gave edge to Sullivan's demand for firmness was the news which he brought Cabinet: a new union was in the process of formation at the major port of New Plymouth. This was what Cabinet members wished to hear. Back came all the excitement of 13 and 14 March. Whakatane, it now seemed, had not been a flash in the pan to be repeated only at minor ports; it had been the beginning of the end for Barnes, Hill, the N.Z.W.W.U., and for a large number of men formerly employed on the waterfront. An overwhelming victory now seemed in sight. As New Plymouth went, so would go the country.

But there was more to Holland's rejection of the watersiders' approach than this. To have accepted their proposals would have necessitated handing at least some of the credit for solving the dispute to Nash and to the Labour Party. And by this time the idea that the National Party might use the waterfront struggle to score an upset victory over Labour was probably taking shape in the minds of Cabinet members. It seems that it was not concern for those new unions that had been registered at minor ports, and which would have to be deregistered if the national union was restored, that concerned the Government on 20 April.[74] Indeed, the total number of men actually at work in the new unions at Whakatane, Tauranga, Tokomaru Bay, Motueka and Opotiki on 20 April was only sixty-five.[75]

Moreover, it seems likely that most of the "new unionists" at Whakatane, Motueka, Tokomaru Bay and Opotiki had been members of the old national union and had been forced to return to work by community pressures at the small ports. It was almost impossible to get relief, and the availability of other jobs[76] in these towns was not sufficient that the men could afford to hold out indefinitely. It was always possible that there would be no jobs to return to. There is no reason, therefore, to believe that those "new unionists" would have regarded reregistration of the national union as unacceptable. Nor is there any indication that the Government sought the men's opinions on this point. The Government's expressed concern for the "new unionists" was more probably a screen for motives that were less worthy of the praise so liberally bestowed by the press. Political considerations were weighing heavily with the Prime Minister and Cabinet when, on 20 April, they took the major decision which lengthened the waterfront dispute by another twelve weeks.

Holland's announcement may have pleased the press. But it shocked Nash. He had known for some time that the Government wanted to see separate port unions established. But he was certain that this goal could only be achieved by a long, drawn-out struggle which would add greatly to the suffering of watersiders' and miners' families. Nash saw the Government's determination to obtain its full pound of flesh as selfish arrogance. He immediately denounced it:

> It is intolerable that the community should have to suffer a continuation and intensification of hardship merely on the ground that the Government wishes to negotiate with individual port unions rather than with a national union.

Although careful not to mention Barnes and Hill, Nash suggested that there would have to be some national body to negotiate on behalf of watersiders who were still fighting on a national scale. He concluded with the assertion that the Government would have to accept "full responsibility" for the continuation of the stoppage which had "already been allowed to drift too far".[77]

It was at this point that the Government's immense political advantage in refusing to agree to the watersiders' letter of the 19th became apparent. From this point onwards the fight against the watersiders could now be broadened to include the Labour Party which shared responsibility with the watersiders for producing plans for a settlement which the Government had chosen to find unacceptable. Holland intended to exploit this

G. THE SILENT THREE ARE McLAGAN, NASH, AND SEMPLE

opportunity to link Nash with the watersiders. "So Mr Nash has shown his hand at last," the Prime Minister replied. "He has aligned himself alongside the deregistered Waterside Workers' Union." With logic that was far from faultless, Holland asserted that Nash's insistence that the national union be reregistered meant that he wanted to see the old leaders heading it, men who were "unscrupulous", and who had "not hesitated to employ the most despicable methods of intimidation and threat in order to prevent decent men from resuming work under the just and fair conditions laid down by the Government".[78] Nash had begun to pay dearly for his solicitude for the watersiders' families.

The Leader of the Opposition was not daunted yet. He issued a further press statement in which he suggested that the Government had gone back on a promise to negotiate if the union would accept the "Seven Points", and he deplored the policy which seemed to be implied in the rejection of the letter of 19 April: that the men would be starved back to work if necessary.[79] But Holland was riding high. His reply was that of a man deliberately trying to cloud the issue:

> For Mr Nash to say that the Government is responsible for the continuation of the strike is as ridiculous as it is untrue. Mr Nash seems determined to move from one blunder to another. He hasn't raised his little finger to help in this trouble and there have been unlimited opportunities for him to have rendered a real and practical help had he wished to do so.

Again Holland set up a straw man: reregistration of the national union would involve restoring Barnes and Hill. Again he knocked it down. This would be unacceptable since the Government was determined to secure a "new order" on the waterfront. And then, to change the subject, he added:

> This is not a political contest between the National Party and the Labour Party, or between the Government and the Opposition. This is just part of a cold war in which a group of wreckers has declared war on the people in an effort to replace orderly, democratic government with anarchy and direct action; to replace the long-established lawful system of industrial conciliation and arbitration with an unlawful system in which direct action and intimidation are the basic ingredients. This is a time when we should all be prepared to rise above party politics and, recognizing the dangers that beset our land, we should all be pulling together united in facing the common danger.[80]

What made Nash appear so unequal in the struggle was the attitude of the press. The *Herald* among the morning papers had been shocked at Holland's apparent hesitation on 19 April,[81] and all the papers were ready to do whatever was necessary to strengthen his nerve. In the weeks following 20 April every daily in the country lavished praise on the Government for refusing to accept the watersiders' letter, and poured editorial scorn on Nash and the Labour Party. Some went further. The sub-editorial device of featuring the Prime Minister's replies in black headlines ahead of the statements to which they were referring, became regular practice for the *Herald* and the *Evening Post*.[82] Early in May the *Evening Post* took an extraordinary step. It published a long anonymous letter attacking Nash as a regular news item.[83] The job of playing watchdog of the nation's interest has always fallen uneasily on New Zealand's newspapers. But in the moment of the country's greatest industrial crisis they were allowing themselves to become virtual propaganda sheets for the National Government and the port employers.

By 24 April it was clear that Nash's efforts to bring about a settlement of the waterfront dispute had failed. Nash issued a third statement saying that the Labour Party had been aiming all along for a commencement of normal work, and added that he believed this would be appreciated once the press was "open" and "everyone is free to speak".[84] For the meantime, however, he retired, bruised, from the fray.

Nevertheless, the Government's decision of 20 April had a very considerable effect on members of the Parliamentary Labour Party. Deregistration, Emergency Regulations and strike ballots were all weapons which the Labour Government had either used, or contemplated using. Smashing a national union was something else altogether, an object which seemed both unnecessary and a sinister portent of things to come. Nash wrote Osborne:

> It looks as if the policy now is submission and humiliation, and personally I do not think that this will succeed in the long run. Submission by the watersiders has been agreed to, and it does not appear to me that good results will come from the present policy of humiliation also.[85]

When it became apparent that at New Plymouth the employers, the Labour Department and the W.I.C.[86] were operating a selection committee which was weeding out the "undesirables" among those deregistered unionists who were applying to return to work, apprehension in the Labour Party turned to indignation.[87] Nash and a number of Labour MPs openly advised the watersiders to refuse such conditions for a return to work. On 3 May a deputation of Labour MPs waited on the Prime Minister, and expressed the view that a settlement would be delayed much longer if watersiders thought they were going to be victimised. They were likely to feel that in unity lay their only chance of re-employment on the waterfront. But by this time Holland was enjoying the dispute too much to listen to any suggestions for a settlement.

Three days later several Labour MPs spoke to Auckland's

13. Members of the new union arriving for work in army lorries, 3 May 1951.

14. Constables at the gates of Princes Wharf, Auckland, with fire hoses ready to be used against deregistered watersiders if any demonstration occurred, 3 May 1951.

deregistered watersiders and reported on Labour's activities. They were warmly received. On the 16th, A.E. Armstrong, MP for Napier, told the Auckland watersiders: "Your cause is right. I will do all I can for you. I would like to be able to give a few thousand quid". Holland's belligerence was restoring some old friendships.[88]

New Unions

Once the Government had taken its decision that no settlement was possible unless separate port unions were formed, every effort had to be made to achieve that end. The longer it took to get these unions operating the greater would be the cost of the waterfront dispute to the country. At no stage was forming new unions an easy task. Only at Timaru where there had been long-standing differences between branch officials and the national office did the watersiders submit easily to Government pressure, most of them returning to work on 26 April.

The Labour Department played a key role in the formation of new unions at other ports.[89] Sullivan and Bockett returned to Wellington from New Plymouth on 20 April; officials from the department remained behind to supervise the final details. On the 26th a new union with fifty-six men was registered, and work began on the waterfront the same day. This number was only about 16 per cent of the figure that was regarded as adequate for normal work there,[90] but the fact that a union was operating had a big impact on the men who were still holding out. Four days later the members of the old union held their usual meeting and decided to register *en masse* with the Labour Department.[91] The screening committee offered work to 132 members of the old union and these men quickly assumed *de facto* control of the new union. On 7 May they decided not to handle cargo for the coastal vessel the *Mamaku*, which was being manned by the Navy.[92] The port employers refused to employ the men if they would not work all ships ("deregistered the registered deregistered", as an Auckland watersiders' *Bulletin* expressed it) and two days later, after a personal visit from Baxter of the F.O.L., who appealed to the men to work all vessels, the new union decided to comply with the employers' terms.⁹³ The waterfront crisis at New Plymouth had finally ended.⁹⁴

At Whangarei the Labour Department also had a hard job. On 20 April a number of members of the deregistered union, as well as some former "seagulls", attended a meeting organised by the Labour Department. Dick Scott reported that before the meeting began a police sergeant read out the conditions the men had to agree to before they could form a new union. "A farmer took the chair, and a police inspector, a detective, a constable and a Labour Department official ranged themselves about the hall."⁹⁵ The meeting lasted for two hours and there was continual uproar. A secret ballot of the sixty-nine men present resulted in a vote of 38:31 to hold over any decision to return to work until Monday 23 April, the new deadline which the Government had provided for deregistered men to apply for work. All but twenty-eight of the men then left the hall and the twenty-eight, who were all "seagulls", formed the new Whangarei Longshoremen's Union. They began work on the 24th.⁹⁶ When the deregistered men met they decided by a large majority (35:6) not to join this new union.⁹⁷ The Labour Department's efforts in Whangarei had been only partially successful.

Auckland was an even tougher nut to crack. The employers and the press had been enthusiastically anticipating the establishment of a new union at the nation's largest port since early in March. Auckland's was by far the largest branch of the N.Z.W.W.U., providing nearly 30 per cent of the total membership of the old union. Moreover, it was Barnes' home base and the place where Drennan, the most prominent Communist in the union, held office. Auckland held the record, too, for industrial holdups prior to 1951. If its union could be cracked it would be some achievement. The task was not easy. Allum, the Mayor, had been optimistic since the beginning.⁹⁸ But the union held firm, and non-union labour was extremely scarce. The *Herald* reported on 26 April that there had not been sufficient registrations with the Labour Department "to meet labour requirements". At the end of April it was claimed that

15. Police struggling with some demonstrators outside Auckland's Town Hall on the morning the new waterfront union was formed (28 April 1951). The crowd consisted mainly of deregistered watersiders plus some members of the public.

more than 500 men had registered, most of them former "seagulls",[99] but the *Star* reported that the Labour Department had found, when checking these, that 250 were names of non-existent people.[100]

Nevertheless, the Government decided to proceed with the ritual of forming a new union in Auckland. On Saturday 30 April a new body was formed in the Auckland Town Hall amid jeers and derision from about 600 members of the old union who were assembled outside. One hundred and ninety-one new unionists joined servicemen at work on the morning of 3 May, having been brought from their homes in closed Army lorries with police escorts. The *Herald* described the scene in Quay Street:

> In addition to hundreds of servicemen arriving by boat and truck for normal port work, large parties of soldiers, sailors, airmen and Royal Marines poured in to assist in defence. Walkie talkie radio communication between control points was established. One of the key points was at Military District headquarters which had all the atmosphere of a wartime command post. Fire hoses were fixed to hydrants and run out near the entrance to Princes Wharf.[101]

Some members of the deregistered union observed proceedings from a distance and then went home peacefully. By early afternoon the police were relaxing playing cards.[102]

During the following week a few farmers, some Maoris,[103] some returned servicemen[104] and general supporters of the Government came forward and volunteered on a temporary basis to raise the numbers employed on the Auckland waterfront.[105] By 9 May over 1,000 men were registered,[106] and with the figure at 1,145 on 26 May the register was closed temporarily. Until servicemen were withdrawn from Auckland on 8 June the volume of work being done was sufficient to cope with shipping needs. By the end of June, however, wharf labour was again in short supply and few ships were fully manned.[107]

The screening procedure that had been pioneered at New Plymouth was used in Auckland, but this time the employers were more careful.[108] A few deregistered watersiders were ultimately let back into the new union, especially if, as in the case of N. Donaldson who had been a vice-president of the Auckland Branch of the N.Z.W.W.U., they had a record of opposition to the policies of the national union.[109] But any new unionists who were found to retain any sympathy for the deregistered men or to be supporting watersiders financially, were liable to be removed from the roll of the new union.[110] As of the middle of October 1951, three months after the deregistered union's leaders had advised members to go back to work, only seventy-nine deregistered watersiders representing 4.3 per cent of the total strength of the new union, had been admitted. More than 90 per cent of the membership of the new union had not previously had any experience of waterfront work.[111]

On 13 June an ex-Grenadier Guardsman, W.F. McMullen, was elected President of the new Auckland Maritime Cargo Workers' Union. The employers worked very closely with McMullen. In return for the work that he did in cementing the foundations of the new union the port employers assisted him in finding accommodation for his family, for they had only recently arrived in Auckland. The port employers also guaranteed an overdraft for him on at least one occasion.[112]

Once some progress had been made with the new union in Auckland the Government turned its attention to other ports. A union was formed at Dunedin on 18 May, fifty men starting work three days later. On the 21st the Lyttelton Waterfront Employees' Union was registered and work for 104 men was offered for the first time on the 28th. Wellington was the hardest centre to deal with. Labour was particularly short in the capital city and the Labour Department found it nearly impossible to round up the necessary men. When the Wellington Waterfront Workers' Union finally began work on 28 May it had only forty-two members, and by early in July this number had risen to a mere 326,[113] which was about 14 per cent of the work force considered necessary.[114] There was considerable difficulty finding anyone to lead this new union. A.K. Bell, who was finally chosen, had a police record known to the deregistered watersiders, who published and distributed a special bulletin on the "virtues" of the new unionists.[115] The Government, however, seemed to be unaware of the calibre of some of the new unionists. F.L.A. Gotz, MP called Bell "a gallant man who has the courage of his convictions".[116]

By the first week in June some nineteen new port unions had been formed, although they were all greatly understocked with members. The Government, nevertheless, felt pleased with its efforts. On 6 June the Prime Minister visited the Auckland waterfront, taking a cup of tea with the new unionists. He spoke of "a new era of industrial harmony", and invited delegates from all the new unions to attend a conference in Wellington to exchange views on the future operations of New Zealand's waterfront industry.[117] The press, too, was delighted at the progress made during the month of May. The *Herald* editorialised on 31 May:

> A new spirit of energy and honesty today animates cargo work on the Auckland waterfront. That spirit, if it can be maintained, will make all the hardships of the strike worth while. It must be maintained.

The Government's determination to fight to the bitter end was slowly bringing results. With every day that passed fewer and fewer jobs remained for the deregistered watersiders to return to. Sullivan's plans were succeeding even if the cost of prolonging the dispute was mounting rapidly.

CHAPTER 7

GOVERNMENT TRIUMPHANT

Tightening the Screws

Forming separate port unions in the major centres was a massive undertaking. Government Ministers, newspaper editors, leaders of the Returned Servicemen's Association and farmers all joined in the effort, calling alternately for the deregistered men to return to work or for non-unionists to come forward and take their places on the waterfront. Leaders of other trade unions also played a part. The Government discovered a number of leading unionists who, because of past differences with Barnes and Hill, or because of their belief in Moral Re-armament (M.R.A.),[1] were prepared to associate themselves with the Government's smashing of the N.Z.W.W.U. Prime broadcasting time was made available to union leaders prepared to give speeches sufficiently critical of the watersiders' leaders. F.W. McNeil, President of the Auckland Harbour Board Employees' Union, was the first to say his piece on 13 April. He asserted that the waterfront dispute was a fight between two forces, "sane labour and honourable trade unionism on the one side, and unpatriotic forces of selfishness and wanton destruction on the other".[2] On the 18th McNeil's fellow Moral Re-armer, J. Freeman of the New Zealand Timber Workers' Union, told radio listeners that if the watersiders did not want to shoulder their responsibilities they should stand aside. They should seek some other occupation and "leave the wharves so vital to our safety and prosperity to better men and better trade unionists."[3]

On 20 April, S.V. Glading, National President of the New Zealand Engineers' Union added his voice to those of the Moral Re-armers. He asserted that if the watersiders returned to work nobody would call them "scabs", nobody but their "power-

16. A procession of watersiders halted by the police in Cuba Street, Wellington, on 2 May 1951. T.G. Wells, President of the Wellington Branch of the N.Z.W.W.U., can be seen advising the men to disperse. Several policemen have their batons drawn.

hungry leaders".[4] Others followed,[5] the radio becoming an important propaganda instrument in the Government's battle with the watersiders. Pleas by T.U.C. officials and Labour Party leaders for an opportunity to put their respective cases over the air were refused by the Prime Minister,[6] and the *Listener* published no letters commenting on any of the speeches made over the air during the course of the dispute. Few acknowledged dictators have possessed more effective control of the mass media than Holland did during 1951.

Frustrated every way they turned, it was inevitable that some of the men out of work would resort to violence. Many watersiders, miners and freezing workers felt themselves to be experiencing privation in the midst of plenty in defence of a cause which the Government refused to let the public know anything about. Incidents began at the end of April. On the day the Auckland Maritime Cargo Workers' Union was formed, A. Farr, a former member of the deregistered union who had applied to join the new union, was struck down by one of the deregistered men as he was leaving the Town Hall.[7] Then on the evening of 30 April three men visited R.S. Belsham, the first president of the new union, and also a former member of the deregistered union, at his home in Eden Terrace. After a brief argument the three men attacked Belsham who was later admitted to Auckland Hospital suffering from concussion and minor scalp wounds.[8] Another member of the new union, H.S.P. Hurst, was assaulted on 1 May; one of his assailants was alleged to have carried a bicycle chain.[9] The new unionists were becoming victims of the frustrations of the old.

On 30 April there was trouble on the coalfields. Some explosives were laid under a small railway bridge at Mahuta, near Huntly, on the Glen Afton line. The explosives did not wreck the bridge, for they had been badly laid.[10] It was assumed that striking miners wishing to disrupt the carriage of coal from the open-cast mines were responsible.[11] Although the press joined Government Ministers and made play of the fact that lives could have been lost had the bridge been wrecked, it seems clear that whoever was responsible had carefully misplaced the charges with the intention only of warning open-cast miners who were working.[12]

The press played up these incidents, for they reflected badly on the watersiders and their allies.[13] Knowing little of the frustration that produced such acts, and predisposed by this time to dismiss the watersiders' case had they known it, the public was ready to believe that the violence was the work of enemies of the people. The *Auckland Star* suddenly lost its customary equilibrium and called for drastic measures. Referring to the incidents arising from the formation of the new Auckland union the editor wrote on 1 May:

> The Government must act rather than talk. A final warning should be issued, and it should take the form of a ban, in the meantime, on any gatherings in the vicinity of the wharves. The Government should announce that crowds on the waterfront will be dispersed without hesitation, and that in view of what has already happened, the Police will be armed. And the Government should make it known, before any further incidents occur, that should individuals or groups defy the ban and challenge the authority of the Police, the Police will shoot.

The Government needed little urging. It seemed to have been anticipating some kind of outbreak of violence.[14] On the evening of 1 May further regulations were gazetted under the Public Safety Conservation Act. These gave the police wider powers to prevent the circulation of illegal pamphlets and to forbid the loitering of strikers or sympathisers. In addition, the property of a deregistered union as well as its liquid assets, could be taken over by the Receiver.[15] In Wellington where some Victoria University students were friendly to the watersiders' cause the annual capping procession was banned. On the evening of 1 May in a national broadcast Holland announced that a Civil Emergency Organisation would be set up "to provide adequate protection for people who are undertaking essential duties". Mayors and County Council chairmen were requested to receive enlistments of volunteers and to arrange small working executives. Emotionalism was running high. In his broadcast Holland, who seemed temporarily to have lost his nerve, claimed that the industrial crisis had "taken a dramatic and grave turn", and that "a very determined effort has been made to overthrow orderly Government by force".[16]

Between them, a handful of strikers, the newspapers and the Prime Minister had conjured up frightening prospects. Volunteers flocked to join the C.E.O.'s, 8,000 men enlisting throughout the country on the first day.[17] By the end of June the numbers had swelled to 28,921.[18]

Labour supporters were sceptical about the whole business. A friend of Nash's wrote him on 2 May:

> Just to convey my reaction to Holland's melodramatic and almost hysterical broadcast last night . . . I am not going this morning to register for Civil Emergency work. Did you notice he never mentioned an age limit, but even talked of organising the women! Really, the overgrown schoolboy has eclipsed himself.[19]

In fact there was little work for the thousands who did enrol. In Cuba Street in Wellington there was a demonstration by more than 1,000 watersiders, freezing workers and seamen on 2 May. But the police handled it with the help of their truncheons, the watersiders' leaders counselling passivity.[20] There were to be further demonstrations in Auckland on the afternoon of 18 May and on the morning of 1 June; from the latter which involved a confrontation with the police outside Myer's Park several men staggered away with cuts, bruises and abrasions. Wellington also experienced several more marches. But Holland's forecast of major civil disturbance proved to be exaggerated. The regular police force was more than equal to the task of maintaining order.

The Government made good use of the crisis atmosphere in the first week of May. On 2 May when T. Magee refused to hand the property of the old Wellington Drivers' Union to the Public Trustee he was arrested. S. Giles, secretary of the deregistered Wellington District Freezing Workers' Union, was arrested on a similar charge. Both men were fined £50.[21]

The following week one of the trustees of the Auckland Branch of the N.Z.W.W.U. was fined £50 for failing to provide an acceptable written answer to a questionnaire from the Public Trustee concerning the withdrawal of £4,900 from the union's bank account on 22 February.[22]

However, at the end of the first week in May the Government and some of its supporters overplayed their hand. The Leader of the Opposition had for some weeks been asking the Government to provide the Labour Party with some broadcasting time to enable Labour to express its point of view. When this was refused, Nash repeated his demand that Parliament be summoned. This too was refused.[23] The Labour Party decided therefore to hold a series of public meetings throughout the country. At the end of April the Auckland Labour Representation Committee approached the Auckland City Council for a May booking of the Auckland Town Hall at which Nash was to be the major speaker. The Council meeting on 3 May rejected the request. According to the deputy Town Clerk, there would be no bookings for political meetings "during the operation of the present emergency regulations".[24]

Suspecting that use of the hall was being banned by the police because of the Emergency Regulations, W.T. Anderton, Labour MP for Auckland Central, approached Superintendent Hall of the Auckland Police on 4 May to ask whether he,

17. Barnes addressing the Auckland Town Hall meeting on 20 May 1951. The chairman is T.J. "Pat" Potter.

Anderton, could hold a "pre-sessional" meeting with his constituents either at the Town Hall Concert Chamber or at another centrally-located hall. Superintendent Hall replied that Anderton could hold a meeting so long as he didn't mention the waterfront dispute or the Regulations. Anderton replied that it was impossible to discuss the economy without mentioning the dispute, and asked Hall to seek a directive on whether or not a meeting, unfettered by the Regulations, could be held. Hall rang back later in the day and told Anderton that "all political meetings are banned". Anderton was "so amazed" that he wired the Prime Minister and rang Nash to protest. He then rang R. McDonald, Labour MP for Ponsonby, who was scheduled to speak in his electorate that same evening. McDonald rang Superintendent Hall and received the same ruling.

Sensing that such rulings might play into the Labour Party's hands, the Government quickly reversed itself. At 7 pm on 4 May, W.H. Fortune, Minister of Police, telephoned Anderton's home to tell him to go ahead with his preparations for a meeting.

He said that some "misunderstanding" had taken place. But it was too late. Anderton clearly believed that Hall had been speaking on Ministerial direction when he had banned the meeting earlier in the day,[25] and Nash believed him. Nash issued a statement strongly criticising the Government which, he claimed, was responsible for the City Council's decision.[26] Over the last two months, he said, "the evidence . . . would suggest that allegedly to prevent the introduction of a form of Government repugnant to the British way of life, the Government is acting in exactly the same way as other Governments which later ended in dictatorship".[27] Both the editor of the *Herald* and the Prime Minister quickly claimed that the decision to prevent Nash from using the Auckland Town Hall had not been made by the Government.[28] Sir John Allum's statement on 6 May that the hall would not be let "while the present conditions prevail, no matter what anyone says" would tend to confirm that he was—at least by this stage—acting as an independent agent.[29]

Nash could not prove that the police had had any hand in the City Council's original decision. In fact, the City Council and the mayor had probably made the decision on their own not to let the hall. Nash did, however, produce strong evidence to suggest that whatever had been the outcome of negotiations for the Town Hall the police had originally had instructions that no meeting was actually to take place. Anderton's original encounter with the police spoke for itself.[30]

This incident with the Town Hall, more than anything else, made the Government more cautious. On 8 May the *Auckland Star* urged that Nash be given access to the radio. About the same time a deputation made up of members of the Public Questions Committees of the Presbyterian and Methodist churches waited on the Prime Minister and asked for repeal or modification of the Regulations.[31] Liberal opinion was clearly concerned at the fact that Anderton, who was the Member for Auckland Central, had been told that he could not address his constituents. As a result, Anderton's decision to go ahead with a meeting in St James' Hall in Wellington Street on the 10th was not challenged by the police.[32] The following evening

Allum, who continued for some days after 4 May to deny Nash the Town Hall, announced that the ban on political meetings in the hall would be lifted. He went so far as to offer the hall to the Labour Party should a projected meeting in the Auckland Domain be rained out. Allum's explanation for the change in the City Council's policy was specious. He claimed that the "recent improvement" in the waterfront position "had exceeded the greatest expectations", and that members of an unspecified "militant organisation" had left the city and it was now safe to lift the ban.[33] It seems more likely, however, that the Government had by this time been exerting considerable pressure on its truculent adjutant.

During the following week the tension relaxed a little. On Sunday 13 May, in rather inclement weather, Nash addressed a crowd of 6,000 people (Nash believed it was 10,000) in the Auckland Domain.[34] The newspapers, smarting perhaps from the stiff criticism Nash had levelled at them in previous weeks, reported the speech fairly carefully. Too carefully, in fact, for Nash had cause to regret what he said at this meeting. Most of the speech was a resumé of Labour's previous statements. Nash wanted to see watersiders able to return to work without victimisation; he argued that wages should be decided by an independent tribunal; and he suggested that the watersiders should consider working under a system of cooperative contracting. He added one thing that was new. The harbour boards, in his opinion, should be the sole employers of waterfront labour, not the shipowners. Speaking of the attempts that had been made to settle the dispute, Nash expressed the opinion that the hold-up could have been solved thrice in the past and it could be settled now if the Government would call a compulsory conference. He added, however, that the Labour Party was not siding with the watersiders. In a sentence that was to do dog him for the rest of his days, Nash said: "we are not for the watersiders nor are we against them", and added that he simply wished to see the matter cleared up as quickly as possible "for the sake of the watersider and every other worker" in the country.[35] When Barnes came forward from the crowd to address the gathering, Nash and members of the Auckland Labour

Representation Committee who had organised the meeting, urged him to respect the fact that this was a Labour Party rally and he should organise his own meeting. Barnes accepted the plea and withdrew.

Holland was quick to comment. He said that under no circumstances would the Government negotiate a settlement with Barnes and Hill. To restore power to the "former officials" would be "a betrayal of the people who had suffered and endured so much". He added that of course the dispute could have been settled earlier: "peace could always be bought at a price".[36] The newspapers, too, lost no time in retaliating against Nash. The *Herald* made much of his "neither for . . . nor against" statement, suggesting that Nash was merely "agin the Government".[37]

The Leader of the Opposition explained his feelings in a letter to Ben Chifley, the Australian Leader of the Opposition, who had written to commiserate over the Town Hall incident:

> You will know that over the years, we, as a Government, had some very difficult times with the Waterside Workers' Union, and they did not always play the game with us, but it does not appear that we would be warranted in supporting a Government that denies all expression of opinion . . . that is not in accord with its own.[38]

In fact, Labour's position could be defended. Until the miners and freezing workers had had their proposals for a settlement of the dispute rejected in March, the Labour Party had not disagreed in substance with Holland's actions. By May, however, the Government had been pursuing its vendetta against the watersiders with an enthusiasm that Labour could not condone. Smashing the national union and blocking many willing men from returning to their old employment, thus prolonging the dispute, was too much for Labour to swallow. Yet in the crisis atmosphere Nash's criticisms did look like quibbles. The publicity given to such Labour statements in May and June was beginning to look more damaging to the party than the suppression practised by the press during April. The press had set public attitudes by May; anything that could be interpreted as equivocation on the issues raised by Holland was now politically dangerous to the person concerned.[39]

Even more damaging to the Labour Party was the fact that the Labour caucus was split within itself and a gulf was also emerging between most of the party, which was loyal to Nash, and the F.O.L. While a number of Labour Members were increasingly critical of Holland's determination to pursue a policy of total victory, a few members of caucus, in particular McLagan (who was still recuperating in Christchurch), A.G. Osborne, R. Macfarlane, Semple and F. Jones, remained above all else hostile to Barnes and Hill.[40] Semple, who was quite close to Walsh, was the only member of caucus who revealed his feelings in public: he issued a statement on 3 June which sounded very similar to his attack on Barnes some years earlier:[41]

> If it is not too late, I would urge the trade unionists not to jettison all that has been gained by the hard work and sacrifice of their great leaders through the years that have gone. I appeal to them to forsake the wreckers, the Communists and the leaders so called, who are aiming to lead them into a way of life that is contrary to our own.

Referring to Barnes, Semple continued:

> [He] is ambitious for personal power. Because of his position as president of a powerful union, because he has adopted the mantle of protagonist for the worker and of trade unionism, and because he is able to sell his story, he constitutes a real threat to the industrial peace and general welfare of the people of this country.[42]

Such statements brought out into the open the divisions which were opening up within the labour movement.

In some ways the uneasiness that existed by May 1951 between the Parliamentary Labour Party and the F.O.L. can be dated back to the Labour Party's loss of power in 1949. While Labour leaders were stripped of power the F.O.L. had to continue to represent its affiliates and to deal as best it could with the new Government. The interests of the two sections of the labour movement were beginning to diverge. Added to this was the fact that the F.O.L. itself was, during 1950, in the process of splitting, the rump organisation feverishly competing

18. Deregistered watersiders meeting in the Auckland Domain, Sunday 3 June 1951. A large contingent of police not shown watched proceedings from under the trees.

with the T.U.C. for the affections of New Zealand's 370 unions. Even before Fraser died there was a suspicion growing amongst the leadership of the F.O.L. that some members of the Parliamentary Labour Party were more friendly than they should be with the T.U.C.[43]

With Nash's election to the leadership of the Labour Party in January 1951 the Parliamentary Party was now headed by a man who had come to mistrust F.P. Walsh because of his role in the Holmes satchel case in 1948.[44] Walsh and Nash never succeeded in establishing the close friendship which the former had enjoyed with Fraser. In fact during the waterfront dispute considerable tension developed between the two. At first, while Nash was still feeling his way, the Labour Party did nothing to upset Walsh's plans for isolating the watersiders. But during March Walsh decided to try and force Nash into making a whole-hearted declaration of support for the F.O.L.'s policies. The meeting at Hamilton on 29 March, which was sponsored by the Waikato Trades Council, and at which K.M. Baxter of the F.O.L. spoke first, was planned in such a way that Nash would find it difficult to do other than support the F.O.L.'s handling of the dispute. When it came to the point Nash eluded the trap, spoke freely, and did not hesitate to condemn the Regulations. But he was furious about the whole affair: in a handwritten note found by the author amongst his papers Nash wrote:

> After arrival at Hamilton, all the evidence tended to show that [the] purpose of [the] Waikato Trades Council was to use the Leader of [the] P.L.P. to attract [a] crowd to hear Mr Baxter boost the F.O.L. . . . Mr Walsh's purpose might have been to associate me with the attack on the Waterside Workers' Union.[45]

A few days later when Nash indicated to Baxter by phone that he was considering writing asking Barnes and Hill to address the Labour caucus, the F.O.L. rushed to the press with a denunciation of the move. By early April relations between the leaderships of the F.O.L. and the Labour Party had descended to an unprecedented low.

For the rest of the dispute there was little contact between Nash and Walsh. As a matter of courtesy Nash had to be invited to address the annual F.O.L. conference at the end of April. Walsh knew that not to invite him would be seen as a needless affront to a man considered by many in the Labour movement as one of its greats. But during May, as the watersiders came to develop a new respect for the Leader of the Opposition (one of Barnes' assistants called Nash's Auckland Domain speech "very fair and all fact"),[46] the F.O.L. kept as clear of the Labour Party as possible. To Walsh it seemed to be in enemy hands. Nash, for his part, did try to maintain some semblance of unity within the Labour movement by holding a combined meeting

of the executives of the F.O.L. and the Labour Party on 30
May. But relations between the industrial and political wings
remained icy.[47]

Early in June Nash hinted publicly at the difficulty which
he was encountering. "The Labour Party," he said, "is a political party that cannot live without the industrial movement.
One cannot go as far as it should without the other."[48] The
implication was there that without the actions of some of
Labour's allies the Leader of the Opposition might have been
able to do more to assist the men for whose cause he now felt
considerable concern.

The Government and the press viewed these differences
within the labour movement with some glee; Nash was again
criticised for his statements.[49] Neither Nash nor the Labour
Party as a whole was deterred. At its annual conference a few
days later T.G. Wells, vice-president of the deregistered
N.Z.W.W.U., was given an opportunity to address the delegates.
Wells told the conference that the feeling for the Labour Party
within his organisation had "never been stronger than it is at
present because our members believe that the party has recaptured the fighting spirit of 1935".[50] The conference decided,
after hearing a full discussion on the question, not to refuse
membership to unions that had affiliations with the W.F.T.U.[51]

The Labour Party's rank and file was much nearer to Nash,
Nordmeyer and the other critics of Government policy than to
Semple and the F.O.L., a fact that afforded the Government
yet another opportunity to mock the party. On the 13th,
Holyoake, the Deputy Prime Minister, claimed that the Labour
Party was moving "hand in hand" with Communism.[52] Labour
was paying dearly for its opposition to the smashing of national
unions and the "screening" of men who wished to join the new
unions. It was of no public moment that it had remained solidly
in favour of the principle of compulsory arbitration throughout
the dispute. Nash began receiving a flood of anonymous letters,
some of them vicious, from Holland's most fervent supporters.
One was addressed to the "Honourable" Comrade W. Nash;
another to Walter Nash, Neither for or against, Hutt; another
called him a "miserable old hypocrite"; many contained copies

of Minhinnick's cartoons belittling Nash from the *Herald*, suitably inscribed by the anonymous donors with filthy epithets.[53] After sixteen years of hard work the newspapers were at last succeeding in denting Walter Nash's reputation.

Collapse

After 20 April when Holland rejected Nash's efforts to solve the waterfront dispute, the watersiders had nobody who could negotiate on their behalf with the Government. A deputation of Labour MPs did wait on the Prime Minister early in May; on 7 May, and again on 30 May, joint meetings were held of the National Executives of the Labour Party and the F.O.L. in an endeavour to work out a common policy to the dispute. Nothing resulted from these meetings. Knowing of the disarray in labour ranks the Prime Minister felt under no pressure to offer or agree to any compromise settlement of the dispute. Meantime the crisis persisted; 20,000 men were still out of work; and no one seemed to be making any significant effort to settle the dispute. When negotiations did take place they were at first accidental, and then the product of necessity. The men were in fact slowly being starved back to work.

A direct meeting between watersiders and the Minister of Labour took place on 11 May 1951, when, following a demonstration outside Parliament Buildings, Sullivan agreed to see Wells, J. Napier and E.A. Napier of the Wellington Branch of the deregistered union. The watersiders had had no direct contact with the Government for months and were uncertain as to the precise terms on which the Government would agree to a resumption of work. Sullivan promised to let the watersiders have these terms in writing, and a letter was duly dispatched to Wells on 14 May. Heading the list of conditions was the acceptance of separate unions at each port. Unions had to be open to all applicants, with Port Conciliation Committees having the power to decide how many workers' names would be placed on Port Registers. The employers at each port would select the names to be placed on the register and if a man was refused he could appeal to the local Port Conciliation Committee, whose decision would be final. There were other points as well—many of them matters which had been raised before by ministers, employers and the press, but never actually set down as conditions for a resumption of work. "Spelling" was outlawed. Of more significance, there was to be completely new machinery set up to control waterfront affairs. Port Conciliation Committees were to consist of an equal number of representatives[54] from employers and employees and they were to be chaired by a Government appointee who was not to be a member of the staff of the W.I.C. The W.I.C. was to consist of one man appointed by the Government and his duties were to be entirely administrative. There was to be a new Waterfront Industry Tribunal in place of the old W.I.A., the W.I.T. to consist entirely of "independent persons" (three in all) who would be appointed by the Government.[55] The Government had moved way beyond the "Seven Points"; even the question of separate port unions was only a part of Sullivan's new terms for a resumption of work.

The watersiders were quite shocked at the severity of the terms. The task of "screening" applicants for jobs on the waterfront which had been handled at New Plymouth and Auckland by representatives of the employers, the Labour Department and the W.I.C., was now to be placed entirely in the hands of the employers. Moreover, the workers were to be deprived of any representative on the W.I.T., which was the final appeal authority on the waterfront. Envisaging that the Government's idea of "three independent persons" for the W.I.T. might well mean three faithful members of the National Party, the Wellington Branch of the N.Z.W.W.U. was quick to denounce Sullivan's terms. At a special meeting of the branch on Tuesday 15 May the men unanimously rejected Sullivan's letter. Instead they moved a resolution reaffirming the policy of their national union and calling for the repeal of the Regulations, no victimisation, recognition of their democratically elected leaders and reregistration of the national union, and the calling of a compulsory conference with a view to obtaining a settlement by conciliation and arbitration.[56]

Once again a stiffening of the Government's terms for a settlement had brought about renewed determination in the men. A settlement seemed further away than ever. Claiming that the waterside workers seemed "not anxious to find a mutually satisfactory settlement to the dispute", Sullivan continued with his search for new unionists.[57] On the 27th the Minister again dismissed Nash's suggestion that a compulsory conference be called as "just silly". "Whom can we have a compulsory conference with [sic]?" he asked. The existence of the new unions removed the need for discussions; the stoppage, he believed "was 80 per cent over".[58]

The Government's refusal to concede anything to the watersiders did make negotiations seem useless. The early hopes which the watersiders had held of toppling the Government had long since faded. There now seemed not even a chance that they could save much face from the dispute. The only question that remained was how long it would take before they acknowledged total defeat. Barnes and Hill tried to keep up morale. On 20 May both were allowed to address large meetings in Auckland and Wellington, although an address by Hill to the Wellington seamen three days later was interrupted by the Police. For the first time what they had to say was widely reported.[59] But the decision to allow them to speak in public was not, as they interpreted, a sign that the Government was weakening. It indicated, as Sullivan bragged, that the Government considered the dispute to be almost over; nothing Barnes and Hill could say would alter that fact.[60]

The watersiders now turned increasingly to the public, and staged several marches and rallies in Auckland and Wellington, hoping that the public would come to appreciate their plight.[61] When the shipowners arbitrarily announced at the end of May that they were intending to clap a 50 per cent surcharge on shipping charges in order to recoup some of the cost of New Zealand's holdup, a move that was universally criticised by the press, the watersiders took new heart. Surely the public would realise at last that the watersiders had been victims of the most ruthless of employers? But it was hopeless. Public attitudes had been set over a number of years. The press had baked them rock hard. By now it seemed that nothing could shake the impression that the watersiders were "enemies of the people".

On 12 June there was a meeting in Wellington of the watersiders' leaders with representatives of those unions striking in protest at the Emergency Regulations. The meeting showed a high degree of unanimity among the delegates. Barnes reported that his National Executive had reaffirmed its determination to "struggle until an honourable settlement is obtained", and he optimistically expressed the hope that now that the Emergency Regulations had been slackened a little, and the watersiders had been given the chance to present their case to the public, the Government might be forced to repeal the Regulations altogether.[62] The freezing workers, too, believed that clouds had silver linings; the Government had been unable to find enough men to bring the new freezing unions up to full strength, and would almost certainly have to give ground. The Wellington drivers' representatives reported that between 400 and 500 drivers were still on strike, and the seamen, some of whom had previously been grumbling about the numbers of watersiders who had taken secondary employment, promised that they would not go back to work until the watersiders had "received a satisfactory settlement".[63] It was the miners who sounded a note of warning. Already there had been press reports suggesting that West Coast miners were anxious that the watersiders should return to work.[64] At the meeting the Waikato miners, while reporting solidarity among the ranks, warned that their financial position was such that the men could hold their position for only about another fortnight. Consequently the meeting decided that another effort must be made to obtain a settlement. A motion was carried:

> That this conference pledges its determination to fight until an honourable settlement is obtained based on the principles of no victimisation of any worker involved and the repeal of the Emergency Regulations. To this end we arrange a conference with the Rt Hon. W. Nash for Tuesday, 19 June, in order that a further approach be made to the Government with a view to obtaining an honourable and just settlement.[65]

The statement that the watersiders would return to work if the Government would agree that there be no victimisation and lifted the Regulations,[66] suggested that the watersiders were prepared to accept separate port unions as well as the Government's refusal to recognise Barnes and Hill.[67] Some small face-saving device was all they now wanted. It would be enough if members of the deregistered union were allowed to join the new unions without impediment.

The Government, however, was determined to deny the watersiders even the smallest of concessions. On the 14th Sullivan said that any suggestion that former watersiders should be allowed to return to their normal work now that their jobs had been taken by others "was absolutely impossible". The Government's condition for a resumption of work "was the formation of new port unions by men prepared to register for work". He added: "That has been done. And that's the end of the waterfront trouble".[68] When Nash met Sullivan, Holyoake and Webb[69] on the afternoon of the 19th he made no progress towards a settlement.[70] He explained that the watersiders' demand for "no victimisation" meant either the deregistration of the new unions or a policy whereby the former watersiders were allowed to join the new unions thereby, in effect, taking them over.[71] The Government would not budge. The next day Holland repeated what was now a familiar refrain: watersiders could appeal to the Port Conciliation Committees if they felt victimised; the men themselves "had the repeal of the Emergency Regulations in their own hands by simply calling off the strike and taking employment".[72]

Once again Holland castigated Nash, and claimed that he had not brought forward "a single new idea" for a settlement.[73] And once again he got away with it. Not one newspaper pointed to the obvious: the watersiders had all but given up the fight and appeared ready to accept almost any settlement that would enable them to return to their old jobs. Only Holland's lust for total victory continued to make accommodation difficult. By this time Nash was at his wits' end to know how to assist in bringing about a settlement. He was receiving many reports of deprivation and hardship among the families of men involved in the dispute. From one watersider's wife he received the following pathetic appeal:

> Dear Mr Nash,
> Why don't you stop this strike? Before this business we were a happy family. Now my husband has started hitting me and my kids . . . .[74]

Caught between Barnes' and Hill's determination not to suffer total humiliation and the Prime Minister's equal determination to achieve it, the Leader of the Opposition had nowhere to turn. On 25 June Nash confided to McLagan:

> I am satisfied the Government does not want to settle except by a complete showdown of the miners, seamen, watersiders and other unions . . . and I do not know what we can do about it.[75]

Moved by the distress which the dispute was causing, Nash instructed a minister within his electorate of Hutt to pay out money to help the families of those in distress as a result of the dispute. When the Emergency Regulations were finally lifted at the end of July Nash sent the minister £21.0.0 of his own money as reimbursement.[76] Like many a concerned Labour supporter he found this the only tangible way left to him to express his concern at the drift of events.

However, the resistance of some of the Government's opponents had almost been worn away. With the failure of Nash's efforts it became apparent that the strike on the coalfields was crumbling. On 22 June the miners independently approached Sullivan about the conditions for their own return to work. Sullivan seized the opportunity to deliver a parting blow to National's old adversaries. He announced a set of conditions which miners would have to accept before they could return to work. As a broad principle, he said, there would be no victimisation, but "full and reasonable safeguards were necessary in the interests of the men working". In particular he announced two conditions: open-cast miners still on strike would not be able to be re-employed at open-cast mines but might be given jobs at other mines; and the management at all mines must have the right to place men "to the best advantage".[77]

The *Herald* enthusiastically endorsed Sullivan's conditions.[78] But 1,000 Waikato miners meeting at Huntly unanimously refused to accept work on such terms and it was only after considerable public protest including a telegram from fifty Huntly businessmen who were alarmed at the prospect of any further prolonging of the strike,[79] that Sullivan modified his demand.[80] The Government held the electorate of Raglan by the narrowest of majorities and Cabinet, however much it might have wanted to punish the miners, was reluctant to do so at the risk of losing a seat.

Over the following week secret ballots were held at most mines where the men were still on strike, and beginning on 4 July the miners streamed back to work. The miners, said A.C. Baxter of Rotowaro, had reached the limit of their economic resources in protesting against the Government's action. Now that Parliament was at last in session they felt they could leave the rest of the protest in the hands of the Labour Party.[81] The strike, during which more than ninety working days had been lost, which had meant that 300,000 tons of coal had not been mined, and which had seen miners forfeit some £250,000 in wages,[82] was over at last.

Meantime, the seamen had been moving towards a return to work. On 15 June finances were so low that strike payments in Wellington had had to be reduced. On 22 June Auckland seamen confirmed an earlier decision to end the strike[83] and a meeting of the National Council of the Seamen's Union on the 25th decided to hold meetings at all ports to consider a resolution to return to work. The union's branches hesitated, deciding to go ahead with ballots only when the miners had ceased their strike.[84] On Friday 6 July New Zealand's seamen voted by large majorities at all ports except Wellington (which decided to wait for some move from the watersiders) to return to work the following Wednesday.

These moves towards a resumption of work involved some recriminations from the watersiders. Barnes, who had advocated street demonstrations and the use of force against the police, only to be overruled by wiser councils within the N.Z.W.W.U.,[85] was bitter in his denunciation of Prendiville and Crook of the U.M.W. when he met them together with F.P. Walsh in Wellington on 29 June.[86] The *Herald* reported euphemistically that

Prendiville and Barnes had exchanged "frank views couched in vigorous language" about the part each had played in the crisis. Walsh had been forced to end the meeting only a few minutes after it started.[87]

However, Barnes' days as a union leader were drawing to a close. He had held his men together with some skill during the first fourteen weeks of the dispute. But by June splits were beginning to show. On 7 June the watersiders at Port Chalmers went back to work *en masse*; their president, N. Crichton, was quoted as saying that it was a decision between keeping the men together or dragging them down to further poverty and degradation. "Somebody had to make the move and, as I saw it, it was my duty". The Government regarded the return to work at Port Chalmers, the first at one of the four main ports, as a major breakthrough.[88] More were to follow. By the last week in June the Wellington Branch of the deregistered union was engaged in its own negotiations with the Government. Brigadier Hunt of the Wellington Civil Emergency Organisation approached Wells and Napier to find out if they intended holding a demonstration to coincide with the opening of Parliament on 26 June. In the course of his discussion he found that the watersiders were still quite uncertain as to the Government's terms for a return to work. He recommended discussions with H.L. Bockett, the Secretary of Labour, and these took place on 25 June.[89] Again the watersiders were asked to put their proposals in a letter to the Minister. But again the watersiders' terms, including as they did "no victimisation", immediate elections of officers in all new unions, conditions of employment on the waterfront similar to those applying pre-February, and an end to the Regulations, were unacceptable to the Government.[90] Sullivan labelled the letter "a complete rejection of the terms that have been announced for a resumption of work". He added: "Some of the conditions you suggest are completely unacceptable to the Government".[91] Negotiations had again broken down, the watersiders protesting once more that they were still unclear about Government policy.[92]

Such a state of affairs could not continue for ever. Clearly the Government was not going to give an inch, particularly now that the watersiders' allies, and the N.Z.W.W.U. itself, were crumbling. Lyttelton was the first of the "big three" ports to topple. On 4 July the deregistered watersiders there decided by a two-to-one majority to return to work. As a result, 152 applications were made to join the new Lyttelton union.[93] The decision to work was reversed the following day[94] but an ultimatum had been delivered to the deregistered national union; a meeting of unions affected by the dispute must meet the following week to consider a return to work. Such a combined meeting duly took place on 9 July and the seamen, watersiders, freezing workers, and drivers unanimously decided to return to work as soon as possible. The statement that was issued said:

> Supremely confident of the conscious discipline of our ranks, we call upon every individual member to return to work and hold up the banner of his union on the job.
>
> We call upon watersiders, seamen, miners, freezing workers, drivers, and all other unionists to stand by their fellow workers in a positive fighting programme to overcome screening, hold conditions, and clean out scabbery root and branch.[95]

On the 11th the National Executive of the N.Z.W.W.U. recommended a return to work and within hours a large number of applications had been lodged for membership of the new waterfront unions. The 1951 waterfront stoppage was over.

It was impossible to view the return to work, wherever it was available, as anything other than a long-delayed acknowledgment of defeat. For months the unions had been holding out, hoping to be able to save a little face. The Government would allow them none. Sheer exhaustion had finally forced the men to call off the fight.

For those involved directly in the 151-day stoppage it had been a searing experience. Finances had been severely strained, family life disrupted. For almost half a year a majority of fathers had either been out of work or in part-time employment. And as time wore on the prospects of victory which had never been good, faded away. The approaching humiliation was, however, collective. As the Government tightened up the pressure the men stood closer together. In spite of the big bonuses being paid to the new unionists,[96] the number of men who "scabbed" was remarkably small. The Wellington Watersiders' *Information Bulletin* on 1 June estimated the number at 500 out of a total union membership of 8,300.[97] Each member of the union carefully kept the lists of his mates who had deserted the cause; the Dunedin branch of the N.Z.W.W.U. called its list the "Roll of Dishonour", a roll that was "inscribed to those despicable individuals who committed the vile crime of scabbing during the Great Lockout". Far from encouraging the men to "reject their misleaders", Government and F.O.L. policies had forged loyalties that only privation could break.

Yet, when the fight was called off in July the Government's victory was total. No guarantee that victimisation would not be practised was obtained from the Government.[98] And in fact many members of the deregistered union did not find their way back on to the waterfront.[99] Of the three main ports only the men at Wellington, where the new union was so much below normal strength, and where it had proved impossible to get enough strike-breakers, went back with their union almost intact;[100] at Auckland and Lyttelton the Port Conciliation Committee kept the port register at below normal strength for some months while deregistered watersiders were forced to seek employment elsewhere in the city. Some occupations, however, were closed to deregistered watersiders. The Government insisted they not be employed by the Railways Department.[101]

The cause of militant unionism had suffered a stunning blow. In place of one national waterside workers' union there were twenty-six small unions padded to varying degrees with members who had never before had experience of waterfront work. With the Wellington freezing workers' and drivers' unions the same was true. The strongest unions in the country had been humbled, their ability to question, oppose or fight Government policies greatly weakened.

The waterfront dispute had been a costly one. More than 1.1 million man days were wasted and the loss of wages to all workers involved in the dispute was £3.1 million, half of this amount being watersiders' wages.[102] The economic loss to the country was more difficult to gauge. Barnes in a speech on 22

July claimed that the cost of the dispute would amount to £100 million.[103] A.H. Nordmeyer estimated that the cost might be as high as £50 million.[104] The Government Statistician concluded that the correct figure was about £42 million.[105] Apart from the coal that had not been mined, some 70,000 tons of cement had not been produced. More than 600,000 cases of apples and pears had either rotted on the trees or in waterfront sheds between February and April. The wool that was not sold at the time of peak market prices was estimated to be worth £31 million. Sugar shortages during the dispute necessitated the importing of 9,500 tons of sugar from the United Kingdom and this sugar had to be subsidised to the extent of £170,000 in order that it could be sold at the regular New Zealand price.[106]

At the same time the Government's action did result in greater efficiency in the waterfront industry. The number of stoppages decreased[107] and the rate of work among the new unionists was higher than that performed by members of the N.Z.W.W.U. This improvement in industrial relations was partly a result of the Government's actions but was also due to the new co-operative contracting system which was introduced and which substantially increased bonus payments to watersiders.[108] To achieve their ends Government and employers had been forced to use the carrot as well as the stick.

The direct beneficiaries of the Government's stern measures were the shipowners. By the end of the dispute they had more compliant unions to deal with and they benefited from the faster rate of work. During the dispute itself, however, they lost a lot of money. Some 3,250 ship days were wasted in New Zealand ports as a result of the dispute[109] and the potential loss to the shipowners was calculated to be £1.5 million. The shipowners made it clear that they supported the Government's handling of the dispute.[110] But they were also determined to make New Zealanders share their costs. In May they announced a 50 per cent surcharge on shipping costs for goods going to and from New Zealand. This move placed the Government in an embarrassing position. Having taken strong action against the union for arbitrary activities it was now faced with employers behaving in the same manner. Government and Opposition protests were loud[111] and the press was hostile.[112] But the shipowners stuck to their guns. When the surcharge was lifted at the end of July it was calculated that they had recouped about 75 per cent of their losses.[113]

Other industries were not in a position to retrieve their losses so easily. The building industry was held up because of the shortage of cement. Plaster, too, was scarce owing to the difficulties in shipping the necessary gypsum from Australia.[114] Confectionary and biscuit producers also suffered due to the shortage of sugar.[115]

Victory had not been cheap.

Parliament Dissolved

What made defeat seem like something less than total humiliation for the watersiders was the fact that on the evening of 11 July the Prime Minister announced that he was going to ask the Governor-General for a dissolution of Parliament. For the first time in New Zealand in the twentieth century elections were to be called before they were due. If the watersiders had not actually toppled the Government, as Barnes had hoped, they had led Holland to seek another mandate to govern. The whole waterfront issue remained—nominally at least—open, even if defeat of the Government seemed most unlikely.

National Party members had, no doubt, been hoping for some months that the Government could benefit directly from the showdown with the watersiders. However, the first public suggestion that the Prime Minister might be thinking in terms of an election came on 8 May when, in reply to criticism which Nash had made about the Government's monopolisation of the radio, Holland stated that he was "prepared to stand or fall by the public assessment of his attitude to the waterfront strike in comparison with that of the Leader of the Opposition".[116] There can be little doubt that Holland was beginning to see the dispute as offering an excellent opportunity to entrench his party in power. The country's overseas balance of trade was healthy, the only serious economic problem being the rapid rise in the cost of living.[117] And attention that might in normal times fasten on this question could probably be diverted away by the waterfront issue. On that question the National Party had everything going its way. The press was unanimous in its support; the Emergency Regulations had made public opposition to the Government virtually impossible; the radio had been used openly for propaganda purposes; and the Government's political opponents were in a state of disarray, some approving of Holland's actions. In Australia, R.G. Menzies had just used emotive opposition to Communism to secure a return of his conservative Government, albeit with a reduced majority in the Federal House of Representatives. The advantages of "snap" elections were almost certainly discussed when Holland visited Canberra in June 1951.

The Labour Party on the other hand was understandably reluctant to face public opinion when Holland first raised the issue. Nash's reply to Holland on 9 May was cautious:

> Mr Holland is content to let the public judge between himself and myself, but how can the public judge correctly when the facts are denied them? Let the facts be brought to the bar of public opinion and then a just verdict may be obtained . . . . When these facilities are provided we could then justifiably be asked to stand or fall by the public assessment of our respective attitudes.[118]

Nash was painfully aware of the disadvantages under which the Labour Party was operating, hence the reason for his frequent requests that Parliament be assembled. In most other countries where provisions existed for the taking of emergency powers it was mandatory that Parliament be summoned, so that government actions could be subjected to careful public scrutiny. No such requirement existed in the Public Safety Conservation Act 1932,[119] so Holland continued to refuse Nash's requests, thereby depriving the Labour Party of its most effective public forum. In fact, Parliament did not meet until 26 June 1951, which was almost the latest possible date in the year on which it could assemble.[120]

After the question of whether Nash was to be allowed to address public meetings had been settled in his favour early in May, and the enforcement of the Regulations was relaxed a little, Labour's position was not quite so difficult. Members spoke freely and regularly, although they were not always reported. Nevertheless, Labour members were increasingly frustrated as time wore on. H.E. Combs, Labour MP for Onslow, was reported as saying that they had "had a tough time sitting around 'sawing wood' as they say in America".[121]

When Parliament did finally meet, the Labour Party moved on to the offensive. Once the formalities had been cleared away, Nash used the Imprest Supply Bill to begin what was to develop into a major attack on the Government's handling of the waterfront dispute. Nash himself was frequently interrupted during the course of his speech,[122] but other Labour speakers in this debate and in a later Want of Confidence debate were able to develop a consistent line of attack: inflation had exacerbated industrial tension; when the February crisis came the Government was duty-bound to call a compulsory conference but did not; at least four subsequent opportunities presented themselves on which a settlement of the dispute could have been made—8 March, 20 April, 12-14 May and 19 June—but on each occasion the Government chose to prolong the dispute; the Emergency Regulations were far too wide and dangerous in their scope. Frequent reference was made to excessive police activity,[123] in particular to the banning of political meetings early in May.[124]

What gave sting to Labour's attack was the arbitrary way in which the shipowners had levied their 50 per cent surcharge. The Government had spent millions of pounds subduing a workers' claim for an extra 3d an hour in wages; the shipowners had been able to raise their charges by a simple statement of intent. Against the workers the Government used everything it had; against the employers it seemed to be powerless. A.H. Nordmeyer expressed the point on 5 July:

> I am asking what the Government really did about this increase of 50 per cent in shipping freights—a far greater increase and a far greater burden on the community than the increase of 3d an hour that the watersiders asked for. The Government has apparently uttered a mild protest about the matter—yes a mild protest. There is no question of submitting the case to arbitra-

tion; there is no question of seven points. There is nothing but a supine acceptance of what the shipping companies propose to do.[125]

The Labour Party did not have it all its own way. A spirited defence of the Government's actions came from National Members who were able to twit their critics with references to Labour's previous encounters with the militants, and with the fact that Labour throughout its fourteen years in office had not seen fit to repeal the Public Safety Conservation Act.[126] Some went further suggesting that Labour was in league with the watersiders and/or the Communists.[127] Nevertheless, for the first time since the dispute had begun the Government had been subjected to consistent public attacks on its policies, and there can be little doubt that many members of the public were beginning to wonder whether the Government had really told the full story.

Some National members seemed to be aware of the fact that the impetus behind the Government's case was slowly ebbing. On 29 June W.S. Goosman, the Minister of Works, publicly expressed the hope that it might be possible to test public opinion on the waterfront issue,[128] and there was evident relief when on the night of 11 July the Prime Minister took the unprecedented move of announcing that he would ask the Governor-General for a dissolution of the House.[129] The *Herald* summed up the position perfectly when it commented that "some will say that Mr Holland's aim is to ride the winning wave following on his successful handling of the strike and to ride it before it breaks on the shortness of public memory".[130] Further delay would have been wasteful.

Holland did not dally. Parliament was immediately dissolved, the Labour Party being thrown back again upon the newspapers to report its case against the Government. And just to sustain the crisis atmosphere until the last possible moment, the Government announced on 19 July that the State of Emergency would continue in spite of the fact that it was now some days since the waterfront dispute had ended. Even the *Herald* regarded the perpetuation of the State of Emergency as excessive,[131] and on 25 July just over five weeks before the date of the

General Election which had been set for 1 September, the Emergency Regulations were at last withdrawn. The Government's opponents had the unenviable task of attempting to counter five months of unchallenged propaganda in the space of five weeks. With the weapons they possessed, defeat was almost a foregone conclusion.

CHAPTER VIII

FINALE

The Election
 Once the date of the election had been finalised a new battle was soon being waged. The Electoral Office was faced with a huge task of preparing the rolls and additional staff had to be employed. For the first time elections for the four Maori seats were to be held on the same day as for the European seats.[1] The political parties encountered more complex problems. Each party had to select its candidates and organise its propaganda in a very short space of time. For the Labour Party, which was perennially short of funds, a second election in twenty-one months was a serious drain on resources. Within a week of Holland's request for a dissolution of Parliament all Labour Party branches were being canvassed for contributions to the central campaign.[2]
 From the beginning there could be little doubt that the Government was in the stronger position. Some people usually sympathetic to National criticised the decision to hold an early election. The *Press* felt that an election would "distract" from the "main task of rebuilding the economy";[3] S.W. Peterson, president of the Associated Chambers of Commerce, regretted the decision; and several Auckland businessmen felt the election was unnecessary. Most of the Government's critics, however, were understanding. One Auckland businessman commented that Holland had obviously decided that the Opposition intended to "rake him fore and aft" for the next eighteen months on the industrial issue and that it was wiser to go to the country now.[4] The rallying of the stock market on 13 July was a good indication that a majority of investors had confidence in National's ability to win through.[5]
 The Government had more going for it than this. While the

cost of living had risen by nearly 6 per cent in the previous six months, the favourable balance in the country's overseas trade was quite considerable and at the end of July it was announced that there had been a surplus of £4.8 million in the public accounts for the first quarter of the financial year.[6] While something could be made of the cost of living issue it would be difficult for the Labour Party to argue that the economy was other than in a sound position. And in fact even the cost of living issue around which Labour planned to centre its campaign had been affected to some extent by the Government's decision at the end of May to pay out a £5 bonus for every child.[7]

The activities of the press also probably had some effect on the general standing of the National Party. Most of the papers had invested much time and energy in bolstering the Government's case throughout the stoppage. They were not now going to desert the National Party in its hour of greatest need. The morning papers, in particular the *Herald* and the *Otago Daily Times*, began to run a series of editorials which, for the savagery of their attacks on the Labour Party, can seldom have been equalled in New Zealand's history. The *Otago Daily Times* began its efforts on 13 July with an appeal "to the organised forces of anti-Socialism in Dunedin" to take advantage of "this opportunity to offer a vigorous contribution towards better government". By the 30th, and with still a month to go, the editor was at fever pitch:

> The part of Mr Nash and his colleagues (including the Dunedin Members of Parliament) in quibbling and nibbling at the edge of the trouble, thereby exacerbating it, will not soon be forgotten . . . Those who were not with the elected Government of this country in its calculated "showdown" with the striking industrial unionists were against it, and no textual prevarications with this fact are admissable. Those who were against the Government in this crisis—and hiring halls and stumping the country in an endeavour to confuse the public—and incidently to encourage the strikers—are not responsible men . . . . Out of office they should remain, until the people of New Zealand are prepared to welcome anarchy and embrace Communism.[8]

The *Auckland Star*, which had followed an erratic editorial policy throughout the dispute, commented in much the same vein. On the eve of the election the editor wrote: "That the Labour Party . . . is susceptible to the taint of association with those who 'take the Communist line' is beyond dispute. It is well that every elector going to the poll on Saturday should understand that".[9] The two weeks at the end of the campaign when Labour was allowed equal broadcasting time were scarcely enough to counter such propaganda.

What made the Labour Party's campaign more difficult was the very forceful support given to the party by deregistered watersiders and adherents of the T.U.C. At a meeting on 20 July of the executive of the Auckland Branch of the deregistered N.Z.W.W.U., Barnes recommended to members that if they wanted to get back on to the waterfront again they should do all within their power to secure the defeat of the Holland Government.[10] Speakers' notes were issued to many watersiders, several organisers were appointed, and a number of street corner and hall meetings were held to "assist" the Labour Party during the campaign.[11] The same people who had not mourned the exit of a Labour Government in 1949 now threw every effort into the fight to return the Labour Party to power. The bitter lesson had been learnt; whatever the drawbacks of a party that contained men such as Semple and McLagan, it could never be as hostile to militant unionism as one full of Hollands and Sullivans.

Such support from men who by now were regarded as industrial outlaws was embarrassing. Dubious press reporting made it worse. On 22 July Barnes and T.J. ("Pat") Potter addressed a large meeting at the Auckland Town Hall. The press quoted Potter as saying:

> The Holland Government has won the first round, but the second round will not be won until 8,000 watersiders are back in their jobs on the waterfront. Let us put Sid out and Walter in. Then we can line Mr Nash up.[12]

It is doubtful whether these were the words actually used by Potter. A typescript of his speech read as follows:

> I am confident you will spare neither time or [sic] energy in the pleasant task of putting Sid in the political garbage can . . . . Ask the Nationals about the open union pledge, making the £ go

19. Holland on the campaign stump, 1951.

further, about the Regulations. Let us put Sid out and Walter in. If they [sic] fail to rectify these things, then we can line Mr Nash up.[13]

However, the damage had been done. From the newspapers' report of the speech the inference was clear; a Labour Government might return the old order to the waterfront.[14]

Coming at a time when there were ominous reports from Auckland that influential adherents of the F.O.L. were considering standing their own candidates in opposition to the Labour Party,[15] such statements as Potter's had to be dealt with firmly. On 24 July Nash was quoted as saying that there was no chance of a pressure group "or any organisation or person lining up either the Labour Party or myself".[16] The price for support of the Labour Party by the F.O.L. was high: a complete renunciation of the defeated watersiders.

Nash's rebuff to the watersiders was enough to prevent a complete rupture of relations with the F.O.L., and as the campaign progressed much of the militants' zeal for the Labour Party evaporated.[17] But somehow Nash's assurances that a Labour Government would be master in its own house failed to carry conviction with the public. National Party candidates kept referring to Potter's reported statement of 22 July, and the Prime Minister in his opening campaign speech on 13 August said:

> I believe that if Mr Nash and his friends go on to the Treasury Benches of New Zealand the old union will be back in a month, the old leaders will be back in their places and we will see a return to the old abuses.[18]

It was the Labour Party that was now being "raked fore and aft" for its role in New Zealand's biggest industrial upheaval.

Labour's frustration showed through as time wore on. At Nelson Nash was quoted as saying:

> The election is just a stunt, a sordid political manoeuvre. Never has an election been brought forward with its purpose so disguised. It is sheer hypocrisy on the part of the Government to go to the country asking support for its handling of the wharf dispute when it knows that by the end of its term in 1952 it will be completely out of favour.[19]

Try as they might to fight the campaign on the wider issues of social security benefits, state housing, price control, protection for manufacturers and foreign affairs,[20] Labour candidates found their opponents returning to the waterfront dispute. Endless insinuations had to be answered as well as possible, but it was well nigh impossible to deal with the many statements made by the National Party suggesting that "a vote for Labour was a vote for the Communists".[21] In the closing stages of the campaign the terms "Fascist" and "Communist" were used freely by parliamentary candidates[22] in what must surely rank as one of New Zealand's most unedifying examples of democratic procedure.

When the election returns were in it was clear that the National Party's decision to hold the election in the emotional atmosphere of the waterfront dispute, had been a shrewd one. Holland's party consolidated its position, winning another four seats (Gisborne, Napier, Lyttelton and St Kilda) from the Labour Party by the narrowest of margins.[23] There was no significant transference of allegiance from Labour to National. What had happened was that the Labour vote declined, many former Labour supporters staying at home and not voting. In fact, the election of 1951 saw the smallest turnout of voters for many years.[24] What was significant for the National Party was the fact that it had managed to "firm up" the support it gained in 1949. The waterfront dispute enabled it to provide its supporters with the more cohesive ideology of anti-Communism and anti-unionism in place of the vague anti-Labourism of 1949. After 1951 Holland looked less like an interim Prime Minister wedged between two periods of Labour dominance, and more like the inaugurator of a lengthy period of National rule. While National had won office in 1949 it was the election of 1951 which saw it fully assume power. The editor of the *Otago Daily Times* saw some of the significance of the election when he wrote gleefully:

> The people have rejected Socialism; not haltingly, not provisionally, but with a clear voice. When they turned out Labour in 1949 there was a disposition on the part of Labour's leaders and Labour's supporters to doubt the validity of their defeat.... Nothing could have been further from the truth ...
>
> The impetus of zealous reform which brought the socialists to power sixteen years ago has expended itself.[25]

The National Party's uncompromising stand against militancy had been the principal agent of this change.

The Election Aftermath and Mr Holland's Legislation

With the election of 1951 the waterfront dispute was finally ended. When Barnes went to prison in September to serve a two-month term with hard labour for criminally defaming a policeman during a June demonstration in Auckland, the power of the old waterfront leaders was extinguished.[26] On

New Zealand's waterfronts the new pattern was establishing itself. At Wellington, there was a period lasting several years when there were two port unions, one led by A.K. Bell with a membership of several hundred, and the other led by the old officers, Wells and the Napier brothers, and containing more than 1,000 formerly deregistered men. The deregistered men quickly gained the upper hand, but only after Wells and the Napiers had dissociated themselves from policy statements of Barnes and Drennan.[27] At Auckland, however, there was no letting down of the barriers to enable the old watersiders to resume work on the waterfront.[28] Within weeks of the election most of the deregistered men had been forced to take employment elsewhere, several of them ultimately rising to positions of leadership within other unions.[29] North Island and South Island associations of port unions were established in 1952, but not until 1959 did any very effective form of federation of the twenty-six port unions begin to emerge. With encouragement from Jim Healy, Secretary of the Waterside Workers' Federation of Australia, several communists had attempted to keep the deregistered national union in existence. But both Barnes and Hill were opposed to this, and they ceased drawing wages from the old organisation early in 1952.[30] The national organisation soon collapsed.

The forced dispersal of Auckland's militants left a legacy of bitterness that took some years to heal. Frequent minor scuffles were reported in hotels near the waterfront, and occasionally assault charges came to court.[31] At the end of October 1951, N. Donaldson, a member of the new Auckland union, told the Royal Commission of Inquiry into the Waterfront Industry, which was again taking submissions, that he was frequently abused by his former colleagues. "In a moment like this," he said,"you have to have blood like crude oil".[32] Strikebreaking usually has ugly consequences, and the 1951 exercise was no exception.

Soon after the election of 1 September the Government indicated that it did not yet regard the industrial crisis as finalised. Holland announced that the Government was considering legislation that would assist the authorities in ferreting out the sources of such "subversive and deplorable" pamphlets as those circulated during the dispute.³³ In due course it became clear that the Government was planning to overhaul the most important Acts regulating industrial activity in the country as well.

As early as April there had been suggestions that the Government might intensify its security precautions against the "red menace",³⁴ and in May the *Otago Daily Times* suggested that New Zealand should follow Australia and hold a referendum on whether or not the Communist Party should be banned. The paper asked for an assurance that there would be "positive action" against the "instigators of trouble", that those who had no claim to residence in New Zealand would be deported, and that all those "whose loyalties are not to New Zealand" should be removed from "official and public positions".³⁵ However, other newspapers were less receptive to the idea of a McCarthyite witch hunt. The *Press* suggested that any banning of the Communist Party would be "repugnant to the democratic principles of government and [could] be justified only in war or in times of the most exceptional civil emergency. Not many New Zealanders", the *Press* added, "will believe their country is yet in such extremity".³⁶ The *Dominion*, too, was opposed to the comments by D.J. Eyre MP³⁷ which suggested that the Government might be considering legislation to outlaw the Communist Party. Yet the *Dominion* did feel that there could be legislation against "subversion".³⁸

The Government, however, was in no hurry to bring forward such legislation. No mention of pending action against "subversion" was made in the Governor-General's Speech from the Throne on 26 June, and only occasional reference was made by National Party candidates to the need for legislation during the campaign. There were hints, nevertheless, that the I.C. and A. Act might be amended. Sullivan told the National Party conference early in July that there was a need for "putting teeth into the I.C. and A. Act".³⁹

When Parliament assembled at the end of September the Government quickly revealed its plans. The Governor-General indicated that changes to the labour laws were to be introduced when he said:

> It has . . . become clear to the Government that industrial legislation needs to be buttressed with provisions designed to ensure that responsible law-abiding working men, who represent the overwhelming majority of the labour force of this country, shall be protected against violence, intimidation, and vulgar insult on the part of a small but noisy minority who have, for too long, been undermining the best interests of the workers of this country.

Secret ballots on all strike issues were to be made compulsory, and picketing was to be made illegal.[40] The Governor-General went on to deal with the question of "subversion", saying that it was the Government's intention to:

> examine existing legislation with a view to strengthening the law so that subversive activities, which tend to stir up ill-will, disaffection, and class hatred amongst our people, may be more effectively dealt with.[41]

Although the Industrial Conciliation and Arbitration Amendment Bill was not given its first and second readings until 12 October, the Prime Minister explained at some length his philosophy on unionism on 2 October. Saying that he had "absolute faith" in the final judgement "of the average working man of New Zealand", he said that his Government wished to give that man the opportunity, with adequate safeguards by way of penalty, to express his opinion. Somewhat disingenuously he added:

> Our opponents said that we were out to crush and destroy unionism. On the contrary, there are more unions in existence than ever before. The Minister [Sullivan] and the Government . . . did this and more. We established the importance of more unions and proved the value of the decentralisation of union control. That is what we have gone in for, and it has been a conspicuous success.

He added: "We want to build up the unions and decentralise them; to give them power to decide their own destinies".[42] Sullivan, as always, was more direct. The National Party, he said, wanted to encourage "sound trade unionism". It was time steps were taken "to check some of those more militant leaders inside of the trade union movement".[43]

Part One, Section Three of the Bill, which had been amended considerably by the Labour Bills Committee, made provision for the election of union officials by secret postal ballot. It was reasoned here, as it was similarly with the provisions for the taking of secret ballots before strike action, that the majority of unionists would always vote for moderation rather than militancy if assured of privacy and freedom from intimidation. But should this fail to be the case further checks were provided. Provision was made for the Registrar of Industrial Unions to refuse to sanction any rule or alteration to a union's rules that might in any way be "unreasonable or oppressive". He could also investigate union affairs such as elections. Ballot papers had to be kept for one year after an election on penalty of a fine of £100 or twelve months imprisonment for a union official who disobeyed.

In the hope of keeping union control decentralised, the Government placed restrictions on any alteration of union rules "for the purpose of extending the membership of the union of employers or workers so as to include employers or workers in, or in connection with, any industry if there is in the same industrial district an existing union . . . registered in respect of that industry".[44]

If all of these measures should still fail to prevent militancy, then the Government would be prepared for any eventuality. The terms "strike" and "lockout" were redefined and new penalties provided. The definition given to the term "strike" was similar to that included in the Waterfront Strike Emergency Regulations 1951, which in turn had closely followed the definition in the Strike and Lockout Emergency Regulations 1939. However, the clause "whether by refusing or failing to work overtime or otherwise", which had been included in the 1951 Emergency Regulations to fit the watersiders' actions on that occasion, was excluded from the new definition. Ceasing to work overtime was covered by a new clause which declared that a strike "means the act of any number of workers who . . . in reducing their normal output or their normal rate of work—the said act being due to any combination, agreement, common understanding, or concerted action, whether expressed or implied, made or entered into by any workers—with intent to compel or induce any such employer to agree to terms of employment or comply with any demands made by the said or any other workers; or with intent to cause loss or inconvenience to any such employer in the conduct of his business . . .". A member of a union who was a party to any such strike that had been declared without a secret ballot was liable to a fine not exceeding £100: an official of the union was liable to a fine not exceeding £500 "unless he proved that he had no means of knowing of the imminence of the strike or that he took every step possible . . . to prevent the strike".[45] The onus of proof had been placed on the unionist and union leader; they would be assumed guilty until they proved themselves innocent.

The I.C. and A. Amendment Bill was as significant for what it omitted as for what was contained within it. There was no mention in the Bill of a removal of compulsory unionism. Sullivan pointed out that the Government had changed its policy concerning compulsory unionism because the F.O.L. and employers' and farmers' associations had all supported its retention. The employers' organisations, said Sullivan, felt that "if compulsory unionism was voted out the control of unions might get into the hands of the few—of the militants, the go-getters, those people in the trade-union movement whom we might call aggressive". He added: "we might be led into more industrial strife than we have ever experienced".[46] National's 1949 election promise to abolish compulsory unionism was quietly thrown away. Under the new scheme of things weakness lay in numbers.

The Labour Party put up a dour fight against the Bill. McLagan claimed that it revealed the sinister side of the National Party's attitude to trade unions:

> They are to be treated as undesirable organisations under the provision of this measure. They are to be tolerated, like an attack of measles or influenza, tolerated until they can be got rid of. In the meantime they are to be hampered and restricted, weakened and regimented in every possible way.

Later he added:

> In my opinion the type of industrial relations conceived in this

Bill was the type pioneered by Hitler and Mussolini. It follows
that parent pattern of regimentation, control, and stultification
of trade unions.[47]

Yet members of the Labour Party found difficulty in refuting
charges made by their opponents that many of the provisions
which they found objectionable had more than ample precedent
in the regulations and legislation of the First Labour Government. What Labour seemed to fear most was the intent behind
the new legislation, and the prospect of that legislation being
administered by the National Party.[48]

The "second leg" of the Government's industrial legislation
was the Police Offences Amendment Bill, a bill which had much
wider implications, and which excited more public controversy
than the I.C. and A. Amendment Bill. The Act as it was finally
passed on 5 December 1951, fell into two major parts. The
first part dealing with "sedition" was not specifically connected
with industrial relations, although it was clear that the provisions
in it had become necessary in the eyes of the National Party
because of events during the waterfront crisis. It was the dissemination of pamphlets containing virulent attacks on Ministers,
the Governor-General and on the executive of the F.O.L. that
justified this Bill, Government members claimed. "Sedition" had
been carefully defined in the Crimes Act, 1908, and it included
"bringing into hatred or contempt or exciting disaffection
against the person of His Majesty or the Government or the
Constitution [sic] of the United Kingdom . . . or the Government or Constitution [sic] of New Zealand or the Parliament
thereof or the Administration of Justice".

Or sedition could also be "raising discontent or disaffection
amongst His Majesty's subjects", or "promoting feelings of ill-will between classes of such subjects". Under the 1951 provisions,
however, the definition of "seditious intention" was "made
wider and at the same time vaguer".[49] It included "to incite . . .
violence, lawlessness or disorder" and "to excite such hostility
or ill-will between different classes of persons as may endanger
the public safety". The question of what was likely to excite
hostility or ill-will which would endanger the public safety
was left entirely to the discretion of the magistrate or judge.

What was most novel about the first part of the Police Offences Amendment Act 1951 was the fact that the penalties it provided (not more than three months imprisonment or a fine of £100 or both) were sufficiently slight as to deny the accused the right to trial by jury. This made it possible for any person charged with sedition to be dealt with summarily by a magistrate and to be detained for three months. When coupled with other clauses of the Act which dealt with the distribution of literature, or of possessing printing equipment "used for seditious purposes", these provisions could become most effective weapons for hampering strike activity. Again the onus of proof was shifted from the Crown to the defendant if he were found in possession of "seditious" literature or of a printing press used to produce same.

The second part of the Police Offences Amendment Act dealt mainly with the use of intimidation during strikes and lockouts. In many ways it embodied in law the povisions of the Waterfront Strike Emergency Regulations 1951. The definitions of strikes and lockouts that were used in the new I.C. and A. Amendment Act were repeated, and the traditional means by which strike action had been made effective in the past—namely picketing, processions, demonstrations and poster displays—were made illegal. Police constables were given the power to seize posters; only sergeants or above could determine whether an offence was being committed under those provisions of the Act covering picketing.

The Police Offences Amendment Act as finally passed seemed severe enough. But it was a greatly toned-down version of the initial Bill that had been presented to Parliament. In its original form the Bill had made it an offence to criticise ministers of governments outside New Zealand, or to assist people in any part of the Commonwealth to change their laws by violence, no matter how tyrannical those laws might be. The provisions relating to picketing, too, were much wider in the original Bill. A constable was given the power whenever he considered that a person was on a road, street or private property with seditious intent, to direct such a person to remove himself.[50]

The Police Offences Amendment Bill 1951 was modified

only after some quite hostile criticism of the Government from unexpected quarters.[51] After the Bill was introduced the Government's grand coalition of party, press and F.O.L. that had handled the waterfront crisis so effectively suddenly fell to pieces. The *Evening Post* agreed that picketing should be outlawed and it wanted the law concerning "subversion" tightened.[52] However, the editor was uneasy about the original Bill: "it might be preferable," he wrote tactfully, "to make the interpretation of 'seditious intention' a little less sweeping".[53] Apart from the *Herald* and the *Otago Daily Times*, which remained faithful to the end, the *Post*'s criticism was the most polite. The *Auckland Star*, which had expressed some support for the Government's intention of strengthening the law against "sedition"[54] was quite critical of the original Police Offences Amendment Bill:

> What remains of paramount importance, of infinitely greater importance than the prevention of strikes or making the detection of sedition easier, is that hard-won and long-established liberties should not be filched away.[55]

The *Dominion* took exception to those clauses in the Bill that shifted the onus of proof to the defendant, calling them "an attack on a long-recognised principle in our system of justice",[56] while the *Press* was more sweeping. The Government, said the editor, had "failed to . . . show an imperative need" for such an Act.[57]

In addition to the newspapers, the law societies,[58] churches, universities and trade unions, including the F.O.L., made submissions to the Statutes Revision Committee opposing aspects of the original Bill. The Committee made more than fifty amendments to the Bill. Some of those people who had opposed the original Bill expressed satisfaction with the amended provisions.[59] Included amongst these was the F.O.L., whose leaders had been principal targets of the illegal pamphlets circulated during the waterfront dispute, and who no doubt wanted some tightening of the law against "seditious" literature.

The Labour Party, however, fought the passage of the Bill vigorously, arguing that fundamental principles of British justice such as the right of trial by jury, and the innocence of the accused until proved guilty, were still threatened even in the amended Bill.[60] A party which during the recent waterfront dispute had found existing legislation stifling, was hardly likely to view with equanimity any addition to it. Some months later Nash called the Police Offences Amendment Act 1951 "a complete negation of many of the basic principles of democracy".[61] Eight years later his Government was to repeal the offending clauses.

Together, the I.C. and A. Amendment Act and the Police Offences Amendment Act rounded off the long line of legislation introduced since 1908 in an attempt to eliminate strike action in New Zealand. In 1894 the basic framework inside which industrial relations were to operate had been established with the passage of William Pember Reeves' I.C. and A. Act. During the next fifty-seven years the provisions of the Act which outlawed direct action for those unions that were registered under it were challenged by two major periods of industrial upheaval, 1912-13 and 1949-51 as well as many minor strikes and lockouts. In some cases unions had simply defied the Act; in other cases they had deregistered themselves from the I.C. and A. Act, hoping thereby to claim the right to strike legally.

But gradually successive governments closed off the avenues along which strike action could be pursued. Ward, Massey, Savage, Fraser and now Holland had all presided over ministries that had passed legislation making strike action outside the arbitration system increasingly difficult.[62] The legislation of 1951 was much the most restrictive, providing the State as it did with an impressive battery of weapons that could be used against recalcitrant unions. It was possible to say after 1951 that the right to strike for an arbitrationist union or a non-arbitrationist union no longer existed.[63]

Yet this legislation has not prevented strikes. Industrial holdups have occurred each year since 1951. They continue, however, on the State's sufferance; a Minister of Labour has possessed the power at almost any moment to use the force of the State against strikers. Only commonsense and political reality have restrained successive Ministers, while at times the pressure to stage a repeat performance of 1951 has been quite strong.[64] The only things that can be said with certainty are that, just as Holland found himself legislatively better equipped to deal with militancy than Massey had been in 1912-13, so the next Government that stages a "showdown" will be even better provided. And nothing seems more certain than that some day a Government will raid the arsenal so temptingly close to hand.

Conclusion

After the passage of the Police Offences Amendment Act relative quiet descended on the industrial scene for the first time for many years. The handful of militant unions lay smashed; and although some people, mostly communists, urged that they be rebuilt, it was to be many years before militancy of the immediate post-war variety reasserted itself.[65] And when it did, the waterfront unions were not as conspicuous as freezing workers and drivers. The T.U.C. faded out of existence in 1952[66] although some of the unions that had been associated with it were not readmitted to the F.O.L. until the late fifties. It was not until 1960 that Toby Hill, by then secretary of another union, was able to attend a conference of the F.O.L. Barnes, by this time, was a successful drain-laying contractor.

In the meantime the F.O.L. reigned as undisputed spokesman for organised labour. F.P. Walsh, the man who personally gained most from the defeat of the militants, assumed formal leadership in 1953 of the body whose interests he had effectively managed for so long.

When the old T.U.C. unions straggled back into the F.O.L. in the late fifties that body assumed a somewhat more militant stance. Dispersing the militants in 1951 ultimately enabled many ex-watersiders to emerge in positions of leadership in other unions. Walsh's utterances, and those of his successor, T.E. Skinner, reflected the new balance within the F.O.L. Relations between Walsh and Nash while the latter was leader of the Labour Party never reached the closeness that had existed between the F.O.L. and Fraser. The result has been a much greater independence on the part of the F.O.L. The position of importance within New Zealand society which the Labour Party gave to organised labour the F.O.L. now exercises in its own right, sometimes to the embarrassment of its former benefactor. One of the militants' aims of the immediate postwar years, that of making the industrial movement its own man, has most certainly been achieved.

Another aim of the militants has also been achieved. The same Arbitration Court the safety of which Walsh and the F.O.L. fought to defend in 1951, has slowly been undermined in the two decades since. Aided by a persistent shortage of labour which has enabled unions to negotiate ruling rates for wages quite independently of the Arbitration Court and substantially above award rates, the stronger unions have succeeded in relegating the deliberations of the Court to the periphery of the industrial scene. In 1951 much public money was spent upholding a system which other aspects of the National Party's economic policy were conspiring to undermine. Some militants of twenty years ago might also argue on this score that in defeat there was ultimate victory.

Perhaps the only enduring aspect of the National Party's victory in 1951 was the hold which it gave to Holland and his successors on power. At first their political anti-unionism was confined to attacks on the handful of militants and the Labour Party which could not divorce itself entirely from their interests. As the F.O.L., National's erstwhile ally, came to adopt a more militant posture, and even as it followed a policy of greater political independence, the movement as a whole was increasingly depicted by the National Party as Labour's Achilles heel. Aided by the press, by the occasional reckless utterance of a militant, and by the Labour Party's inability to control the genie which it had conjured up, National adroitly edged the entire union movement into a position of substantial public odium. 1951 was a most significant date for the National Party in this process of political and ideological consolidation. All trade unions, even those that helped the Government in the dispute, were lowered a peg in the public's esteem as a result of that massive upheaval. Neither has the Labour Party since that event been able to restore itself in the eyes of the electors. Barnes, Hill and their militant followers might have won some points in the years after 1951. But in other respects they did untold damage to the cause which workingmen still hold dear.

BIBLIOGRAPHY

PRIMARY MATERIAL: The primary material is scattered. Some of it, such as the Walter Nash Papers (National Archives, Wellington), the Seamen's Union Papers (University of Auckland), the F.P. Walsh Papers (Alexander Turnbull Library), the W. McAra Papers (University of Auckland), the Auckland Labour Party Papers, 1949-51 (University of Auckland) and several incomplete collections of illegal pamphlets (Auckland Public Library; General Assembly Library) has found its way into libraries. Much material still remains with the organisations concerned (Minutes and Correspondence of the New Zealand Labour Party; Minutes of the N.Z.F.O.L.) or with individuals. Messrs H. Barnes, R.E. Jones and Dick Scott, all of Auckland, possess some material relating to the dispute. Mr H.O. Roth, Deputy Librarian at the University of Auckland, possesses the best private collection of general material (especially good files of illegal documents) in the country. The Labour Department was prepared to cooperate up to a point: material relating to the *Mountpark* dispute, to the W.I.A.'s activities in 1950, and submissions made by A.E. Bockett and W. Sullivan to the Royal Commission of Inquiry in 1951, were readily made available to the author.

The General Assembly Library is useful not only for the complete files of New Zealand's newspapers, but also for its good files of union journals and its bound volume of press clippings. Bound volumes of press clippings relating to waterfront affairs are also kept in the University of Auckland Library.

A major collection of papers, the S.G. Holland Papers, could throw a different light on some aspects of the dispute. It is not yet open to the public.

SECONDARY MATERIAL: Secondary material is sparse. Dick Scott's *151 Days* (Auckland, 1952) is the fullest account of the dispute but is written from a highly partisan viewpoint. W.B.

Sutch has quite a lot on the dispute in his *Quest for Security* (Wellington, 1966). The errors contained in Sutch's account were repeated in his later *Poverty and Progress* (Wellington, 1968). The first book is discussed by the author in a review in *Landfall*, Vol. 81, March 1967, pp. 111-7. There are two short summaries of the dispute: Michael Bassett, "Labour's Leg Iron?", *Dispute*, No.3 (1965) (reprinted in A. Haas [ed.] *The Right to Dissent*, NZUSA, Wellington, 1965 pp.67-74) and L.G. Lukey, "The 1951 Waterfront Crisis", *Historical News*, No.21 (August 1970).

Unpublished theses with material of relevance to 1951 are:

R.M. Martin, "Compulsory Unionism in New Zealand", Victoria U.W., 1954

R.N. McDonald, "Historical Survey of the Actions and Policy of the N.Z.W.W.U., 1937-1951", Victoria U.W., 1955

R. McLuskie, "Militancy within the N.Z.F.O.L. during the Post-war Years", Victoria U.W., 1954

L.G. Lukey, "Industrial Conflict in New Zealand, 1951-1961", University of Canterbury, 1966.

NOTES

Notes to Introduction

1. See K. Sinclair, *William Pember Reeves,* Clarendon Press, Oxford, 1965, p.206.
   See also N.S. Woods, *Industrial Conciliation and Arbitration in New Zealand*, Government Printer, Wellington, 1963.
2. R.C.J. Stone, "The Unions and the Arbitration System, 1900-1937", in R. Chapman & K. Sinclair (eds.) *Studies of a Small Democracy*, Blackwood Paul, Auckland, 1963, p.201.
3. Woods, *op. cit.*, pp.93-4.
4. For a detailed discussion of this point see R.M. Martin, "Twenty Years of Compulsory Unionism", *Political Science*, Vol.8, September 1956, pp.104-121.
5. D. Scott, *151 Days: History of the Great Waterfront Lockout and Supporting Strikes* New Zealand Waterside Workers' Union (deregistered), Auckland, 1952, p.203.
6. *Auckland Star*, 9 July 1951.

Notes to Chapter I

1. L.F. Crisp, *Ben Chifley*, Longmans, Melbourne, 1961, p.344.
2. For comments on the American labour scene see Joel Seidman, *American Labor from Defense to Reconversion*, Chicago University Press, Chicago, 1953, pp.213-253; Eric Goldman, *The Crucial Decade—And After: America, 1945-1960*, Vintage Books, New York, 1961, pp.19-45.
3. See D.W. Oxnam, "The Incidence of Strikes in Australia", in *Australian Labour Relations*, eds. J.E. Isaac and G.W. Ford, Sun Books, Melbourne, 1966, p.22
4. For a discussion of New Zealand's labour legislation see N.S. Woods, *Industrial Conciliation and Arbitration in New Zealand*, Government Printer, Wellington, 1963.
5. J.B. Condliffe, *The Welfare State in New Zealand*, Allen and Unwin, London, 1959, p.99. See also J.V.T. Baker, *The War Economy*, Government Printer, Wellington, 1965, p.533; J.W. Williams, "Recent Economic Developments in New Zealand", *Pacific Affairs*, Vol.20, June 1947, pp.141-151.
6. Baker, p.535.
7. See reactions to the budget, *Otago Daily Times, (O.D.T.)*, 17 August 1946, p.8

8. See "Report of Royal Commission of Inquiry into the Waterfront Industry", *A.J.H.R.*, 1952, H-50. M.E.R. Bassett, "The 1951 Waterfront Dispute", unpublished M.A. thesis, University of Auckland, 1961, chapters 1 and 2.
9. See P.N. Pettit, *The Wellington Watersiders: The Story of Their Industrial Organisation*, Standard Press, Wellington, 1948.
10. Pettit, pp.65-102.
11. For a general discussion of union problems see R.C.J. Stone, *loc. cit.*, pp. 201-220.
12. Pettit, pp.132-137.
13. *New Zealand Transport Worker (N.Z.T.W.)*, 1 July 1938; 7 October 1938.
14. *N.Z.T.W.*, 1 April 1927.
15. Baker, pp.393-99.
16. "Spelling" was the practice where watersiders' gangs worked on a rotation basis taking spells from difficult work. It is described in detail in Baker, pp.398-99.
17. *N.Z.T.W.*, 1 November 1940.
18. *Ibid.*, 10 December 1943.
19. See George Fraser, "Barnes versus Rex", *Here & Now*, Vol.4, 1950, p.11; *Freedom*, 20 June 1951; reprinted in *N.Z.T.W.*, 13 April 1951, and in Fraser's *Ungrateful People*, Price Milburn, Wellington, 1961, pp.55-57.
20. *N.Z.T.W.*, 5 October 1944.
21. *Ibid.*, 5 May 1944. The clearest statement of watersiders' aims in relation to the waterfront industry is to be found in J.J. Mitchell's proposals, September 1945, W. McAra Papers, University of Auckland.
22. *O.D.T.*., 3 July 1946.
23. The magazine of the General Labourers' Union, *Challenge*, 1 September 1945, carried the following rhetorical question:
    > We sowed the seeds of victory.
    > We tended them through the
    > nightmare years.
    > Now the reward of all our toil has
    > ripened for the reaping.
    > Is it going to bring social advancement,
    > raised standards of living, democracy
    > and international co-operation?
24. *O.D.T.*, 21 February 1947.
25. *Ibid.*, 6 March 1947.
26. Walsh is believed to have had advance warning of New Zealand's intention to revalue the currency in 1948 and to have indulged in speculation in Australia. (Information supplied to the author by an Australian contact of Walsh's.)

27. *O.D.T..*, 1 August 1946.
28. *Ibid.*, 8 July 1946.
29. The final result in the Raglan electorate could not be counted as a Labour win till the Courts finally decided on several disputed votes in May 1947. In addition to this problem, D.G. Sullivan, Minister of Industries and Commerce, died in April 1947; J. O'Brien, Minister of Transport, was seriously ill in the early months of 1947 and died in September; A.S. Richards, MP, died in the middle of 1947 after some months of illness.
30. Barnes had made submissions to the W.I.C. in October asking that the guaranteed daily minimum wage being paid at the main ports be also paid at the secondary ports. Judge Ongley awarded a monthly minimum in a decision on 28 November 1946. See submissions and comments, W. McAra Papers. T. Hill produced a pamphlet in October 1946 entitled "The Case for Guaranteed Daily Attendance Money".
31. W.J. Jordan to P. Fraser, 20 November 1946; J.G. Barclay to P. Fraser, 18 December 1946, Walter Nash Papers, File 1215. S.G. Holland, Leader of the Opposition, had long been in the habit of attacking militant unions (see *N.Z.T.W..*, 4 August 1939; 1 September 1939). After the election of 1946 he stepped up his attack with a strongly-worded statement at the time of the overtime ban (see *Herald*, 18 December 1946). The editor of the *Herald* had already called the Government "weak-kneed" on 30 November. The attacks were to continue during 1947. At the end of March Holland accused the Government of "complete and undisputed surrender" to the watersiders (*O.D.T.*, 1 April 1947). This line was pursued again in a by-election address in the Avon electorate on 26 May when Holland asserted that the Government was "running away" from the watersiders (*O.D.T.*, 27 May 1947). On 1 April the Acting Dominion President of the Federated Farmers, Mr H.E. Blyde, called the state of industrial relations "a disgrace", and demanded that the Government take stronger measures to counter union militancy. (*ibid.*, 2 April 1947.)
32. *Herald*, 21 December 1946. There are some notebooks recording some of what transpired at these meetings in the W. McAra Papers.
33. A perusal of membership returns to the Dominion office of the Labour Party reveals that branch membership declined drastically between 1947 and 1950. To take some random samples: membership of the Belmont-Bayswater branch in Auckland had fallen to 40 per cent of the 1947 figure by 1950; in the Karori Branch in Wellington it fell to 25 per cent of the 1947 figure; in some of the more solid Labour areas such as Riccarton, the fall was

less drastic, although in the Prime Minister's own electorate of Brooklyn "the apathy and general lack of interest among the greater majority of the Branch members [had] spread alarmingly". (Brooklyn Branch File, N.Z.L.P., 1947-48, Annual Report.)

34. *O.D.T.*, 6 June 1947. At closed sessions within the Labour movement comments were less tactful. At the special conference of the F.O.L. early in 1947 Fraser was reported to have called the watersiders "political blacklegs", while McLagan compared them with Japanese generals dictating surrender terms. *N.Z.T.W.*, 12 March 1947.
35. McLagan, a dour Scot, had been a Communist in the 1920s during his active mining days. He had held many positions in the Miners' Union and was president of the Federation of Labour from 1937 until elected as MP for Riccarton in 1946.
36. *O.D.T.*, 2 May 1947; 17 May 1947. The union's case was outlined in T. Hill to P. Fraser, 16 May 1947, Nash Papers, File 1215.
37. *O.D.T.*, 12 June 1947.
38. *Ibid.*, 17 June 1947.
39. *Ibid.*, 1 July 1947.
40. See Fraser's statements, *ibid.*, 25 August 1947; also Semple's *N.Z.P.D.*, vol.278, 1947, pp.39-42.
41. See the strong statement of the Amalgamated Society of Railway Servants (A.S.R.S.), *N.Z.T.W.*, 8 October 1947.
42. The 1948 conference of the F.O.L. eventually endorsed the strike ballot, *O.D.T.*, 1 May 1948.
43. The Government proposed to appoint deputy judges of the Arbitration Court; the F.O.L. wanted greater powers given to conciliation commissioners to make decisions in disputes. See *O.D.T.*, 8 August 1947.
44. *O.D.T.*, 4 May 1948. Later in the month Semple published a pamphlet "Why I Fight Communism", Wellington, 1948. This did not mention the watersiders by name, but by this time few could doubt that he had them in mind.
45. The hatches were claimed to be too heavy and awkward to lift by hand. The dispute is described briefly by R.N. McDonald, "Historical Survey of the Actions and Policy of the N.Z.W.W.U., 1937-51" (unpublished M.A. thesis, Victoria University, 1955) p.76ff. See also the W.I.C.'s file, "Port of Auckland, Mountpark Dispute".
46. *O.D.T.*, 26 June 1948. See "Our Union Is Attacked, a Report to Members by the National Executive, N.Z.W.W.U.", [1949]. See Barnes' comments about the W.I.C. and its chairman, Judge Dalglish, *O.D.T.*, 28 and 29 July 1948.
47. See for instance, the statement by the Federated Farmers, *ibid.*,

26 June 1948; also the statement by S.G. Holland, *ibid.*, 6 July 1948.
48. *O.D.T.*, 1 July 1948.
49. The tribunal was presided over by the Chief Justice, Sir Humphrey O'Leary. It found that the watersiders were justified in refusing to lift the hatches on the *Mountpark* on 20 February 1948 and awarded the men $935-12-10 in lost wages to cover the period 20-25 February. The decision of the W.I.C. on 25 February was adjudged incorrect and the men were awarded a further $363-14-8 for wages lost. However, on all matters concerning the dispute between May and July the watersiders were found to be at fault, and the W.I.C.'s rulings were upheld. The inquiry was widely reported (see *O.D.T.*, 28 July-7 August 1948). See also W.I.C.'s file "Port of Auckland, Mountpark Dispute".
50. *O.D.T.*, 16 July 1948.
51. The deregistration was announced on the evening of 25 March, nearly six weeks after the men had been dismissed, and approximately one week after some supporting unions, notably the Drivers' Union, had decided to resume normal work. For the F.O.L.'s account of the carpenters' dispute see the National Executive's report, *The History of the Carpenters' Dispute, 1949*, N.Z.F.O.L., Wellington, 1949. The Carpenters' case was expressed by Roy Stanley, *Fighting Back! The True Story of the 1949 Carpenters' Dispute,* Forward Press, Auckland, 1950.
52. McLagan insisted that it was not right that a new union should be recognised until a majority of carpenters had indicated that they wanted it. Interview with H.L. Bockett, former Secretary of Labour, 23 April 1969.
53. See Captain M.T. Holm to P. Fraser, 5 April 1949, Nash Papers, File 2232.
54. "Our Union Is Attacked", *op. cit.*; H. Barnes and T. Hill, "The Attack Continues", [1949].
55. *O.D.T.*, 5 April 1949.
56. *Ibid.*, 30 June 1949.
57. *Ibid.*, 19 July 1949.
58. *Ibid.*, 11 August 1949.
59. See the account of the meeting in McLagan's White Paper, "Statement Concerning Recent Disputes Affecting Waterfront Work", issued by the Government Printer, September 1949.
60. *Herald*, 19 August 1949.
61. See "Jock" Barnes and J.A. Lee, *Resist Peace Time Conscription,* Universal Printing Products, Wellington, 1949.
62. Not only were several Labour MPs, notably G.H.O. Wilson, W.W. Freer, P. Kearins, F. Langstone and A.M. Finlay known to oppose peacetime conscription, but Langstone, a former Labour Cabinet

Minister who campaigned against conscription, proceeded to resign from the Labour Party immediately after the referendum, taking with him the Three Kings Branch of the party and the Roskill electorate organiser from the most marginal seat in Auckland. In the South Island the North Canterbury L.R.C. was known to oppose conscription, and on 5 August, H.G. Kilpatrick, Labour's candidate for Hurunui, resigned from the party. On 13 August the Canterbury Builders' and General Labourers' Union passed a motion of no-confidence in Fraser because of his attitude to conscription. In Dunedin, the Otago Trades Council, which had opposed conscription, urging its members to vote against it, was particularly lukewarm in its support for Labour when the general election approached.

63. Barnes' activities during the 1949 election were discussed during a court case in October 1950. See *Herald*, 11, 12, 13 October 1950; *Star*, 30 November 1950. See also Nash Papers, File 2235.
64. *N.Z.T.W.*, 11 November 1949. The New Plymouth Branch of the N.Z.W.W.U. remained solidly behind the Labour Party and contributed £173-10-6 to Labour's campaign. See J.S. Harris to A.J. McDonald, 18 November 1949, N.Z.L.P. File, (New Plymouth).
65. *O.D.T.*, 11 November 1949.

Notes to Chapter II

1. See for instance Holland, *N.Z.P.D.*, Vol.277, 1947, p.797.
2. *Ibid.*, p.801. See also Sutherland, *N.Z.P.D.*, Vol.280, 1948, p.219.
3. See the comments by Austin Mitchell, *Politics and People in New Zealand*, Whitcombe & Tombs, Christchurch, 1969, pp.106-8. Little has been written about Holland. Apart from a flattering short biography in *An Encyclopaedia of New Zealand*, Government Printer, Wellington, 1966, Vol.2, p.107ff, most comments about him have been unkind. See for instance, J.C. Beaglehole, "New Zealand Since the War", *Landfall* No.58 (June 1961), pp.140-2; Sir George Mallaby, *From My Level*, Hutchinson, London, 1965; also *Herald*, 27 March 1965.
4. See particularly the speech reported in the *O.D.T.*, 9 June 1949.
5. *Ibid.*
6. *Ibid.*, 28 October 1949.
7. *Herald*, 1 November 1949.
8. Sullivan was a building contractor aged fifty-nine in 1949, who had been elected member for Bay of Plenty in 1941.
9. Barnes was quoted in the *Herald*, 26 April 1950, as saying that Sullivan could not be more hostile to strong unionism than was McLagan.

10. See his statement, *Herald*, 12 October 1949.
11. *O.D.T.*, 10 December 1949.
12. *Herald*, 19 January 1950. Hill called the meeting "very pleasant". *O.D.T.*, 19 January 1950.
13. See Captain Holm to W. Sullivan, 25 January 1950, Labour Department Files.
14. *O.D.T.*, 26 April 1950.
15. *Herald*, 5 May 1950.
16. *Herald*, 29 April 1950, also *O.D.T.*, 11 May 1950.
17. K.M. Baxter, the Secretary of the F.O.L., suggested that there might be some "secret arrangement between the Government and the watersiders". *O.D.T.*, 28 April 1950.
18. Baxter was critical of the watersiders for their tactics throughout the dispute. *Herald*, 30 December 1946.
19. See R. McLuskie, "Militancy within the N.Z.F.O.L. during the Post-War Years", unpublished M.A. thesis, Victoria University, 1954. At the 1949 Conference, Walsh beat Richards for the vice-presidency by 203 to 87.
20. See *N.Z.T.W.*, 10 February 1947; 12 March 1947. Also "Dispute between the N.Z.W.W.U. and the F.O.L.", F.O.L. Bulletin 1950, p.2
21. *The History of the Carpenters' Dispute*, 1949, p.22.
22. McLuskie, p.73ff. There is a description of the 1949 conference in the minutes of a Special Meeting of the Wellington Seamen's Union, 7 June 1949, Seamen's Files, University of Auckland.
23. *N.Z.T.W.*, 9 April 1949.
24. See Barnes' justification for this, *ibid.*, 10 March 1950.
25. *Ibid.*
26. Minutes of the National Council of the F.O.L., February 1950, p.2.
27. Scott, *151 Days,* pp.18-24.
28. See Walsh to T.F. Anderson, 24 January 1950; 8 March 1950. F.P. Walsh Papers, Seamen's Union 1950-55, Folio 571, Alexander Turnbull Library.
29. See the protests by J. Roberts and A.B. Grant of the Canterbury Trades Council, *Herald*, 31 January 1950, and of the Otago Trades Council, Scott, p.20. Only the Wellington Trades Council under the expert guidance of its president F.P. Walsh, who refused to allow Barnes a chance to address the February meeting (*Herald*, 15 February, 1950), endorsed the National Executive's decision. See also Walsh's statement *O.D.T.*, 16 February 1950.
30. *Herald*, 1 February 1950.
31. Minutes of the National Council of the F.O.L., February 1950, p.5.
32. *Herald*, 31 March 1950.
33. *O.D.T.*, 18 April 1950.
34. See McLuskie, pp.92-106.

35. The unions which withdrew from the F.O.L. conference on 19 April were: New Zealand Freezing Workers' Association
New Zealand Drivers' Federation
New Zealand Hotel Workers' Federation
New Zealand Waterside Workers' Union
New Zealand Carpenters' and Joiners' Union
New Zealand Tramways Employees' Union
New Zealand Railway Tradesmen's Association
New Zealand Bakers' Union
New Zealand Wood Pulp Workers' Union
Auckland General Labourers' Union
Taranaki General Labourers' Union
Canterbury General Labourers' Union
Poverty Bay General Labourers' Union
Canterbury Clothing Trades Union
Otago and Southland Clothing Trades Union
Christchurch Rubber Workers' Union
Auckland Rubber Workers' Union
Christchurch Painters' Union
Wellington Painters' Union
Auckland Woollen Mill Workers' Union
Auckland Boilermakers' Union
Christchurch Biscuit Workers' Union
Auckland Moulders' Union
Auckland Fruit Preservers Workers' Union
36. *O.D.T.*, 20 April 1950. The events following the walkout are discussed by R.M. Martin, "Compulsory Unionism in New Zealand", unpublished M.A. thesis, Victoria University, 1954, p.180ff.
37. *O.D.T.*, 21 April 1950.
38. Chairman: F.G. Young; Vice-Chairman: John Roberts; Secretary: P.A. Hansen (NZ Tramways Employees' Union); Committee: A.C. Melville and F. Muller (NZ Drivers' Federation); H. Kay and T.J. Potter (NZ Labourers' Federation); S. Giles and H.G. Kilpatrick (NZ Freezing Workers' Association); H. Barnes (N.Z.W.W.U.); W.B. Richards (NZ Tramways Employees' Union); F.L. Langley (NZ Carpenters' and Joiners' Union).
39. *O.D.T.*, 21 April 1950.
40. Principally the bulletin "History of the Dispute between the N.Z.W.W.U. and the F.O.L.", *op. cit.* Examples of the T.U.C.'s case were A.B. Grant's "Report to the Unions" Trade Union Congress, Christchurch, 1950, and T.J. Potter, "Machine Made Majorities" Trade Union Congress, Auckland, 1950.
41. *O.D.T.*, 27 April 1950; 1 May 1950.
42. In some cases the vote was by show of hands (watersiders) or

secret ballots (Christchurch Tramways and Christchurch Carpenters).
43. *O.D.T.*, 29 May 1950.
44. See minutes of Meeting of T.U.C. supporters, Auckland, 11 May 1950.
45. Minutes of the Inaugural Congress of the T.U.C., Wellington, 9 August 1950.
46. Potter had been chairman of the Auckland Provisional Council of the T.U.C., the rival to the Auckland Trades Council.
47. In a ballot held by all branches of the Tramways Union in August, the proposal to leave the F.O.L. was defeated by 2½ to 1. *O.D.T.*, 9 August 1950. P.A. Hansen, the secretary of the Wellington Tramways Union and interim secretary of the T.U.C., was forced to relinquish his interim secretaryship by a resolution of his union. *Herald*, 27 May 1950.
48. The unions represented at the August conference are listed in the Minutes of the Inaugural Congress. They were:

NZ Waterside Workers' Union	(8 delegates)
NZ Carpenters' and Joiners' Union	(4 delegates)
Auckland Drivers' Union	(2 delegates)
Hawke's Bay Drivers' Union	
Auckland General Labourers' Union	(3 delegates)
Otago General Labourers' Union	
Christchurch Biscuit Workers' Union	(2 delegates)
Wellington Painters' Union	(2 delegates)
Christchurch Painters' Union	
Stockton Miners' Union	(2 delegates)
Millerton Miners' Union	(2 delegates)
Runanga Miners' Union	(2 delegates)
Grey Valley Miners' Union	
Brunnerton Miners' Union	
Blackball Miners' Union	
Waikato Miners' Strike Committee	(2 delegates)
Wellington Drivers' Union	(2 delegates)
NZ Drivers' Federation	
NZ Freezing Workers' Association	(2 delegates)
Christchurch Rubber Workers' Union	
Dunedin Tramways' Union	
Auckland Hotel Workers' Union	
Wellington Watersiders' Union	
NZ Workers' Union (Mangakino)	
Auckland T.U.C.	

They represented only 22,765 workers, *ibid.*, p.21. The National Council of the NZ Freezing Workers' Association decided to deregister from the F.O.L. in August 1950. But a Court Order

early in 1951 sought by the Auckland branch (see *Southern Cross*, 1 February 1951) prevented it from joining the T.U.C. The N.Z.F.W.A. represented 16,000 workers. See Minutes of Federation of Labour, 1951, 12 February 1951, p.1066.
49. See Walsh's warning *O.D.T.*, 16 February 1950; Baxter's warning, *O.D.T.*, 1 May 1950.
50. *O.D.T.*, 29 April 1950.
51. *Ibid.*, 28 April 1950. Roberts was, of course, referring to Walsh and one of the important points which the initial T.U.C. supporters agreed on was that their organisation, unlike the F.O.L., would not have a Wellington residential requirement for members of the National Executive.
52. When the Otago District Council of the T.U.C. was finally formed on 11 September only six organisations were represented and the watersiders dominated the executive (*O.D.T.*, 12 September 1950).
53. *N.Z.T.W.*, 12 September 1950.
54. *O.D.T.*, 11 May 1950.
55. Lampblack was a constant cause of industrial trouble. It was imported from Texas for use in the manufacture of tires, and it came in bags that were not sufficiently protective to prevent the noxious carbon black from penetrating into the clothing and skin of those handling it. See *O.D.T.*, 17 June 1950.
56. *O.D.T.*, 19 June 1950.
57. *Ibid.*, 21 June 1950.
58. *Ibid.* This amounted to an extra 2/6 per hour plus the provision of protective clothing, and 10/- at the completion of the job for the cleaning of clothes.
59. *Ibid.*, 22 June 1950.
60. *N.Z.P.D.*, Vol.289, 1950, p.54.
61. *Herald*, 7 July 1950.
62. *Ibid.*
63. *Herald*, 3 August 1950.
64. *Ibid.*, 4 August 1950. See also *Auckland Star*, editorial, 4 August 1950.
65. The industrial correspondent to the *O.D.T.* suggested that this was Walsh's motive, *O.D.T.*, 4 August 1950.
66. The fullest account of activities on 3 August 1950 was that circulated to Trades Councils and Affiliated Unions by the F.O.L. on 9 August 1950.
67. See copy of letter from the union to Judge Dalglish, 25 August 1950, in the N.Z.W.W.U.'s "Circular to Branches", confidential, 12 September 1950, p.2.
68. See the "Circular to Branches", confidential, *op. cit.*, where it is stated that Hill and J. Napier from the union heard the captain

state in Marchington's presence that he had received such orders from the latter. The Press Association carried a rather confusing version of the same allegation, *O.D.T.*, 14 September 1950.
The charge was repeated by Dick Scott, p.28, and by Barnes in a broadcast entitled "Dispute", on the YA stations, 24 November 1968. To the writer's knowledge the allegation has never been denied by either Marchington or the Port Employers' Association.

69. *O.D.T.*, 9 September 1950.
70. See footnote 68.
71. *Herald*, 12 September 1950.
72. *O.D.T.*, 13 September 1950.
73. *O.D.T.*, 15 September 1950.
74. *Herald*, 16 September 1950.
75. *New Zealand Observer*, 20 September 1950.
76. *O.D.T.*, 5 August 1950.
77. *O.D.T.*, 14 September 1950.
78. Fraser did ask a detailed question of Sullivan in the House on 14 September.
79. *O.D.T.*, 15 September 1950.
80. *Ibid.*, 16 September 1950.
81. *Ibid.*
82. *O.D.T.*, 19 September 1950.
83. *Ibid.*
84. The *Otago Daily Times'* Special correspondent was not entirely correct when he guessed what was being discussed with the Commissioner of Police. He believed that the Cabinet was simply discussing the watersiders' desire for an inquiry into police methods on the waterfront. Clearly more important matters were also being discussed. See *O.D.T.*, 19 September 1950.
85. *O.D.T.*, 19 September 1950.
86. *O.D.T.*, 20 September 1950. The circumstances under which the Governor-General could declare a State of Emergency were when "any action has been taken . . . on so extensive a scale as to be calculated by interfering with the supply and distribution of food, water, fuel, or light or with the means of locomotion, to deprive the community . . . of the essentials of life, or if at any time it appears to the Governor-General that any circumstances exist . . . whereby the public safety or public order is, or is likely to be imperilled". *Statutes*, 1932, No.3, p.17.
87. *Herald*, 20 September 1950.
88. *Ibid., N.Z.P.D.*, Vol.291, 1950, p.253ff.
89. See Moohan's report of the meeting, *N.Z.P.D.*, Vol.294, 1951, p.58. There is another account of the meeting in the Minutes of

the Stop Work Meeting of the Wellington Seamen's Union, 3 October 1950, Seamen's Files, University of Auckland. The Industrial Relations Act 1949 contained a section enabling a Conciliation Commissioner to call a compulsory conference of parties where any matter causing industrial unrest was not covered in an award or industrial agreement. Lampblack clearly came into this category.
90. *O.D.T.*, 21 September 1950.
91. The State of Emergency was initially introduced for a fourteen-day period. It was revoked on 4 October.
92. *O.D.T.*, 22 September 1950.
93. The National Executive of the Labour Party congratulated Fraser for his part in settling the dispute (National Executive Minutes, N.Z.L.P., 26 September 1950). But Barnes refused to give any credit to Fraser for the settlement. He claimed that the idea of a compulsory conference had been put to the Government by the union on 14 September, (*O.D.T.*, 22 September 1950). This was probably correct. Yet it is clear that the Government had no intention of acting on such a suggestion until Fraser made it again on the 19th.
94. See the comment of the editor of the Transport Worker, *N.Z.T.W.*, 11 October 1950, and of the *O.D.T.*'s special correspondent, 22 September 1950.
95. *N.Z.T.W.*, 11 October 1950. In fact the compulsory conference of September 1950 had undoubtedly been called under the Industrial Relations Act 1949 only because the matter under dispute—lampblack rates—was not covered under the Waterfront Industry Agreement.
96. *O.D.T.*, 22 September 1950.
97. *Herald*, 22 September 1950.
98. *N.Z.T.W.*, 11 October 1950. The terms of reference of the Commission had been published on 22 September.
99. *O.D.T.*, 20 October 1950. The same insistence that negotiations should involve some acceptance of arbitration was made by the port employers in a ships' carpenters' dispute in November 1950. See *O.D.T.*, 8 November 1950.
100. *N.Z.T.W.*, 5 December 1950.
101. *Ibid.*, 15 January 1951.
102. *NZ Observer*, 11 July 1951; see also *N.Z.T.W.*, 5 December 1950. The *O.D.T.*, 1 December 1950, carried a report of Belford's submission which omitted these words. The watersiders' leaders met briefly with Belford and Marchington on 19 December 1950 and Belford reaffirmed what he had said before the Royal Commission. Barnes reported Marchington as adding that he wished to see Barnes and Hill in gaol. See *N.Z.T.W.*, 15 January 1951.

Notes to Chapter III

1. The employers' submissions to the Royal Commission in November and December were given much publicity, as were the comments of Sir John Anderson, the Chairman of the Port of London Authority, who while on a visit in February 1951 expressed the opinion that the real cause for the slow turn-round of ships was that watersiders did not work hard enough. *Star*, 20 February 1951.
2. See the complaints of the union, *Herald*, 24 June 1950; 15 August 1950.
3. *O.D.T.*, 20 September 1950.
4. *Outlook*, Vol.57, No.43, 25 October 1950.
5. *O.D.T.*, 23 September 1950.
6. Fraser died on 12 December 1950.
7. John Gordon (which was the pseudonym for John Gordon McLean, an officer of the National Party) wrote a pamphlet after the 1951 dispute that was entirely favourable to the Government entitled *Crisis on the Waterfront*. In it he wrote (page 5): "The National Government . . . was determined to take a stand and, if necessary, to 'have a showdown' with the militant element on the waterfront."
8. See Belford's statement p.56.
9. Barnes told a meeting of watersiders and the executive of the Auckland General Labourers' Union on 12 June 1952 that he knew the "Holland Government was heading for a showdown". See the minutes of the meeting in the possession of Dick Scott.
10. Several people interviewed by the author have attested to this.
11. Total export receipts increased by 24 per cent in 1950 and by another 36 per cent in 1951. These increases were due almost entirely to high wool prices. See *Official Year Book*, 1953, p.247. The Consumers' Price Index began to rise very sharply in the latter half of 1950. See *ibid.*, p.787.
12. See *O.D.T.*, 1 December 1950.
13. *Ibid.*, 20 November 1950.
14. *N.Z.T.W.* 15 January 1951.
15. *Ibid.*, 5 December 1950.
16. *Southern Cross*, 21 December 1950; quoted in *N.Z.T.W.*, 15 January 1951.
17. See the tables in W.B. Sutch, *The Quest for Security in New Zealand, 1840-1966*, Oxford University Press, Wellington 1966, p.459.
18. See the report of the meeting between a deputation of F.O.L. leaders and Cabinet Ministers, 9 February 1951, Minutes of the F.O.L., pp.1055-1067.
19. The railway strike by the Railway Tradesmen's Association

(R.T.A.) and the Amalgamated Society of Railway Servants (A.S.R.S.) is described in the *Railway Review,* January 1951. See also George Broad, "The Railway Strike", *Here and Now,* No.5, January-February 1951.
20. For a worker on the average wage at this time of £8.10.0 these claims amounted to 34 per cent and 41 per cent respectively.
21. *Herald*, 1 February 1951.
22. *Southern Cross*, 1 February 1951.
23. *Ibid.* Barnes made a very critical statement which was quoted in *People's Voice*, 7 February 1951.
24. See *Herald*, 14 February 1951. It was announced that the freezing workers were believed to have negotiated an additional 15 per cent increase in spite of the fact that they had been excluded from the Arbitration Court's order in view of a rise of 12 per cent granted them in January. See also editorial, *Evening Post*, 15 February 1951.
25. *Herald*, 10 February 1951.
26. These were the words used by Judge Dalglish, *W.I.A. Agenda*, No.A-8, Dis. No.1, 5 July 1950. See Scott, p.33.
27. The Meeting of 8 February is discussed in T. Hill to J. Healy, 26 February 1951, Nash Papers, File 2235. For a report on the state of the dispute, *Evening Post*, 10 February 1951.
28. See Minutes of a meeting of the National Executive of the N.Z.W.W.U., 13-14 February 1951.
29. See the *Order of the W.I.C.*, Wellington, 1947, pp.47-48.
30. The meeting lasted three-quarters of an hour. *Evening Post*, 14 February 1951.
31. *Herald*, 14 February 1951; *Evening Post*, 14 February 1951.
32. At ports where overtime had been refused on the 14th, no work was offered the following day. At Wellington, Auckland, Westport, Greymouth and Bluff normal work was provided on 15 February because no overtime call had been made the previous night. *Evening Post*, 15 February 1951.
33. He was, of course, incorrect on one point. The overtime ban was a contravention of the W.I.C.'s order.
34. *Herald*, 16 February 1951; *Evening Star*, 15 February 1951.
35. *Ibid.*
36. Holland was still overseas.
37. *Evening Post*, 16 February 1951.
38. So far the details of this meeting have come from the "Factual Survey of the Waterfront Strike, 1951", submitted to the Royal Commission by the General Manager of the W.I.C., October 1951, p.5.
39. These details of the meeting were given to the author by Barnes in

an interview in 1960. See also N.Z.W.W.U. "Circular to Branches", 21 February 1951, and T. Hill to W. Nash, 6 April 1951, Nash Papers, File 2235.
40. See the "Factual Survey", p.5.
41. The Government treated the W.I.A. as still being in existence, despite the union's withdrawal of its members the previous September.
42. Sullivan to Hill, 16 February 1951, in "Factual Survey", pp.5-6. In his statement to the press, Sullivan spoke of "thousands of innocent people" possibly suffering. *Evening Post*, 17 February 1951.
43. See "Statement by the Minister of Labour, Hon. W. Sullivan, on the 1951 Waterfront Strike", 2 July 1951, p.3. Nevertheless, Sullivan, from the way he presents the wage claims on p.2., would appear to have considered the employers' offer reasonable. On 23 March Holland claimed in a broadcast that the wage of 4/7½ included "the full 15 per cent". See Chapter V, p.123.
44. *Herald*, 17 February 1951.
45. *Herald*, 7 February 1951.
46. Fendalton was Holland's electorate.
47. See two pamphlets issued by the N.Z.W.W.U. during the dispute: "A Call to ALL New Zealanders: Your Freedom Is in DANGER", and "Holland Must be Defeated, Nationalists are in League with a Foreign Power", both published in Auckland, 1951.
48. See Scott, p.37, and *Evening Post*, 19 February 1951. The telegram was sent on Saturday morning after Holland's statement had appeared in the morning press.
49. See Scott, p.38. A representative of the employers told the author that these notices were displayed by their authority.
50. See Scott, pp.37-39.
51. *Evening Post*, 19 February 1951.
52. *Ibid.*
53. Hill to Sullivan, 19 February 1951, in "Factual Survey", p.7.
54. *Press*, 20 February 1951.
55. The farmers were Holyoake, McDonald and Corbett. The employers were Sullivan, Bowden, Fortune, Holland and Goosman, the last two also owning farms. Holland's farm had been financed by Goosman, see *Herald*, 18 January 1969.
56. Broadfoot, Bodkin, Algie, Webb, Watts and Marshall were lawyers. The other member was Doidge (journalist).
57. H.L. Bockett, then Secretary of Labour, doubts there was any discussion of the matter.
58. *Herald*, 20 February 1951.
59. Blakely's statement read: "It is completely unrealistic to state, as the union leaders have stated, that men may individually decline

overtime. The conditions of employment, while embodying this factor, also state that men shall not collectively refuse overtime, but this is exactly what the union leaders initially directed their members to do". *Evening Post*, 21 February 1951.
60. Sullivan to Hill, 20 February 1951, see "Factual Survey" p.8.
61. *Southern Cross*, 21 February 1951.
62. *Evening Post*, 21 February 1951.
63. The telegram sent to Holland from the Auckland Manufacturers' Association, is published *Herald*, 22 February 1951.
64. A strong plea was made by the Auckland Harbour Board. See *Herald*, 21 February 1951.
65. *Evening Star*, 15 February 1951.
66. *Auckland Star*, 15 February 1951.
67. *Evening Post*, 15 February 1951.
68. *Ibid.*, 20 February 1951.
69. *Star-Sun*, 22 February 1951.
70. *Herald*, 16 February 1951.
71. *O.D.T.*, 16 February 1951.
72. *Press*, 20 February 1951. This confusion persisted. See editorial 23 February 1951; *Dominion*, 21 February 1951.
73. *Press*, 20 February 1951. The *Southland Times* remained a little uneasy about whether the dispute was a "lockout", and as late as 5 June felt called upon to repeat the argument that it was not.
74. *Auckland Star*, 22 February 1951.
75. *Herald*, 24 February 1951.
76. *Landfall*, Vol.6, No.2, June 1952, p.151.
77. See Chapter II, footnote 86.
78. *Statutes*, 1932-3, No.3, p.18. For a general discussion of the Act see Bassett, *op. cit.*, p.116ff.
79. *N.Z.P.D.*, Vol.279, 1947, p.979.
80. This was the same definition that was contained in the 1939 regulations. It covered the 1951 situation adequately.
81. See *Gazette*, 1951, Vol.1. Also *Herald*, 23 February 1951.
82. *Herald*, 23 February 1951.
83. *Press*, 24 February 1951.
84. The *Herald* on 22 February suggested that the Government might deregister and "permanently dissolve" the N.Z.W.W.U., and that its leaders could be prosecuted for "conspiring against the public safety". Those who were not New Zealand-born might be deported. The Government could also use the Armed Forces both to protect and work New Zealand's waterfront.

Notes to Chapter IV

1. *Evening Post*, 23 February 1951.

2. See for instance *Southland Times*, 20 February 1951; *Timaru Herald*, 22 February 1951; *Nelson Evening Mail*, 22 February 1951.
3. The only time Barnes justified belonging to the W.F.T.U. he said that "its power for good and as a bastion against evil is enormous. Its value to us in the event of any major dispute is incalculable." *N.Z.T.W.*, 10 March 1950. During the dispute the watersiders made little effort to invoke the W.F.T.U.'s assistance. In November 1952 a leading member of the Communist Party criticised the N.Z.W.W.U. (deregistered) for having paid lip service only to the W.F.T.U. See typescript, "Lessons of the N.Z. Waterfront Dispute of 1951", in hands of H.O. Roth.
4. See for instance Sullivan's statement, *Herald* 8 March 1951; *Auckland Star* 24 February 1951. On 4 April Sullivan also claimed to see some sinister significance in the fact that the London *Daily Worker* had endorsed the watersiders, *Evening Post*, 4 April 1951. See also *Freedom*, 18 April 1951:
   > The strike which began on February 13 and has continued ever since, is not an industrial dispute. It is part of the cold war, engineered by Communists to advance their cause and the cause of Russia.

   A Minhinnick cartoon of 27 February 1951 showed New Zealand watersiders in the palm of the W.F.T.U.'s hand. The slogan was: "Hands up all those who vote for a strike".
5. See *Waikato Times*, 3 March 1951.
6. See New Zealand Communist Party, *The Waterfront Situation*, Auckland, 1952, p.4. Also the reviews of Scott's *151 Days, People's Voice*, 28 January 1953; 18 February 1953. Some Communists had been advising caution since the middle of 1950. See *N.Z. Labour Review*, Vol.6, No.7 (September, 1950) pp.26-29; *People's Voice*, 13 December 1950.
7. S.W. Scott, *Rebel in a Wrong Cause*, Collins, Auckland, 1960, p.187.
8. *Press*, 28 February 1951.
9. *Herald*, 27 February 1951.
10. See Eric Goldman, *The Crucial Decade—and After*, Vintage Books, New York, 1961, Chapter 6.
11. A.H. Nordmeyer won Fraser's old seat with an increased portion of the poll. Fraser took 61 per cent of the valid votes cast in 1949, Nordmeyer taking 63 per cent in the by-election of 17 February 1951. This victory was achieved despite poor organisation on Labour's part. See A.G. Osborne's report to the National Executive, N.Z.L.P., 8 March 1951.
12. *Evening Post*, 7 July 1951. It will be noted that there were no Communist Party members in Parliament. Sim must have been referring to the Labour Party.

13. *O.D.T.*, 22 February 1951.
14. *Ibid.*
15. N.Z.F.O.L. Minutes, National Executive, 19 February 1951, p.1068.
16. *Evening Post*, 24 February 1951.
17. The unions represented were the Harbour Board Employees, Tally Clerks, Foremen and Stevedores, Seamen, Cooks and Stewards, Boilermakers, Hotel Workers, Fire Brigadesmen, Coach Workers, Rubber Workers, Shipwrights, Cool Store Workers, A.S.R.S., Engine Drivers, Firemen and Cleaners Association, British Seamen and Clothing Trade Workers. N.Z.F.OL. Minutes *op.cit.*
18. *Ibid.* Also *Evening Post*, 26 February 1951.
19. N.Z.F.O.L. Minutes, *op. cit.*, p.1081.
20. *Ibid.*
21. *Press*, 24 February 1951.
22. *Evening Post*, 24 February 1951.
23. *Evening Post*, 26 February 1951.
24. *Evening Post*, 26 February 1951.
25. See typescript, "Report on Interviews with Representatives of the Waterside Workers' Union, Concerning Dispute", in hands of H.O. Roth. Also N.Z.F.O.L. Minutes, *op. cit.,* p.1082ff. See also *Evening Post*, 9 July 1951.
26. *Ibid.*
27. *Evening Post*, 26 February 1951; *Herald*, 27 February 1951.
28. See statement by Sir John Allum, *Press*, 27 February 1951.
29. For a description of the powers of these and other emergency committees see "Statement by the Minister of Labour", *op. cit.*, p.36ff.
30. When the Auckland branch applied for a Town Hall booking, the Mayor, Sir John Allum, informed the branch that there was no union at present. In any case, he added, somewhat obscurely, the Town Hall was "the people's hall" and could not be used for any meeting affecting the waterfront. *Press*, 3 March 1951.
31. "Statement by the Minister of Labour", p.9.
32. *Ibid.; Herald*, 1 March 1951.
33. *Herald*, 1 March 1951.
34. Minutes of the Auckland branch of the N.Z.W.W.U., Special Meeting, 1 March 1951.
35. A meeting of the Committee of the New Zealand Press Association on 2 March advised newspapers not to publish any statement attempting to justify the "strike" or inciting others to strike. Nor should any resolution emanating from a union meeting be published unless authenticated. There should be no reference published to "preparations by the Government to deal with the strike" other than official statements. The committee believed that editorial articles and letter columns were covered by the

Emergency Regulations but advised that statements by the Leader of the Opposition should not be suppressed. See Nash Papers, File 2235. Of all the newspapers in the country, only the *Evening Post* (20 April 1951) published a letter (written by six Victoria University academics) criticising the Emergency Regulations.

36. *Herald*, 28 February 1951. The miners wrote a parody of this speech:

> *We could knuckle down to your Fascist*
> *Regulations, Holland—but we won't.*
> *We could scab on the wharfies, Holland—but we won't.*
> *We could support you, Holland, by going back to work—*
> *but we won't.*
> *We could stop fighting for higher*
> *wages and price control, Holland—*
> *but we won't.*
> *We could lie down to your Regulations,*
> *Holland, and let you smash our union—*
> *but we won't.*
> *You can sell yourself for Yankee dollars,*
> *Holland—but WE won't.*
> *We can demand the resignation of you and*
> *your Government, Holland—we are going*
> *to do that.*

See *Miners' News*, Huntly, March 1951.

37. *Evening Post*, 1 March 1951.
38. *Herald*, 2 March 1951; *Evening Post*, 2 March 1951.
39. "Statement by the Minister of Labour", p.18. Also *Evening Post*, 26 February, 27 February, 28 February 1951.
40. *Evening Post*, 28 February, 12 March 1951.
41. *Evening Post*, 27 February 1951. For a discussion of the strike at Mangakino see Cynthia Hasman, "Hydro Development on the Waikato", unpublished thesis, Auckland University, 1965. Chapter V.
42. The national Executive Council of the Federated Seamen's Union met on 27 February with the Napier brothers of the N.Z.W.W.U. The executive then decided to recommend that seamen not work ships that were loaded or unloaded by servicemen. Ferries, however, should be worked provided they carried no cargo. The executive also proposed that a compulsory conference should be called to settle the waterfront dispute. Wellington seamen endorsed these proposals on 28 February. See minutes of a special stopwork meeting of the Wellington Seamen's Union, 28 February 1951, Seamen's Files, University of Auckland.

43. See Minutes of the Auckland Branch of the N.Z.W.W.U., 28 February 1951.
44. *Herald*, 1 March 1951.
45. *Evening Post*, 28 February 1951.
46. See Grant's statement, *Press*, 1 March 1951.
47. Minutes of a Special Meeting of the National Executive of the N.Z.F.O.L., 1 March 1951, p.1073.
48. *Herald*, 2 March 1951.
49. See for instance *Evening Post*, 2 March 1951.
50. *Press*, 28 February 1951.
51. *Evening Post*, 1 March 1951.
52. *Ibid.*, 3 March 1951.
53. *Press*, 5 March 1951.
54. Minutes of a Special Meeting of the National Executive of the N.Z.F.O.L., 5 March 1951, p.1072.
55. See "Statement by the Minister of Labour", p.9. An account of these meetings is contained in the U.M.W.'s "Circular to all Branches", 12 April, 1951.
56. Sullivan to Giles, 7 March 1951, "Statement by the Minister of Labour", p.10.
57. See full text of letter, Bassett, thesis, *op. cit.*, p.275.
58. "Statement by the Minister of Labour", p.11.
59. *Ibid.* This was confirmed in a conversation with H.L. Bockett, January 1965.
60. See also Giles' statement, *Southern Cross*, 10 March 1951; *Herald*, 13 March 1951.
61. "Statement by the Minister of Labour", p.12; *Herald*, 14 March 1951.
62. *Herald*, 3 March 1951.
63. *Evening Post*, 8 March 1951.
64. *Herald*, 9 March 1951.
65. *Herald*, 1 March 1951.
66. *Herald*, 13 March 1951; *Evening Post*, 13 March 1951, p.10.
67. Chifley to Nash, 14 May 1951, Nash Papers, File 2235.

Notes to Chapter V

1. Wool sales were suspended early in March because of the waterfront upheaval.
2. *Evening Post*, 13 July 1951.
3. Although the Government made extensive use of the radio for its purposes, no letter or editorial on the dispute appeared in the *Listener* during the period February to July.
4. A decade later, a pamphlet issued by the National Executive of the F.O.L. entitled "Survey of the Development of the Trade Union

Movement in New Zealand", (Wellington, 1961) commented: "In 1951 the country was saved . . . not by the Government which had permitted the crisis to develop, but by the Federation of Labour".

5. Minutes of Special Meeting of the National Executive, N.Z.F.O.L., 7 March 1951. The watersiders declined the offer to Barnes stating that the dispute was "now in the hands of the United Mine Workers' and Freezing Workers' organisations". Scott, p.63.
6. Headed "For or Against?" the leaflet read: "It's not a question of the merits or demerits of the Waterside Workers' claims. It's not a question of tactics—be they good or bad. It's not a question of personalities be they Barnes, Walsh, Hill, Baxter or Potter. It is a question of For or Against (a) the regulations (b) workers engaged in the struggle (c) the Holland Government". Scott, p.63.
7. A summary of Walsh's speech is included in the Minutes of the Special Conference of the N.Z.F.O.L., 8-9 March 1951, pp.1076-1080.
8. Minutes of the Special Conference, pp.1076-1080. An abbreviated report of the meeting with Holland is in the *Evening Post*, 10 March 1951. See also the *Evening Post*, 12 March 1951.
9. J. Freeman of the Timber Workers' Union wanted an immediate return to work. P. Hansen of the Tramways Union wanted support given to the efforts of the miners and freezing workers on behalf of the watersiders.
10. Minutes of the Special Conference, *loc. cit.*
11. *Herald*, 9 March 1951.
12. Minutes of the Special Conference, *loc. cit.*
13. *Herald*, 10 March 1951. A statement issued by Grant on behalf of the T.U.C. stated just a little prematurely that the F.O.L. had "deserted the labour movement", *Press*, 10 March 1951.
14. *Herald*, 13 March 1951.
15. *Evening Post*, 14 March 1951; Scott, p.67. See also U.M.W.'s "Circular to all Branches", 12 April 1951, which comments on the discussions of the period 5-25 March.
16. *Herald*, 14 March 1951.
17. *Evening Post*, 14 March 1951. The Government had been trying hard to get work going again at the smaller ports. The previous week an attempt was made to persuade Nelson watersiders to break with their national body and return to work in order that fruit, which was deteriorating badly in the sheds on the Nelson waterfront, might be hastily shipped to markets. The men had remained solid.
18. *Evening Post*, 15 March 1951.
19. On the 12th it was announced that the Southland Trades Council would help with the formation of a new union at Bluff.

20. Interview with H.L. and A.E. Bockett, Wellington, 20 May 1969.
21. "Factual Survey", p.17.
22. Seamen's Union, NZ Workers' Union, Cooks' and Stewards' Union, A.S.R.S., R.T.A., E.F.C.A. and the Harbour Board Employees' Union.
23. *Herald*, 17 March 1951.
24. See U.M.W.'s "Circular to all Branches", 12 April 1951.
25. See Bassett, thesis, *loc. cit.* p.277.
26. They preferred to keep their separate arbitrationist body, the W.I.A.
27. The bulk of the members of the union had previously been in the "A" category—that is, those who were medically fit. The men in "B" category—that is, those who were old or infirm, received no guaranteed wage.
28. See Barnes' report to the Auckland Branch, Minutes, Auckland Branch N.Z.W.W.U., 20 March 1951.
29. See "Statement by the Minister", pp.12-13. The strongest advocates of point 5 were believed to be the Bockett twins, both of whom argued for an "open" union. See Watersiders' "Speakers Notes", (July 1951) p.119. The Bocketts recall that Holland was the one who was most insistent about an open union. He was concerned about stories that entry into the old union had been something of a racket whereby some executive members benefited financially. Interview with H.L. and A.E. Bockett, Wellington, 20 May 1969.
30. See U.M.W.'s "Circular to all Branches", *op. cit.*
31. *Herald*, 21 March 1951.
32. *Herald*, 22 March 1951.
33. *Ibid.* The Director-General of the Post Office later claimed that only four packets were opened by the Post Office, all of them containing illegal material. They were opened, he said, under Section 31 (1) of the Post and Telegraph Act 1928. See M.M. Cryer to W. Nash, 20 August 1951, Nash Papers, File 2233.
34. *Herald*, 22 March 1951. The T.U.C. was similarly prevented from holding a meeting in Wellington the following week. *Evening Post*, 27 March 1951.
35. This was a misleading statement. The 4/7½ did represent a 15 per cent advance on the 4/- which had been paid watersiders in May 1950. But the watersiders' position, owing to the fact that the July 1950 award had been "final" was not the same as unionists' covered by the Arbitration Court. It would not, however, have sounded so impressive to have said that the wage to be offered the new unionists was 4/7½ which included only 9 per cent instead of the recent 15 per cent award granted to other unions.
36. *Herald*, 24 March 1951; *Evening Post*, 26 March 1951.
37. *Evening Post*, 10 March 1951.

NOTES

38. *Herald*, 13 March 1951.
39. Cool store workers in Auckland returned to work on 28 March.
40. *Evening Post*, 13 March 1951; 16 March 1951.
41. *Herald*, 22 March 1951.
42. *Evening Post*, 21 March 1951.
43. *Herald*, 22 March 1951.
44. The figures for New Zealand were: for normal work: 7291; for helping the watersiders: 4139. See pamphlet "The Story of the Railway Strike", Dunedin [1952]; also *Evening Post*, 31 March 1951.
45. See Minutes, Auckland Branch N.Z.W.W.U., 19 March 1951.
46. "The Story of the Railway Strike", *op.cit.* To some watersiders the substantial wage rise awarded the railwaymen early in May 1951 looked like a kind of Government bonus for "scabbing" on fellow workers.
47. See "Statement by the Minister", pp.25-28. In Wellington on 29 March Walsh made a strong plea to the seamen to return to ordinary work. But there was opposition by the men to a secret ballot. So Walsh, fearing he would not carry an open ballot, decided on 5 April to recommend that seamen reaffirm their stand of 28 February. This would allow the ferries to continue so long as they did not carry cargo loaded by servicemen. When this recommendation was placed before the Wellington seamen it was rejected by 207:149. The position of Wellington seamen remained confused for some weeks while in the meantime no work was done. See Minutes of Meetings of Wellington Seamen's Union, 28 March, 29 March, 5 April and 10 April 1951.
48. *Herald*, 13 March 1951.
49. *Ibid.*, 16 March 1951.
50. This opinion has been expressed firmly by Leicester Webb, "Trade Union at the Crossroads", *New Zealand Journal of Public Administration*, Vol.14 (March 1952), pp.1-13.
51. *Herald*, 28 April 1951.
52. During the debate on the Police Offences Amendment Bill, 1960, J.T. Watts, who had been a junior Minister in 1951, referred to a deputation led by Walsh in May 1951 which appealed for more intensive action against wreckers and lawbreakers who had been "menacing the public". *N.Z.P.D.*, 8 July 1960, p.450.
53. *Dominion*, 22 March 1951.
54. *Taranaki Daily News*, 10 March 1951.
55. *N.Z.P.D.*, 18 August 1960, p.1634.
56. Tuohy had been Walsh's original surname.
57. *Evening Post*, 17 March 1951.
58. *Ibid.*, 16 March 1951.
59. "Statement by the Minister", p.19.

60. *Herald*, 5 April 1951.
61. See cyclostyled "Brief Outline of Events in Connection with the Waterside Workers' Dispute as they affected the officials and members of the Wellington Drivers' Union", Auckland, 1951.
62. "Statement by the Minister", pp.20-22.
63. *Ibid.*
64. *Ibid.*
65. Scott, p.98; see also cyclostyled information bulletin, "Mr Sullivan's New Drivers' Society". This pamphlet, presumably issued by the striking drivers, claimed that the office holders in the new union were either shareholders in, or related to the owners of, a Wellington carrying company.
66. See R.M. Martin, "Twenty Years of Compulsory Unionism", *Political Science*, Vol.8 (September 1956), pp.104-121.
67. The I.C. and A. Amendment Act 1936, stated that "while the award continues in force it shall not be lawful for any employer bound thereby to employ, or continue to employ in the industry to which the award relates, any adult person who is not for the time being a member of an industrial union bound by that award". *Statutes*, 1936, p.77.
68. *Evening Post*, 13 April 1951; Martin, *op. cit.*, p.112.
69. *Dominion*, 19 May 1951.
70. The legal questions involved in the Minister's actions are described fully in R.M. Martin, *op. cit.*
71. Later in the year officials of the old union were elected to control the new Wellington (thirty miles radius) Drivers' Union. But attempts to amalgamate the smaller unions were blocked by the Labour Department.
72. "Statement by the Minister", pp.22-23.
73. Scott, p.75.
74. See *Herald*, 11 April 1951. At a meeting of Wellington seamen on 18 April Walsh reported that he had written to the Australian Seamen's Union asking for a refund of a £2,000 loan made to it in 1922. In the middle of June he managed to raise £500 in a gift from an unidentified source. This enabled seamen's relief to be continued. See Minutes of Meeting of Wellington Seamen's Union, 18 April and 20 June 1951.
75. Telegrammed to all branches on 20 March.
76. *Herald*, 4 April 1951. The open-cast mines in Canterbury, Otago and Southland worked throughout.
77. Only 23 per cent of all miners in the dominion did hold a secret ballot. See *Dominion*, 29 March 1951; *Press*, 2 April 1951.
78. The new group continued efforts to force the resignations of Prendiville and Crook. A majority of the old National Council (including those who were on the new strike committee) met

early in May and voted to suspend them (*Dominion*, 17 May 1951). But Prendiville and Crook refused to surrender the national office of the U.M.W., despite many votes of no-confidence that were carried against them, until secret ballots on the strike issue were held. And these ballots were not held until the strike ended in July.
79. *Evening Post*, 5 April 1951.
80. Late in June *Taupo* was withdrawn from Westport to be refitted for action in Korea. The survey ship *Lachlan* replaced her, *Herald*, 28 June 1951. An account of the Navy's activities on the West Coast is given in the *Evening Post*, 14 July 1951.
81. *Evening Post*, 29 June 1951.
82. *Evening Post*, 9 June 1951.
83. "Statement by the Minister", p.25.
84. *Evening Star* (Dunedin), 25 June 1951.
85. See Scott, pp.82-87.
86. *Herald*, 14 April 1951.
87. See Scott, p.84.
88. *Evening Post*, 12 April 1951. The charge laid under the Regulations was finally withdrawn.
89. *Evening Post*, 19 May 1951.
90. Holland had withdrawn from the National Cabinet in 1942 because Fraser's Government had not prosecuted striking miners, See F.L.W. Wood, *The New Zealand People at War*, Government Printer, Wellington, 1958, pp.232-237.

Notes to Chapter VI

1. This statement was issued at the end of a meeting of the National Council of the N.Z.W.W.U. on 3 April. *Evening Post*, 4 April 1951.
2. *Evening Post*, 12 April 1951.
3. The activities of the Wellington Supplies Committee are described in the *Evening Post*, 3 March and 20 July 1951.
4. One fatality was a naval rating at Westport; the other was a soldier employed in an overseas vessel at Wellington.
5. The report by A.E. Bockett, General Manager of the W.I.C., to the Royal Commission attempts to interpret the servicemen's rates of work in the most favourable possible light pp.47-51. The figures provided do show evidence of improvement, although they are not quite so dramatic if one makes any kind of allowance for a novelty-of-work factor, for the degree of public encouragement given, and for the general conditions provided.
6. There is no doubt that the servicemen enjoyed the change of routine. R.N.Z.A.F. officers and men who remained at Ohakea were reported to feel "very much back-seaters and speak of the water-

front as though it were the front line". *Evening Post*, 24 April 1951.
7. The ships used were the *Arawa, Tamaroa, Mataroa, Wahine, Gothic, Rangitata, Rangitane, Monowai* and *Ruahine*. See *Evening Post*, 14 July 1951.
8. *Ibid.*
9. "Factual Survey of the Waterfront Strike", p.51.
10. See Scott, pp.159-181.
11. *Evening Post*, 9 April 1951.
12. *Ibid.*, 10 April 1951.
13. The police did not disperse a meeting of 1,500 men which was held outside the Trades Hall in Hobson Street, Auckland on the morning of 10 April.
14. This was the cause of some bitterness among members of the relief committees, and was subsequently criticised by Potter in his "Report to Area Conference", 12 June 1952.
15. *Evening Post*, 20 September 1951. It was later reported that Australian sympathisers had contributed nearly A£50,000 in all, including A£40,000 from the Australian watersiders, A£6,664 from Australian miners, and A£1,500 from Australian seamen, *Star*, 19 December 1951.
16. *Evening Post*, 13 July 1951. See J.G. Aitken to W. Nash, 2 August 1951, Nash Papers, File 2233.
17. Occasionally livestock was "appropriated" from farms. Several farmers in the Waikato reported stock losses during April.
18. The Waikato miners organised fishing excursions from Whangamata. Interview with A.C. Baxter, formerly MP for Raglan, and Rotowaro miners' president in 1951.
19. See J.G. Aitken to W. Nash, 2 August 1951, *loc. cit.*
20. *The Labour and Employment Gazette,* Vol.1 (February 1951) p.7, estimated that male vacancies in Wellington and the Hutt represented between 8 per cent and 12 per cent of the surveyed male labour force. In Auckland the figure was 6.2 per cent and was above 5 per cent at Christchurch and Dunedin. The figures were much lower in the smaller ports.
21. The *Herald*, 5 April 1951, claimed that about 1,000 of Wellington's 2,300 watersiders had found some other employment.
22. The Auckland City Council under Allum's guidance took action against watersiders occupying A.C.C. transit houses at Western Springs who were in arrears with their rent. *Herald*, 4 May 1951.
23. Several watersiders mentioned these details in discussions with the author. C.V. Bollinger of Wellington also provided supporting information.
24. Minutes of a special meeting of the Auckland Branch, N.Z.W.W.U., 14 March.

25. *Ibid.*, 27 March 1951.
26. *Ibid.*, 20 March 1951. This motion was finally carried at the executive meeting on the 28th and a meeting of the National Council was held in Wellington on 3 April.
27. The first arrest for distributing literature was in Wellington on 7 March. The man was charged with inciting people to be parties to a declared strike. He was granted bail at £50 on the assurance that he would not distribute any more. *Evening Post*, 7 March 1951.
28. R. Adams, Secretary of the Wellington Painters' Union, was warned on 8 March that a special meeting to discuss the Emergency Regulations could not be held. See *Evening Post*, 8 March 1951. Four days later he was charged by summons under the Regulations for printing a circular "likely to encourage the continuance of a declared strike". See *ibid.*, 12 March 1951.
29. So outraged were watersiders that on 10 April the Auckland Branch decided to appeal to the United Nations to take action against the Government of New Zealand for violating the Declaration of Human Rights. See *Herald*, 11 April 1951. A cable was dispatched from the N.Z.W.W.U. on 12 April and the text was printed in the N.Z.T.W., 13 April 1951. It referred to the various articles of the Declaration of Human Rights that had been infringed by the Emergency Regulations and by the activities of the police. The United Nations, of course, had no power to intervene in this domestic dispute within one of its member countries.
30. *Herald*, 2 May 1951.
31. I am indebted here to Jack Elder whose research essay, "The Publicity Committee of the Waterside Workers' Union during the 1951 Dispute" amplifies some of these points.
32. R.M. Martin, *op. cit.*, p.111.
33. Besides McLagan, A.G. Osborne, R. Walls, R. McKeen and W.E. Parry, all of them members of the Parliamentary Labour Party, were ill for much of the period of the waterfront dispute.
34. See correspondence between Nash and A.E. Bockett, February 1951, Nash Papers, File 2235.
35. See "New Zealand Labour Party: Waterfront Dispute", cyclostyled summary of statements, 1951, pp.7-8. *Herald*, 1 March 1951.
36. *Press*, 2 March 1951.
37. *Southland Times*, 10 March 1951.
38. *O.D.T.*, 2 March 1951. Less extreme criticisms are to be found in the *Dominion*, 1 March 1951; *Marlborough Express*, 1 March 1951; *Taranaki Daily News*, 2 March 1951; *Daily Telegraph* (Napier) 1 March 1951; *Evening Press*, 2 March 1951.
39. Labour's paper, the *Southern Cross*, 3 March 1951, conceded that reforms were necessary.

40. N.Z.L.P., National Executive Minutes, 30 March 1951.
41. *Evening Post*, 30 March 1951.
42. *Ibid.; Herald*, 30 March 1951. Nash's speech notes and his comments on the meeting are to be found in the Nash Papers, File 2235.
43. *Evening Post*, 31 March 1951. See also *Star*, 30 March 1951.
44. Baxter to Nash, 2 April 1951. "Statement by the Minister", pp.29-30. Also printed in the *Evening Post*, 6 April 1951. Nash's attitude to the watersiders at this point is discussed in W. Nash to A.G. Osborne, MP, 12 April 1951, Nash Papers, File 2234.
45. *Evening Post*, 5 April 1951.
46. *Ibid.*; the text of the letter is also contained in the cyclostyled summary, *op. cit.*, p.9.
47. See for instance the *Star*, 6 April 1951.
48. *Herald*, 6 April 1951.
49. *Evening Post*, 6 April 1951.
50. See A.G. Osborne, MP to Nash, 10 April 1951; Nash to A.G. Osborne, 12 April 1951, Nash Papers, File 2234.
51. Nash gave several accounts of his activities during April. See particularly *N.Z.P.D.*, Vol.294, 1951, p.97. The fullest account is in Nash's own handwriting in the Nash Papers, File 2235.
52. See Nash Papers, File 2235; Scott, p.125.
53. See *ibid.*, Nash to Holland, 19 April 1951, cyclostyled summary, *op. cit.*, pp.12-19. See also *N.Z.P.D.*, Vol.294, 1951, pp.109-110.
54. Barnes *et. al.* to Nash, 18 April 1951, cyclostyled summary, *op. cit.*, pp.16-19.
55. Barnes *et. al.* to Holland, 19 April 1951, "Statement by the Minister", pp.13-14.
56. *Herald*, 20 April 1951; cyclostyled summary, p.15.
57. *Herald*, 21 April 1951.
58. Interview with H.L. and A.E. Bockett, 20 May 1969.
59. Scott, p.91.
60. R.L. Macalister was Mayor of Wellington.
61. *Herald*, 7 April 1951.
62. The Government's lists of watersiders' names were not up to date. Some people who were dead and others who had never had any association with the waterfront received letters. Several *bona fide* watersiders did not receive letters. See Wellington Watersiders' *Information Bulletin*, No.14, 16 April 1951. See also circular from T.U.C. to its affiliates [April 1951].
63. *Herald*, 10 April 1951. The letter dated 7 April is included in "Factual Survey", *op. cit.*, p.31.
64. *Herald*, 10 April 1951.
65. *Ibid.*, 11 April 1951.
66. *Herald,* 11 April; 13 April 1951.
67. *Ibid.*, 13 April 1951.

68. *Ibid.*, 14 April 1951.
69. *Ibid.*, 17 April 1951.
70. *Ibid.*, 18 April 1951.
71. *Ibid.*
72. *Ibid.*, 26 April 1951.
73. This interpretation of the Government's actions of 19-20 April was derived partly from the author's discussions with H.L. Bockett, former Secretary of Labour, and J.P. Lewin, former president of the Public Service Association.
74. Sullivan gave as the main reason for rejecting the letter of 19 April the fact that reregistering the national union would have involved the Government in breaking faith with the new unionists at the minor ports. See "Statement by the Minister", p.15. See also Holland's statement and letter, *Evening Post*, 23 and 24 April 1951. The *Press* also argued strongly against "breaking faith" with the new unionists, *Press*, 21 April 1951.
75. See "Factual Survey", p.35. A new union was registered at Gisborne on 17 April with thirty-four men in it, but work did not begin at Gisborne until 23 April.
76. See the figures in the *Labour and Employment Gazette,* Vol.1 (February 1951) p.7.
77. *Herald*, 21 April 1951.
78. *Evening Post*, 21 April 1951.
79. *Ibid.*, 23 April 1951.
80. *Herald*, 23 April 1951; *Evening Post*, 23 April 1951.
81. See editorial, *Herald*, 20 April 1951.
82. See *Herald* from 20 April until mid-May 1951. See also *Evening Post*, 21 April 1951; 23 April 1951.
83. *Evening Post*, 9 May 1951.
84. *Herald*, 26 April 1951. The fullest press report of the statement is in the *Evening Post*, 24 April 1951. See also cyclostyled summary, p.20.
85. Nash to A.G. Osborne MP, 30 April 1951, Nash Papers, File 2234.
86. The Dunedin *Evening Star*, 26 June 1951 said that the Police also had an "interest" in the screening committee.
87. Fifty-six men, several of whom were deregistered watersiders, were allowed to work in the New Plymouth Waterfront Employees' Union on 26 April. A number of deregistered men joined the new union after a meeting on 30 April. *Herald*, 1 May 1951. For comments on the procedure at New Plymouth see *N.Z.T.W.*, 15 May 1951.
88. The Auckland meeting on 6 May is reported in Minutes of Meeting of Auckland Branch, N.Z.W.W.U. The Members present were F. Hackett, W.T. Anderton, R. McDonald and W.W. Freer. Hackett told the men that since the "New Plymouth affair" he

would not recommend a return to work. "The Government", he said, "has reached such a state of fascism that it can't go back." See also the reported statements of A.E. Armstrong MP, 16 May 1951, in W. McAra Papers, Folder 6/4.
89. The role of the Labour Department and the W.I.C. is discussed in *Freedom*, 20 April 1951.
90. See "Factual Survey", pp.35-37.
91. *Herald*, 1 May 1951.
92. The secret ballot on the issue of refusing to handle cargo from the ship saw 132 votes cast in favour of refusing. The vote for normal work was 112. *Evening Post*, 9 May 1951; Scott, p.105.
93. Scott, p.107.
94. On 3 July a secret ballot among the new unionists at New Plymouth saw control formally restored to the hands of men who had been members of the N.Z.W.W.U. *Evening Post*, 3 July 1951. As of 17 October 1951 some 66.5 per cent of the membership of the new union had been members of the deregistered union. See "Factual Survey", p.38.
95. Scott, p.103. The farmer was Mr W. Wrack from near Whangarei. See *Press*, 21 April 1951.
96. *Herald*, 21 April 1951; "Factual Survey", p.35.
97. Scott, p.103.
98. See Chapter IV.
99. *Herald*, 28 April 1951.
100. *Star*, 3 May 1951.
101. *Herald*, 4 May 1951. The Royal Marines were armed. See Scott, p.110.
102. *Star*, 3 May 1951.
103. By mid-June there were 400 Maoris in the new Auckland union. Only eighty had belonged to the old. *Evening Post*, 18 June 1951.
104. One volunteer was seventy-eight-year-old Major Judson, V.C.
105. The *Evening Post*, 28 June 1951 reported that 200 men had joined the Auckland union, worked a short time, and then departed.
106. *Herald*, 10 May 1951.
107. *Ibid.*, 20 June; 28 June 1951.
108. The author discussed the matter of screening with a former secretary of the Auckland Port Employers' Association.
109. Donaldson formally joined the new union on 4 July 1951. In 1950 he had been suspended from the N.Z.W.W.U., and in October of that year he claimed £1,000 from the union as damages for wrongful dismissal. He was awarded £250 by the courts. See *O.D.T.*, 5 July 1951.
110. *Herald*, 26 May 1951.
111. See "Factual Survey", p.38. This figure of 4.3 per cent was the

lowest for any of the new unions in the country. About 43 per cent of the total members of the N.Z.W.W.U. had found their way back on to the waterfront by October 1951. At Westport and Greymouth it was 100 per cent; at Port Chalmers 94 per cent; at Timaru 84.3 per cent; at Wellington 81 per cent; at Lyttelton 44.8 per cent; at Dunedin 20.3 per cent; at Bluff 60.1 per cent.

112. This information was given to the author by a former secretary of the Auckland Port Employers' Association. It was alleged in the House of Representatives (see *Herald*, 11 July 1951) that the port employers had brought McMullen out from England and that he had been given preferential treatment in securing a state house. McMullen denied the latter suggestion (*Evening Post*, 11 July 1951) and it appears that he had been in New Zealand for some time before 1951.
113. *Evening Post*, 4 July 1951.
114. See "Factual Survey", pp.35-37. This difficulty finding men for the new union made it possible ultimately for most of Wellington's deregistered men to get employment on the waterfront again.
115. See cyclostyled bulletin, "For Whom the Bell Tolls", Wellington, 1951. A song written by the watersiders called the "Arthur Kingsley Bell Song", was to be sung to the tune of "The Hand-out on Panhandle Hill". The first four verses went as follows:

> Come away, boys, and scab with me
> Oh come down with Bell
> And your life will be hell
> There'll be brawlers and maulers
> And plenty of crawlers
> At the handout on Parliament Hill.

> Come away, boys, and scab with me
> Come down to the ships
> And get in the chips.
> There'll be cops to protect us
> (And then disinfect us)
> At the handout on Parliament Hill.

> Come away, boys, and scab with me
> For Holland has said
> It's not nice to be Red
> And there's money and perks
> For the joker who works
> At the handout on Parliament Hill.

> Come away, boys, and scab with me
> For unloading boats
> Means plenty of notes

>   Your mates will admire you
>   Their pasts will inspire you
>   At the handout on Parliament Hill.
>
> See *Freezing Workers' Bulletin*, 26 June 1951.

116. *N.Z.P.D.*, Vol.294, 1951, p.117. This solicitude for the new unionists was particularly galling to deregistered watersiders. For it was Sullivan who had claimed in a broadcast on 9 April that the deregistered union had occasionally given membership preference to applicants with police records. *Herald*, 10 April 1951.
117. *Herald*, 7 June 1951.

Notes to Chapter VII

1. M.R.A. had always been strongly opposed to strikes or to other "divisive" movements. All non-Communist countries should maintain a solid front against Communism, a term which was frequently used so widely in M.R.A. propaganda that it covered almost anything left-wing.
2. Part of the speech is reprinted in "Statement by the Minister", p.33.
3. *Ibid.* The *Herald*, 19 April 1951, printed the report, with a large photo of Freeman, as its main news item.
4. "Statement by the Minister", p.33; *Herald*, 21 April 1951.
5. Principally A.W. Croskery of the F.O.L., J.T. Paul, R.S. Belsham, and A.K. Bell.
6. On 17 April the Government announced that it no longer recognised the T.U.C. which had "done their utmost to spread and prolong the trouble". *Herald*, 18 April 1951.
7. Scott, p.108.
8. See *Herald*, 1 May 1951. His wounds required three stitches. *Herald*, 2 May 1951. After appealing to the deregistered men in a broadcast to go back to work, Belsham resigned the presidency of the new union. W. Cain, formerly vice-president, assumed the presidency with A. Farr as his vice-president. W.F. McMullen succeeded to the presidency in June.
9. *Herald*, 2 May 1951. There was a similar incident in Christchurch on 5 July. See *O.D.T.*, 6 July 1951.
10. *Ibid.*, 1 May 1951.
11. See statement by D. Stewart, secretary of Waikato Central Committee of Miners' Unions, *ibid.*, 2 May 1951.
12. This point was made by a leading miner at a public meeting some time later. A tape of his speech was included in the N.Z.B.C. production, *Dispute*, broadcast on 24 November 1968. For press comments see *Evening Post*, 2 May 1951; *Herald*, 1 May 1951; *O.D.T.*, 2 May 1951.
13. The editor of the *O.D.T.* said on 1 May: "The explosion with which

the New Zealand Communists attempted to kill working men at Huntly is indistinguishable from the shell bursts directed by Chinese Communists against New Zealand soldiers in Korea."
14. A.C. Baxter, president of the Rotowaro Miners' Union, said on 1 May that he had warned two Government Members two weeks before that, in his opinion, acts of violence might occur. *Herald*, 2 May 1951.
15. *Herald*, 2 May 1951.
16. *Ibid.* For activities at Victoria University, see also the letter sent to the *Evening Post*, 20 April 1951, by J.C. Beaglehole, R.S. Parker, F.L.W. Wood and others about the Regulations and their violation of the U.N.: Declaration of Human Rights.
17. "Statement by the Minister", p.42.
18. *Ibid.* In Wellington the staff of the Dutch Legation was accepted into the C.E.O.
19. See J. Malton Murray to W. Nash, 2 May 1951, Nash Papers, File 2234.
20. *Herald*, 3 May 1951.
21. The Supreme Court dismissed Magee's fine. The Wellington Drivers' Union had been reregistered under the Trades Union Act 1908 on 13 April. It was not deregistered again by Sullivan until 4 May. Thus on the date of his arrest, Magee's union could not be classified as "deregistered" under the terms of the Emergency Regulations. See Scott, p.101.
22. *Herald*, 11 May 1951. Early in July F.J. Balchan, Secretary of the Lyttelton Branch of the N.Z.W.W.U. was fined £50 for failing to deliver £2,000 of the union's funds to the official Receiver. *Evening Post*, 5 July 1951. On 3 July the Wellington police armed with a warrant, and later an electric drill, raided the offices of the deregistered Wellington Freezing Workers' Union. They seized documents and drilled open the safe in which they found nothing of consequence. *Dominion*, 4 July 1951.
23. See Nash's statement, *Herald*, 7 May 1951.
24. For a full account of the Town Hall incident see W.T. Anderton MP to W. Nash, 13 May 1951, Nash Papers, File 2235. See also F.J. Gwilliam to Auckland L.R.C., 4 May 1951, Nash Papers, File 2235.
25. See Anderton to Nash, *op. cit.*
26. *Herald*, 8 May 1951; see also *Press*, 8 May 1951.
27. The full text of the statement is in the cyclostyled summary, *op. cit.*, pp29-30. See also Scott, p.130.
28. *Herald*, 8 May 1951.
29. *Ibid.*, 7 May 1951. On 9 May Allum told an *Evening Post* reporter that he was worried about possible damage to Town Hall furniture.
30. See Nash's statement, *ibid.*, 10 May 1951; *Evening Post*, 9 May 1951.

See also Nash's comments, *N.Z.P.D.*, Vol.294, p.46 and Anderton's *ibid.*, p.129. See also Scott, pp.130-131.
31. See copy of *Contact* (Westport Methodist Church) Nash Papers, File 2235. See also the comments of A.M. Richards, *Outlook*, 15 May 1951, p.3.
32. *Herald*, 11 May 1951.
33. *Ibid.*, 12 May 1951.
34. Scott, p.134, also claims the number present was 10,000. The figure 6,000 was the *Herald*'s.
35. *Herald*, 14 May 1951; *Evening Post*, 14 May 1951.
36. *Herald*, 14 May 1951.
37. *Ibid.* The *Press*, 15 May 1951, voiced similar sentiments, though with less vitriol.
38. W. Nash to Ben Chifley, 14 May 1951, Nash Papers, File 2235.
39. The press was not always consistent in its reporting of Labour statements during May. On 27 May Nash, referring to suppression of Labour statements, called the newspapers "a menace to the country". *Evening Post*, 28 May 1951.
40. Both McLagan and Jones had backed Prendiville and Crook in their struggles against the Miners' National Strike Committee. See Scott, p.81. See also R. Macfarlane to W. Nash, 30 April 1951, Nash Papers, File 2234.
41. See Chapter I, p.25.
42. *Herald*, 4 June 1951. Baxter had been in touch with Nash on 2 June (see Baxter to Nash, Nash Papers, File 2235) requesting that he urge the watersiders to return to work. When Nash failed to do so it seems likely that the F.O.L. approached Semple.
43. See for instance Croskery to the Chairman of Directors, *Southern Cross*, 27 June 1950; Croskery to P. Fraser, 4 July 1950, Nash Papers, File 263.
44. For a discussion of the Holmes satchel case see W.B. Sutch, *The Quest for Security*, pp.347-8.
45. See handwritten notes, Nash Papers, File 2235.
46. See the reported statement contained in P. Curran to W. Nash, 15 May 1951, Nash Papers, File 2235.
47. See for instance Croskery to Nash, 8 May 1951; Baxter to Nash, 2 June 1951, J.R. Scott (Wellington Trades Council) to Nash, 28 June 1951. Nash Papers, File 2235.
48. *Herald*, 8 June 1951.
49. *Evening Post*, 8 June 1951.
50. *Ibid.*, 13 June 1951. Hill and Baxter also addressed the conference. See Christchurch *Star-Sun*, 13 June 1951. The conference had originally been planned for the end of April but had been delayed because of the industrial trouble.

51. The main speaker in favour of denying membership to anybody affiliated to the W.F.T.U. was K.M. Baxter of the F.O.L. who managed to arrange for himself the credentials of the Printers' Union so that he could attend. *Evening Post*, 13 June 1951.
52. *Herald*, 14 June 1951.
53. A collection of these letters is to be found in the Nash Papers, File 2091.
54. The precise number was not specified.
55. Sullivan to T. Wells, 14 May 1951, "Statement by the Minister", pp.15-16. Also *Herald*, 15 May 1951.
56. See Wells *et al.* to Sullivan, 15 May 1951, "Statement by the Minister", pp.16-17. Also *Herald*, 16 May 1951.
57. See Sullivan's comments, "Statement by the Minister", p.17.
58. *Herald*, 28 May 1951.
59. Both speeches were lengthy analyses of the origins of the dispute. For Barnes' speech see *Herald*, 21 May 1951; for Hill's see *Evening Post*, 21 May 1951. Collections were made at these meetings, the money being used for relief purposes.
60. The *Evening Post* commented on 1 June: "The fact that the Government feels that the time has arrived when the revocation either in whole or in part of the Emergency Regulations can be considered is a welcome indication that the purpose for which the regulations were designed has very largely been achieved". The Regulations were not removed entirely till the end of July.
61. A large rally (Scott, p.158, claims 17,000) was held in the Auckland Domain on 3 June at which watersiders and miners spoke. See *Herald*, 4 June 1951. The size of the rallies was interpreted by the watersiders as evidence that their support was growing. See Wellington Watersiders' *Information Bulletin*, No.31, 5 June 1951.
62. Minutes of Meeting of Unions directly involved in the Waterfront Dispute, Wellington, 13 June 1951, p.2.
63. *Ibid.*, pp.3-4.
64. *Evening Post*, 12 June 1951.
65. Minutes of Meeting of Unions, *op. cit.*, p.4; Scott, p.197.
66. The decision of the meeting was reported in the *Dominion*, 14 June 1951.
67. Barnes had told the meeting on the 12th that he didn't mind separate port unions. In his view there was not much difference between a national union and a federation of port unions. See Minutes of a Meeting of the Wellington Seamen's Union, 20 June 1951.
68. *Evening Post*, 15 June 1951. In fact, most of the unions in the major ports were still well below normal strength.
69. Clifton Webb was Attorney-General.
70. *Herald*, 20 June 1951.

71. Scott, p.197.
72. *Herald*, 21 June 1951.
73. See "Statement by the Minister", p.17.
74. See Nash Papers, File 2234.
75. Nash to McLagan, 25 June 1951, Nash Papers, File 1526.
76. See Nash Papers, File 2235.
77. *Herald*, 23 June 1951.
78. *Ibid.*, 23 June 1951.
79. See *ibid.*, 27 June 1951.
80. The *Dominion*, 29 June 1951 criticised him for being too lenient.
81. *Herald*, 3 July 1951.
82. *Waikato Times*, 30 June 1951. The Government Statistician estimated the amount of coal lost as 400,000 tons. See *A.J.H.R.*, 1952, H-45, p.5.
83. See Minutes of a Meeting of the Wellington Seamen's Union, 20 June 1951; "Statement by the Minister", p.28.
84. *Herald*, 4 July 1951.
85. See Potter's comments, Minutes of Meeting between Watersiders and General Labourers, 19 June 1952.
86. *Evening Post*, 30 June 1951. As the miners' strike collapsed, Prendiville and Crook, who had remained in control of the U.M.W.U.'s national office, found themselves leading the miners once again.
87. *Herald*, 30 June 1951.
88. Chrichton resigned from the National Executive of the N.Z.W.W.U. *Evening Post*, 8 June 1951.
89. *Evening Post*, 30 June 1951.
90. T.G. Wells, *et al.* to Sullivan, 27 June 1951, "Statement by the Minister", p.28.
91. Sullivan to Wells *et al.*, 29 June 1951, "Statement by the Minister", p.29.
92. *O.D.T.*, 3 July 1951; *Dominion*, 3 July 1951.
93. *O.D.T.*, 5 July 1951.
94. "Statement by the Minister", p.29.
95. Wellington Watersiders' *Information Bulletin*, No.45, July 1951; Scott, p.198.
96. *Herald*, 6 June 1951.
97. Wellington Watersiders' *Information Bulletin*, No.30, 1 June 1951. However, there were reports during June and early July that fewer and fewer watersiders were attending the daily meetings of their branches. Many had taken employment elsewhere. In the first week of July only 350 instead of the full muster of 700 to 800 men attended the Lyttelton branch meetings. See *O.D.T.*, 5 July 1951.
98. Sullivan stated on 4 July that there would not be work on the water-

front for "a substantial number" of members of the old union, and these men could thank no one but their leaders, who had prevented their return to work, for the loss of their employment. *O.D.T.*, 5 July 1951.
99. As of 17 October 1951 only 43 per cent of the total membership of the new unions had been members of the deregistered union. See "Factual Survey", p.38.
100. Two groups of workers, members of the old and new unions, worked alongside each other in Wellington for several years until the leaders of the deregistered union (the Napier brothers) gained the upper hand.
101. As of 17 October 1951 only 4.35 per cent of the members of the new union in Auckland had been members of the deregistered union. This was the lowest percentage for any port. See "Factual Survey", p.38. See also Auckland Watersiders' *Information Bulletin*, No.55, 8 September 1951. For the situation at Lyttelton see *O.D.T.*, 6 July 1951. In Auckland the pressure against admitting deregistered men came partly from the leaders of the new union. See A. Drennan and J. Connors, "Representations on the question of Auckland deregistered Waterside Workers", typescript, November 1952, in hands of H. Roth. Protests about the Railways Department's refusal to employ deregistered watersiders are to be found in the Nash Papers. File 2235.
102. *Official Year Book*, 1953, p.891.
103. *O.D.T.*, 23 July 1951.
104. *Ibid.*, 6 July 1951.
105. *A.J.H.R.*, 1952, H-45, p.5.
106. *Ibid.*
107. Over the country at large, 1952 saw fewer man-days lost in industrial disputes than in any year since 1943. *Official Year Book*, 1953, p.890.
108. *A.J.H.R.*, 1952, H-45, p.5.
109. *O.D.T.*, 26 July 1951.
110. *Ibid.*, 6 July 1951.
111. *Ibid.*
112. See for instance, *Herald*, 30 May 1951.
113. *O.D.T.*, 26 July 1951.
114. *Ibid.*, 21 July 1951. See also *Freedom*, 27 June 1951; *Taranaki Daily News*, 29 June 1951.
115. *Labour and Employment Gazette*, Vol.II, February 1952, p.27.
116. *Herald*, 9 May 1951.
117. The Consumers' Price Index showed a rise of 5.7 per cent between 31 December 1950 and 30 June 1951. See *Official Year Book*, 1953, p.787.

118. *Herald*, 10 May 1951.
119. In the Public Safety Conservation Amendment Act, 1960, Nash's Labour Government made it essential that Parliament be called within seven days of the declaration of a State of Emergency.
120. Since 1951 only the session of 1968 has met as late in the year as 26 June.
121. *Dominion*, 26 June 1951.
122. *N.Z.P.D.*, Vol.294, 1951, pp.42-46.
123. On 13 July both Nash and C.F. Skinner, his deputy, alleged that telephones had been tapped during the course of the dispute. *Dominion*, 14 July 1951.
124. Neither McLagan nor Semple took any part in the debates.
125. *N.Z.P.D.*, Vol.294, 1951, p.136. See also Nash, *ibid.*, p.99.
126. See for instance the speeches by Sullivan, Webb and Shand, *N.Z.P.D.*, Vol.294, 1951, p.46ff.
127. See for instance the speeches by Holland, *ibid.*, pp.106-112; Johnstone, *ibid.*, p.129ff.
128. *N.Z.P.D.*, Vol.294, 1951, p.70.
129. See *ibid.*, p.262.
130. *Herald*, 13 July 1951.
131. *Ibid.* 20 July 1951.

Notes to Chapter VIII

1. The Labour Government had allowed the practice of holding the Maori elections the day before the European to continue, mainly because it felt the announcement of four Labour seats on the morning of the European elections was good for Labour's morale. Weekday elections were thought to encourage a high turn-out of voters. The National Party also appears to have believed this. In his report to the National Executive of the Labour Party on 20 September 1951, A.J. McDonald, National Secretary, gave Saturday voting as the main reason for Labour's defeat. He thought it had contributed to the big non-vote.
2. *O.D.T.*, 19 July 1951. All Labour Representation Committees were asked in special telegrams sent on 12 July 1951 for suggestions about election candidates and policy.
3. *Press*, 13 July 1951.
4. *Evening Post*, 13 July 1951.
5. *O.D.T.*, 14 July 1951.
6. *Ibid.*, 31 July 1951.
7. See *Herald*, 23 May 1951.
8. The *Otago Daily Times* did more than editorialise. It ran several articles which purported to show that between 1949 and 1951 people had become much more prosperous. See for example

O.D.T., 8 August 1951; the letter columns were filled with letters signed by "Tory Always", "Happy Tory" and other anonymous eulogists of the Government.
9. *Auckland Star*, 29 August 1951.
10. Minutes of Auckland Branch, N.Z.W.W.U., 20 July 1951.
11. *Evening Post*, 25 August 1951.
12. *Herald*, 23 July 1951; *O.D.T.*, 23 July 1951.
13. Typescript in the hands of R.E. Jones, secretary Auckland Branch, N.Z.W.W.U. (deregistered). In an election broadcast on 25 August 1951, T.C. Webb, Attorney-General, claimed that Potter's version of his speech made no difference to what he had initially been reported as saying. See typescript, "1951 Election Broadcasts", N.Z.L.P. File.
14. Drennan was to make a statement in August which also suggested that Labour would return deregistered men to the waterfront. See *Evening Post*, 24 August 1951.
15. *Herald*, 25 July 1951; *O.D.T.*, 25 July 1951.
16. *Herald*, 24 July 1951. A similar statement appeared in the *O.D.T.*, 15 August 1951, and again on 25 August. Other Labour candidates went further. J.M. Deas (Otahuhu) said on 28 August that "Barnes was a spent force on the labour and industrial front". P.T. Curran (Roskill) was reported to have said that he did not want the votes of the 500 watersiders in his electorate. See Typescript "Summary of Events of 1951 Dispute", in the hands of R.E. Jones. Nash wrote Potter on 24 July telling him he didn't like Potter's initial statement or his qualification. See Nash Papers, File 2235.
17. See the comments on the election, Auckland Watersiders' *Information Bulletin*, No.55, 8 September 1951. Rebuilding relationships with the F.O.L., however, was not easy. Fewer unions contributed directly to electorate organisations for the 1951 election than had been the case in 1949. See J.T. Head to A.J. McDonald, 8 October 1951, N.Z.L.P. Files (North Shore).
18. *Herald*, 14 August 1951. The *Otago Daily Times* quoted Holland as saying: "To vote for Mr Nash and his team, is to vote for Barnes, Hill and Drennan. It is a vote for appeasement and surrender of the way of life we hold dear. It is a vote for those who would 'line up' Mr Nash." *O.D.T.*, 14 August 1951.
19. *Ibid.*, 27 July 1951.
20. See Nash's statements, *O.D.T.*, 3 August, 15 August 1951. The tapes of other Labour speeches show that the major part of each speech was devoted to discussion of the state of the economy. N.Z.L.P. Tapes of Election Speeches.
21. See for instance the statement by W.A. Bodkin, *O.D.T.*, 16 August 1951 and that by Sir Donald Cameron, *ibid*. Holland in a broad-

cast on 30 August claimed that Nash, since he wasn't opposed to the Communist wreckers, was obviously for them. N.Z.L.P. Tapes of Election Speeches.
22. See P.G. Connolly's usage of the label "Fascist", *O.D.T.*, 18 August 1951.
23. Two of the four Labour members defeated were ex-Cabinet ministers, T.H. McCombs (Lyttelton), and F. Jones (St Kilda).
24. See *Official Year Book*, 1951-52, p.965. For comments on the election results see R.M. Chapman, "Politics and Society", *Landfall*, September 1962, pp.252-277; R.M. Chapman, "The Response to Labour and the Question of Parallelism of Opinion, 1928-1960", in *Studies of a Small Democracy, op. cit.*, pp.221-252.
25. *O.D.T.*, 12 September 1951.
26. Hill was to emerge again in the 1960s as a more moderate trade union leader in the Wellington area. Barnes, who became a very successful drainlayer in Ellerslie, Auckland, took little further part in trade union activities.
27. *Evening Post*, 24 August 1951.
28. See statement by W.G. Hopkins, Secretary of the new Auckland union, *Herald*, 25 August 1951.
29. G.H. Andersen, secretary of the Northern Drivers' Union; W.J. Knox, secretary of the F.O.L.; R.E. Jones, organiser of the Auckland General Labourers' Union; J.J. Mitchell, president of the Auckland Boiler Makers' Union; and F.E. Barnard, president of the Auckland Freezing Workers' Union are but a few deregistered watersiders from 1951.
30. See correspondence between Healy, Hill and Drennan, 1951-2, in the possession of H. Roth. Healy believed that if the National Union were retained there would in time be enough supporters in the new unions for a merger to be arranged.
31. See *Evening Post*, 17 September 1951; 24 September 1951; 13 October 1952.
32. *Evening Post*, 31 October 1951.
33. *Ibid.*, 3 September 1951.
34. *Waikato Times*, 14 April 1951; *Southland Times*, 16 April 1951.
35. *O.D.T.*, 3 May 1951.
36. *Press*, 8 June and 22 June 1951.
37. *N.Z.P.D.*, Vol.294, 1951, p.81.
38. *Dominion*, 7 July 1951.
39. *Dominion*, 9 July 1951.
40. *N.Z.P.D.*, Vol.295, 1951, p.6; Holland had promised to outlaw picketing when he spoke in Hamilton during the campaign. (30 August). Tape of his speech, N.Z.L.P. Files.
41. *Ibid.*
42. *N.Z.P.D.*, Vol. 295, 1951, p.67.

43. *Ibid.*, p.835.
44. *Statutes,* 1951, No.61, pp.343-4.
45. *Statutes,* 1951, No.61, Sections 20-33.
46. *N.Z.P.D.*, Vol. 295, 1951, pp.835-836. The F.O.L. was later to claim that it was responsible for persuading the Government not to alter the law concerning compulsory unionism. See N.Z.F.O.L. *Fifteenth Annual Report*, 31 January 1952, p.5.
47. *Ibid.*, pp.841-2.
48. See C. Carr's comments, *N.Z.P.D.*, Vol.296, 1951, p.880.
49. Nigel R. Taylor, "Public Order and Police Powers in New Zealand", *Political Science*, Vol.4 (1952), p.15
50. *Ibid.*, pp.19-20.
51. See Shirley Smith, "The Police Offences Bill: Public Opinion in Action", *Political Science*, Vol.4 (1952) pp.21-31.
52. *Evening Post*, 27 September 1951.
53. *Ibid.*, 29 October 1951.
54. *Star*, 30 October 1951.
55. *Star*, 13 November 1951.
56. *Dominion*, 14 November 1951.
57. *Press*, 15 November 1951.
58. See comments of C.J. Garland, president, Auckland District Law Society, *Herald*, 20 October 1951, and *Star,* 29 October 1951.
59. See Shirley Smith, *op. cit.*
60. See Nash's speech, *N.Z.P.D.*, Vol.296, 1951 p.1218. *Standard,* 7 November 1951 called the Bill "fascist" and suggested that, having won an election on the issue of communism, Holland was now trying to prove that the menace did actually exist.
61. *Evening Post*, 30 April 1952.
62. See R.M. Martin, *op. cit.*; also Willis Airey, *New Zealand Foreign Policy Related to New Zealand Social Development*, Valley Printing, Petone, 1954, pp.6-17.
63. See W. Rosenberg, "The Right to Strike", *Here and Now*, (July 1953) p.9ff; Michael Bassett, "Labour's Leg-Iron?", *Dispute*, No.3 (March 1965).
64. See press comments at the time of the "no decision" by the Arbitration Court in June 1968.
65. An attempt was made to keep the deregistered Auckland Branch of the N.Z.W.W.U. alive, but it gradually faded out, the men no longer having jobs in common. In 1954 the old union's affairs were wound up and remaining funds donated to charitable causes. See *Evening Post,* 31 May 1954.
66. See T.J. Potter, "Report to Area Conference on the National Industrial Scene", (November 1951) in hands of K.M. Baxter. Much of this report was written by R.A.K. Mason, Assistant Secretary of the Auckland General Labourers' Union at the time.

INDEX

Allum, Sir John, Mayor of Auckland, 1941-53; false optimism, 111, 119; Ben Chifley's scorn for, 112; truculence over Town Hall issue, 123; tries to prevent Nash speaking, 174-5.
Anderton, W.T., Labour MP for Eden and Auckland Central 1935-60; Minister of Internal Affairs, 1957-60; and Town Hall incident, 171-174.
Arbitration Court, see Industrial Conciliation and Arbitration Act.
Armstrong, A.E., Labour MP for Napier 1943-51, and dispute, 161.
Ascuncion de Larrinaga, and Lampblack dispute, September 1950, 52-59.
Auckland City Council, and Town Hall incident May 1951, 171-174.
Auckland Domain, meeting, 13 May, 174; meeting 3 June, 177.
Auckland Star, and statements against watersiders 1950, 61; comments, 80, 82; loses its cool, 169; urges slackening of Emergency Regulations, 173; campaign against Labour, 198; criticise Police Offences Bill, 209.
Barnes, Harold ("Jock") President Auckland Branch N.Z.W.W.U., 1942-4; President national union 1944-52; education, 19; personal grievances, 19; attitude to Stabilisation 20; relationships with Fraser, McLagan and Semple, 24-7; *Mountpark* dispute, 1948, 27-29; removal from W.I.A. 1949, 32; participation in anti-conscription campaign 32; support for National Party, 32; early friendship with Sullivan, 38-39; break with F.O.L. April 1950, 39-44; deteriorating relations with Government, 48-52; Lampblack dispute, September 1950, 52-60; photo with T. Hill, 44; belligerence of, 65-66; and February dispute, 69-77; pleas for support, 92-98; rejects Butler's and Croskery's approaches, 98; negotiations with miners and freezing workers, 108-112; invited to F.O.L.'s special conference, 115; supreme confidence, 139-142; discussions with Labour Party 148-150 and Holland's *volte face*; at Nash's Domain meeting, 174-5; some Labour MPs critical of, 176; struggle to keep up morale, 182; Auckland public meeting, 182; advocates violence, but overruled, 186-7; days numbered, 187; recommends support of Labour, 198; goes to prison after Labour's defeat 201; spurned by Wellington leaders, 202; finally leaves deregistered union, 1952, 202; final gains, 212.
Baxter, A.C., Labour MP for Raglan, 1946-49; Rotowaro Miners' president 1951, 186; 247.
Baxter, Ken McL., Secretary, F.O.L., 40; statement for F.O.L., 1 March, 106; and Nash, March, April, 178.
Belford, K.A., Employers' representative on W.I.A., 30; comment on "showdown", 60.
Bell, A.K., Leader new Wellington Union, 165; 202; 245.
Belsham, R.S., First President Auckland Maritime Cargo Workers' Union, May-June 1951, attacked, 168-9; 246.
Blakely, V.P., General Secretary New Zealand Port Employers' Association, comment 79.
Bockett, A.E., General Manager W.I.C., 1948-, doubt about new unions, 151; in New Plymouth, 154.
Bockett, H.L., Secretary of Labour, 1946-64, meets Prendiville, 109; talks with Giles, 110; doubt about new unions, 151; in New Plymouth, 154; discussions with Wells and Napier, 187.

INDEX

Brookes, Walter, comment on dispute, 82.
Brooklyn by-election, February 1951, 91.
Butler, P.M., Member, National Executive, F.O.L. appeals to Watersiders, 97-8.
Cabinet, National's membership of, and occupations, 229; photo 36.
Calcott, T.W., Ohura Miners' President, 134.
Carpenters' Dispute, 1949, 29-30; later significance for struggle within F.O.L., 40.
Cement Workers, Portland and Golden Bay still on strike, 125; deregistered, 130-131.
Chifley, Ben, Labour Prime Minister of Australia, 1945-49; Leader of the Opposition, 1949-51; 13; comments on J.A.C. Allum, 112; Nash's letter to, 175.
Chrichton, N., President, Port Chalmers Branch, N.Z.W.W.U., returns to work, 187.
Civil Emergency Organisation (C.E.O.), established 1 May, 170.
Clarke, A.E., Project Engineer, Mangakino hydro works, 104.
Communism, charges of "communism" against watersiders, 1948, 26-27; 37; and W.F.T.U., 41; F.O.L. warnings on, 45; Holland on Lampblack dispute, 57; O.D.T.'s charge, 61; *Herald's* charge, 81; Sullivan's accusation, 82; Government's accusations discussed, 86-92; Walsh's charges, 115; National campaign issue, 200; Government plans to check, 203-206.
Compulsory Conference, Nash calls for one, 105; miners and freezing workers call for one, 108.
Compulsory unionism, militants' hostility to, 38; National Party policy changes, 206.
Conscription Referendum, August 1949, and Barnes, 32; effect on Labour Government, 219-220.
Controls, wartime, pressure to relax, 14-16.
Cool Store Workers, Auckland's walk out, 99; vote to stay out, 116; New Plymouth's return, 124.
Combs, H.E., Labour MP for Onslow, 1938-54, comment, 193.
Cost of upheaval, 189-91.
Crook, F., Secretary, United Mine Workers' Union, 121.
Croskery, A.W., President, Federation of Labour, 1946-53, 44; appeals to watersiders, 98; special conference, 115; absence, 116.

Dalglish, Judge D.J., Chairman Waterfront Industry Authority, 1948-51, and watersiders' wage demand 1949, 30-1; watersiders' contempt for, 1950, 53.
Dellaway, A.C., Watersiders' representative on W.I.A., 1950, 56.
Department of Labour, role in establishing new unions, 152-5.
Deregistration of unions; of the N.Z.W.W.U., 28 February, 100; union reaction to, 101; of freezing workers, 128; of drivers, 129; of cement workers, 130-31.
Dominion Wellington, comments 81; wants legislation against subversion, 203; criticises Police Offences Bill, 209.
Donaldson, N., critic of Barnes' leadership, 27; allowed to join new union, 164; comment 202; 244.
Drennan, Alex, President, Auckland Branch, N.Z.W.W.U., 1950-51, communist affiliations, 88-9; 142; leadership spurned, 202.
Drivers' unions, reaction to Emergency Regulations, 104; reaction to Barnes, 107; Dunedin returns to work, 124; Auckland and Hastings return to work, 124; Wellington holds out, 125; ballots, 129; deregistration of Wellington Drivers' Union, 129; six new unions, 129-30; position of strikers by June, 183; joint meeting and declaration 9 July, 188.

Emergency Regulations, 83-85. See also Public Safety Conservation Act, and State of Emergency; unions reaction to, 93-98; Regulations enforced 26 February, 99; further Regulations gazetted, 122; 170; full usage, 171; and Town Hall meeting, 171-174; relaxed a little, 173-4; continued for two weeks beyond dispute, 194; lifted 25 July, 194; some provisions included in I.C. and A. Amendment Act 1951, 205; also in Police Offences Amendment Act, 1951, 208.

Evening Post, Wellington, comments, 80; criticises Nash, 146; bias against Labour, 158-9; comments on subversion, 209.
Evening Star, Dunedin, comments, 80.
Eyre, D.J., National MP for North Shore, 1949-66, Minister of Defence, 1960-66; 203.

Farr, A., attacked by watersiders, 168.
Federation of Labour (F.O.L.) and militants, 21-31; and Labour Government, 23-30; moves against N.Z.W.W.U., 39-43; fight with T.U.C., 45-52; and Lampblack, 55; F.O.L. calculations late 1950, 64; and February dispute, 93-98; demand for sole control of dispute, 105; temporarily retires from dispute, 106; plans special conference, 107-9; special conference 113-116; isolates watersiders, 118; accepts seven points and counsels return to work, 120-121; difficult relations with Labour Party, 176-179; joint meetings with Labour Party, 180; threatens Labour, 199-200; opposes Police Offences Amendment Bill, 209; sees T.U.C. unions return late 1950s, 211; final comments, 211-12.
Flood, J., Watersiders' representative on W.I.A., 1950, 56.
Fortune, W.H., National Minister of Police, 1949-54, and Town Hall incident, 172-3.
Fraser, Peter, Labour's Prime Minister, 1940-49; Leader of the Opposition, 1949-50; 14; 15; photo, 17; 19; 22; 24; hostility to militancy, 25; 28; threats to watersiders 1948-9, 28-32; involvement in Lampblack dispute, 57-58; death December 1950.
Freeman, J., Secretary, N.Z. Timber Workers' Union, 167.
Freezing Workers, attitudes to Emergency Regulations, 93; 103; N.Z. Freezing Workers' Association enters dispute 108-112; Westfield returns to work, 123; Southland, too, 123; Kilpatrick resigns from negotiating committee, 124; Wellington district still out, 125; ballots, 127-8; Sullivan deregisters Wellington District Freezing Workers 26 March, 128; twelve new unions 128; discrimination, 129; strikers meet other strikers, 183; joint meeting 9 July recommends return to work, 188.

Gas workers, vote for normal work, 123.
General Election, 1951, 194-201.
Giles, S., National Secretary, N.Z. Freezing Workers' Association, 44; 108; and negotiations with Sullivan 108-12; arrested, 171.
Gilmour, J.A., Industrial Magistrate and Lampblack settlement, 58; 73.
Glading, S.V., President N.Z. Engineers' Union, 167.
Goosman, W.S., National's Minister of Works, 1949-57; 1960-63; 194.
Gotz, F.L.A., National MP for Otahuhu and Manukau, 1949-63, comment on A.K. Bell, 165.
Grant, A.B., Secretary Christchurch Rubber Workers' Union, Secretary T.U.C., 47; comment on Arbitration Court's decision, 1951, 68; February dispute, 95; approach to Labour Party, 104-5; deputation to Holland, 107.

Hall, Superintendent, Auckland Police, and Town Hall incident, 171-173.
Hamilton Town Hall meeting, 29 March, 178.
Harbour Board Employees' Unions, reaction to February dispute, 94; 104; vote for normal work, 123; 124.
Harrington, G., Runanga miner, President National Strike Committee, 132.
Healy, J., Secretary, Waterside Workers' Federation of Australia, 13, 202.
Hill, Toby, Secretary N.Z.W.W.U., loyalty to Barnes, 20; statement 1946 on trade, 20; comment on election 1949, 32; photo with Barnes, 44; comment on Arbitration Court's decision, 1951, 68; and February dispute, 73-4; plea with Barnes for support, 92-3; addresses Wellington watersiders 26 February, 97; discussions with Labour Party, 148-50; some Labour MP's critical of, 176;

INDEX 259

struggle to keep up morale, 182; address in Wellington, police difficulties, 182; finally leaves deregistered union, 202; returns to F.O.L., 211.

Holland, Sidney, Leader of the Opposition, 1940-49; National's Prime Minister, 1949-57; education, 35; views on militancy, 36-7; comment on relations with watersiders, April 1950. 39; photo, 50; and Lampblack dispute, 54-58; with Dulles, 66; arrival back in New Zealand, 75; statements on foreign policy, 75-76; charges about "communism", 87; 92; meeting with F.O.L., 26 February, 98; first broadcast on dispute, 102; meeting with T.U.C., 27 February, 107; meets F.O.L. 9 March, 116; Seven Points, 119-120; broadcast, 23 March, 123; pleasure at harassment of miners, 134-5; discussion with Nash, 17 April, 149-50; rejection of settlement and reasons, 150-157; attack on Nash, 157-8; and Civil Emergency Organisations, 170; criticism of, 170; comment on Town Hall incident, 173; criticism of Nash, 175; meets Nash, 19 June, 184; criticism of Nash, 184; calculations about possible election, 191-193; visit to Australia, 192; refuses request early meeting of Parliament, 192; announces dissolution, 194; election charges, 200; victory, 201; post-election legislation, 204-211.

Holm, Capt. M.T., Secretary New Zealand Port Employers' Association, statement on Lampblack dispute, 56; comment on February dispute, 68.

Holyoake, Keith J., Deputy Prime Minister 1949-57; National's Prime Minister, 1957 and 1960-; Leader of the Opposition, 1957-60; and February dispute, 72-3; praise of F.O.L., 127; Labour and communism, 179; meets Nash, 184.

Hotel Workers' Federation, see F.G. Young; attitude to February dispute, 93.

Huntly, bridge damaged, 169; businessmen pressure Government, 186.

Hurst, H.S.P., attacked by watersiders, 169.

Hunt, F.L., Brigadier; Wellington C.E.O., discussions with Wellington Branch, N.Z.W.W.U., 187.

Industrial Conciliation and Arbitration Act, 1894, 8; Amendment, 1932, 9; Amendment, 1936, 9; Amendment, 1939, 10; Changing attitudes to, 8-12; 16; 18; 21; 23; Amendment, 1947, 26; and Carpenters' Union, 29-30; National Party attitudes to, 34; Arbitration Court's award, 1945, 15; "interim" award 1950, 49; award of 15% January 1951, 67-8; deregistration of affiliated unions, 100; Amendment Bill, 1951, provisions, 204-6; Labour fights 206-7; compulsory unionism retained, 206; Arbitration Court undermined, 212.

Inflation, post war, 14-16; National Government's encouragement of, 50-51.

Jones, F., Labour's Minister of Defence, 1935-49, MP for St Kilda, opposes watersiders, 176.

Kilpatrick, H.G., Secretary, Canterbury Freezing Works Union, 121.

King Neptune dispute, May 1950, 48.

Korean War, economic effects of, 63.

Labour Disputes Investigation Act, 1913, 10.

Labour Government, 1935-49; post-war problems, 13-16; relations with watersiders, 16-30; carpenters' dispute, 29-30; conscription, 32; election defeat, 32-33; declining electoral support, 1946-9, 217-8.

Labour Party, New Zealand (N.Z.L.P.) see Labour Government; Labour and Lampblack dispute, 57-8; Nash's first statement, 105; party enters dispute, 143-161; establishes caucus committee, 145; divisions in party, 145; Nash's activities, 148-159; deputation to Holland, 159; MPs in Auckland support watersiders, 160-61; difficult relations with F.O.L., 176-179; annual conference, June 1951, 179; joint meetings with F.O.L., 180; performance in Parliament, 193-195; faced with general election, 196-201; Opposition to post-election legislation, 206; final assessment, 211-12.

Macalister, R.L., Mayor of Wellington, 1950-56, 152.

McDonald, R., Labour MP for Ponsonby and Grey Lynn, 1946-69, and Town Hall incident, 172.

Macfarlane, R.M., Labour MP for Christchurch Central, 1939-1969; Speaker House of Representatives, 1957-60; opinion on watersiders, 176.
McLagan, Angus, President F.O.L. 1937-46; Minister of Labour 1946-49, 25; attitude to watersiders 1947, 25; *Mountpark* dispute 1948, 27-29; Carpenters and watersiders 1949, 30-32; 38; criticism of Sullivan, 1950, 49; illness 1951, 144; opposition to watersiders, 176; Nash writes to, 185; fights I.C. and A. Bill, 206.
McMullen, W.F., President Auckland Cargo Workers' Union, 164-5; 246.
McNeil, F.W., President, Auckland Harbour Board Employees' Union, 167.
Magee, T.M., Secretary, Wellington Drivers' Union, 129-130; arrested, 171.
Mahuta, bridge explosion 30 April, 169.
Marchington, T.A., Employers' representative on W.I.A., 30; and Lampblack dispute 1950, 53; 60; 224-225; comment about Barnes, 226.
Menzies, Robert G., Liberal Party Prime Minister of Australia, 1949-65, 91; 192.
Methodist Church, Public Questions Committee opinion, 173.
Miners, see United Mine Workers' Union.
Minhinnick, G.E.G., Cartoonist, *New Zealand Herald*, campaign against watersiders, 35; vicious attacks, 143; used by opponents of Nash, 179-80.
Mitchell J., communist affiliations, 89.
Moohan, M., Labour MP for Petone, 1946-67, and Lampblack dispute, 58; discussions Barnes and Hill, 148.
Moral Re-Armament, activities by union members, 167.
Mountpark dispute, 1948, 27-29.
Myrtlebank dispute, June 1950, 48; 51-52.
Nash, Walter, Labour's Minister of Finance 1935-49; Leader of the Opposition 1951-7; 1960-63; Prime Minister of New Zealand 1957-60; budget 1946, 14; and Lampblack dispute, 58; initial reaction to 1951 dispute, 105; becomes closely involved, 143; speaks at Hamilton, 145-6; letter to Holland 5 April, 147; Holland's reply, 147; letter to A.G. Osborne, 148; attempts to mediate, 148-9; meeting with Holland 17 April, 149; confidence 150-52; denunciation of Holland, 156; further criticism, 157-8; trouble with press, 158-9; shock at Government's behaviour, 159; and Auckland Town Hall incident, 171-173; domain meeting, 174; "neither for . . . nor against", 174-5; press criticism, 175; distrust of F.P. Walsh, 176-9; comments on relations with F.O.L., 178-9; anonymous letters, 179-80; suggests compulsory conference, 182; distressed by suffering, 184-5; contributes to relief, 185; requests calling of Parliament, 192; performance in Parliament, 193; embarrassed by Potter, 198-200; shows frustration, 200; election defeat, 201; opposes post-strike legislation, 210.
Napier, E.A., Secretary, Wellington Branch, N.Z.W.W.U., photo, 63; comment, 97; sees Sullivan, 180; discussions with Brig. Hunt and H.L. Bockett, 187; leads majority watersiders, 202.
Napier, J.E., comment on 1951 dispute, 77; sees Sullivan, 180; leads majority watersiders, 202.
National Government, 1949-57. Cabinet Members, 36; initial caution in office, 37; economic problems 1950, 50-51; attitudes to watersiders over Lampblack, 54-8; to employers, 60; political difficulties, 63-64; showdown, 62; intervention in February dispute, 72-77; declares war, 77; decides to prolong it, 113; refuses to negotiate with Barnes, Hill, Drennan, 116; prepares for lengthy battle, 118-119; Seven Points, 119-20; deregisters remaining strikers, 127-130; Holland and April political issues, 143-166; use of violence, 167-175; further conditions for return to work, 180; determined on total victory, 184; wears down strikers, 188-9; calculations about political gain, 191-193; new elections called, 194-5; campaign, 196-201; National's strong position, 197; returned with increased majority, 201.
National Party, political use of the issue of militancy, 24; 33; election victory, 32-3;

INDEX

attitudes to compulsory arbitration, 34-35; leadership of Holland, 35; see National Government.

New Unions, waterfront: first at Whakatane, 14 March, others by 20 April, 152; further attempts to establish, 151-156; New Plymouth, 161; Whangarei, 162; Auckland, 162-5; screening procedures, 164; Dunedin, 165; Lyttelton, 165; Wellington's difficulties, 165; Holland's friendship, 165; press euphoria, 165; Port Chalmers resumes, 187; see also Drivers' unions, Freezing Workers, Cement workers.

New Zealand Herald Auckland; encourages National Government to take strong measures, 1950, 51; 54; 57; 59; campaign against watersiders, 1950, 61; comments on February dispute and Communism, 81; comments, 85; urges "clean sweep", 111; activities 19-21 April, 158; editorial activity, 158-9; delight over new unions, 165; defends Government, 173; attacks Nash, 175; defends Sullivan over miners, 185; uneasy over continuation of State of Emergency, 194; begins electioneering against Labour, 197.

New Zealand Listener, used as propaganda weapon, 114; 168.

New Zealand Observer, comments on Lampblack dispute 1950, 54.

New Zealand Press Association Committee meeting decision, 2 March, 232-3.

Nordmeyer, Arnold H., President of N.Z. Labour Party 1950-55; Leader of the Opposition, 1963-65; Brooklyn by-election victory 1951, 91; discussions, with Barnes and Hill, 148; speech in Parliament, 193-4.

Ongley, Judge F.W., Chairman Waterfront Industry Commission, 1946-47, 23-24.

Order of the Waterfront Industry Commission, Section 47(b), 71; Cabinet's lack of knowledge of, 86.

Osborne, A.G., Labour MP for Onehunga, 1936-63; Nash writes to, 148; 159; opinions, 176.

Otago Daily Times, criticism of Labour Government, 29; pleas for strong action, 54; 59; criticism of watersiders, 61; attacks Labour Party, 144-45; begins electioneering against Labour, 197; comments on communism, 203; supports Government, 209.

Outlook, Presbyterian monthly, comment on watersiders, 62.

Parliament, Nash requests calling of, 146; Government rejects, 146; further request by Nash, rejected, 192; meets 26 June, 192; Holland announces dissolution, 194; Election 1 September, 196-201.

Peterson, S.W., President, Associated Chambers of Commerce, criticises holding of election, 196.

Police Offences Amendment Bill, 1951, provisions of, 207-8; opposition to, 208-210; modified, 209; Nash opposes and subsequently repeals, 210.

Port Conciliation Committees, announced by Sullivan, May, 180-181; keep registers below strength, 189.

Port Employers, New Zealand, representation on W.I.C. 1926, 23-24; and *Mountpark* dispute, 27; hostility to watersiders, 1949, 29-31; criticism of Sullivan, 1950, 49; and Lampblack dispute, September 1950, 52-59; refusal to enter direct negotiations on wages, October-December, 1950, 60; testimony to Royal Commission, 60; meeting with watersiders, February 1951, 68-9; enforce two-day penalty, 71-2; terms for resumption of work, 76-77; deny "lockout", 79; Government takes over control from, 86; encouragement to men to join new unions, 154; screening procedures, 164; and W.F. McMullen, 164-5; introduce 50% surcharge, 182; recoup 75% of losses, 191.

Post and Telegraph Department, special powers to open mail, 122.

Potter, T.J. ("Pat"), President, Auckland General Labourers' Union, Chairman T.U.C., 1950-52, 46-47; deputation to Holland, 107; distributes pamphlets to F.O.L., 115; photo, 172; embarrasses Nash, July, 198-200.

Prendiville, A.V., National President, United Mine Workers' Union, and negotiations with watersiders and Sullivan, 108-112; discussions with Barnes, 121; breaks with watersiders, 122.
Presbyterian Church, Public Questions Committee opinion, 173.
Press, The, Christchurch, comments, 81; uneasy about snap election, 196; opposes extreme action against communism, 203; 209.
Public Safety Conservative Act, 1932, 10; declaration of State of Emergency, 21 February 1951, 83-4.
Railway unions, A.S.R.S., R.T.A., reactions to Emergency Regulations, 104; votes throughout country on return to work, 125.
Rangitoto dispute, July-August 1950, 51.
Reeves, W.P., I.C. and A. Act, 8; 210.
Returned Servicemen's Association, intervention in dispute, 154; 167.
Richards, W.B., President Dunedin Tramways Union, unseats Walsh, 23; sceptical about T.U.C., 46.
Roberts, J., Canterbury Trades Council, 44; comment on F.O.L., 46.
Ross, R., Wallsend miner, secretary Miners' National Strike Committee, 132.
Royal Commission into the Waterfront Industry; establishment announced August 1950, 52; appointment and terms of reference, 58-9; watersiders refuse to co-operate, 59; resumes taking submissions, 202.
Seamen's Union, reaction to Emergency Regulations, 104; confusion in "back to work" votes, 125; not deregistered, 131; position of strikers, June, 183; move to return to work, 186; joint meeting drivers, watersiders, freezing workers, 9 July, return to work, 188.
Semple, Robert ("Bob"), Minister of Works, 1935-49, attitude to Barnes 1947, 25-6; similar criticism June 1951, 176.
Servicemen, placed on waterfronts, 27 February, 99; work mines, 132-3; conditions of work, 136-138.
Seven Points, Holland's proposals of 15 March, 119-20; watersiders' reactions, 121.
Sim, Sir Wilfred, President of N.Z. National Party 1944-51, comment on "communist menace", 92.
Skinner, C.F., Labour MP for Motueka and Buller, 1938-62; deputy-leader of the Labour Party, 1951-62, and Lampblack dispute, 58; discussions with Barnes and Hill, 148.
Skinner, T.E., Labour MP, Tamaki, 1946-9; President F.O.L., 1963-, 211.
Southern Cross Labour daily, 1946- March 1951; prints Barnes' statement, 79-80.
"Spelling", 216.
Stanley, Roy, Carpenters' leader in 1949, 144.
Star-Sun Christchurch, comments, 80-81.
State of Emergency, declared under Public Safety Conservation Act 1932, 20 September 1950, 58; 225; powers not put into effect, 58; declared 21 February 1951, 83; Regulations announced, 84; continued till 25 July, 194.
Strike and Lockout Emergency Regulations, 1939, 10; 84; 205.
Strikes, post war, comparisons between New Zealand, Australia, Canada, Finland, France, India, United States, Great Britain, 13; causes, 14.
Students, some support for watersiders, 170.
Sullivan, William, Minister of Labour, 1949-57, background, 37; comments on militancy, 37; early friendship with Barnes and Hill, 38-9; criticism of, 49; Lampblack dispute, 55; February dispute, 72-74; accusations of "communism", 90; prepares to fight, 99; deregisters N.Z.W.W.U., 100-101; meeting with T.U.C., 107; rejects further dealings with Barnes and Hill, 100; negotiations with Giles and Prendiville, 108-12; anticipates long fight, 122; tightens Emergency Regulations, 122-3; strengthens Holland's nerve, 151-155; role in establishing new unions, 151-5; sees Wells and the Napiers, 180; new conditions, 180; rejected,

INDEX

181; abuses Nash, 182; rejects settlement offer, 184; meets Nash, 184; meets miners, 185; modifies demands, 186; tough with Wellington Branch N.Z.W.W.U., 187.

Town Hall (Auckland) incident, May 1951, 171-4.

Trade Union Congress (T.U.C.), formed April 1950, 44; provisional officers, 45; early difficulties, 45-46; competition with F.O.L. 1950, 48; August conference membership, 223; and Lampblack dispute, 57; claim before Arbitration Court, 67-8; reaction to Regulations, 104-5; meeting with Holland, 107; support for Labour, 198; Potter's speech, July, 198; fades out 1952, 211.

Transport Worker, official publication of the New Zealand Waterside Workers' Union, 18; 19; claims about Lampblack settlement, 59; threats, 65.

Transport Workers' Federation, New Zealand, and watersiders, 1948, 28; 40.

United Mine Workers' Union of New Zealand, (U.M.W.U.) attitude of members to Emergency Regulations, 102-3; leaders meet Barnes and Hill, 108; negotiations with Sullivan, 108-112; Prendiville's further discussions with, and break from Barnes, 121-2; most branches remain out, 125; split within U.M.W.U., formation of national strike committee, 132; battles, 131-135; Ohura, 133-135; Kamo, 134; Denniston, 132; Seddonville, 132; Ngakawa, 132; Buller, 133; Huntly open-cast return to work, 132; underground remain out, 132; strikers' position weakening, 183; approach Sullivan, June, 185; meet Huntly and reject his conditions, 186; hold ballots and return to work 4 July, 186.

United Nations, watersiders' appeal to, April 1951, 241.

University, Victoria University College, students friendly to watersiders, 170; staff protest, 247.

Violence, watersiders attack new unionists, 168-9; bridge explosion Mahuta, 169; *Auckland Star*'s reaction, 169; Holland establishes Civil Emergency Organisation, 170; reaction, 170; Government tightens up, 170-171; demonstrations, Auckland and Wellington, 171-2.

Walsh, F.P., Vice-President Federation of Labour, 1948-53. President 1953-63, 12; 22; loses vice-presidency 1947, wins 1948, 23; domination of Seamen's Union and Wellington Clerical Workers' Union, 23 also 216; close friendship with Fraser, 22; advocacy of stabilisation, 23; photo, 47; moves against Barnes and N.Z.W.W.U., 41-43; and *Rangitoto* dispute, 51; and events late 1950, 62-64; February dispute, 93-98; demands for F.O.L. sole control of dispute, 105; masterminds special conference, 113-118; agrees to Seven Points, 120-121; urges tough measures, 126-7; praise of and hatred for, 127; distrust of Nash, 176-9; gains most from dispute, 211; uneasy relations with Nash after dispute, 211.

Waterfront Control Commission (W.C.C.), 1940-46, 19; 23-24.

Waterfront dispute, financial cost of, 189-91.

Waterfront Industry Authority (W.I.A.), established October 1948, 28; difficulties 1949, 32; restoration by Sullivan, 1950, 38; award to watersiders, July 1950, 49; watersiders' hostility to, 50; and February dispute, 1951, 68-9; abolished May, 181.

Waterfront Industry Commission (W.I.C.) established 1946, 23-24; and *Mountpark* dispute, 27; administrative and judicial powers separated, October 1948, 28; commission control removed from waterfront, February 1951, 78; W.I.C. reconstructed, 181.

Waterfront Industry Tribunal (W.I.T.), to replace W.I.A., May 1951, 181.

Waterside Workers' Union, New Zealand, (N.Z.W.W.U.), historical background, 16-19; attitudes to compulsory arbitration 1920s, 18; 1930s 18-19; attitude to political action, 18; election of Barnes to presidency 1944, 19; post-war demands, 20-23; 1946 dispute, 24-25; attitude to Waterfront Industry Commission, 24-25; *Mountpark*, 27-29; and Carpenters' Dispute, 29-30; attitude to Labour Government, 32; to new Government, 37-39; break with F.O.L. and formation of

T.U.C., 39-47; confrontations with employers and Government, 1950, 48-60; photo of leaders, 63; continued militancy in face of danger, 65; February dispute, 1951, 66-72; reject Government ultimatum of 16 February, 77; watersiders' case, 79; support from N.Z. Communist Party, 89-90; pleas for support, 92-98; reject ultimatum 26 February, 95-97; deregistered 28 February, 100; Public Trustee controls funds, 101; negotiations with miners and freezing workers, 108-112; watersiders' routine, 138-143; funds seized, 138; assistance from Australia, 138; fate of national union sealed, 151-2; new port unions formed, 161-6; criticism of old union, 167; Semple's appeal to watersiders, 176; Wells' praise of Labour, 179; Wellington Branch sees Sullivan, 180; reject conditions, 181; stiffening of morale, 181-2; appeal to public, 182; meeting with striking freezing workers, seamen, miners, drivers, June, and effort to settle dispute, 183; Port Chalmers breaks, 187; Wellington Branch's separate negotiations, 187; Lyttelton Branch topples, 188; meeting with seamen, freezing workers, drivers, 9 July, statement, 188; recommend return to work, 11 July; *Information Bulletins* and number of 'scabs', 189; conditions of employment, 189; decides to support Labour, 198; folds up 1952-4, 202, 255.

Webb, T.C., National's Attorney-General, 1949-54, meets Nash, 184.

Wells, T.G., Vice-President N.Z.W.W.U., 1950-51, photo, 63; 95; discussion with Labour Party, 149-150; praise of Labour Party, 179; sees Sullivan, 180; discussions with Brig. Hunt and H.L. Bockett, 187; leads majority of Wellington watersiders, 202.

Workers' Union, New Zealand (N.Z.W.U.) reaction to Emergency Regulations, 104; return to work, 29 March, 124-5.

World Federation of Trade Unions (W.F.T.U.), and N.Z.W.W.U., 41-42; "communist" directions to watersiders, 87-89; Walsh's comments, 115; Labour Party decision on, 179.

Young, F.G. Secretary New Zealand Hotel Workers' Federation, 43; initial chairman T.U.C., 46; is replaced, 46; and Lampblack dispute, 58; and February dispute, 93; discussions with Barnes and Hill, 149-150